MAY '68: COMING

UNIVERSITY OF READING EUROPEAN AND INTERNATIONAL STUDIES

This new series will include books which discuss some of the major contemporary European and international issues from a comparative perspective. National experiences with a relevance for broader European and international issues will also be covered by this series.

The collection is interdisciplinary in nature with the aim of bringing together studies that emphasise the role of political, economic, historical and cultural factors in shaping the course of international co-operation and international conflicts, particularly from the point of view of Europe and its relations with the rest of the world.

The influence of the processes of European integration (economic, political, cultural) on both the European polity-economy and the rest of the world, as well as the impact on Europe of global integration processes and non-European integration schemes, will be some of the themes that will run through the volumes planned for inclusion in the series.

THE ASSOCIATION FOR THE STUDY OF MODERN AND CONTEMPORARY FRANCE

The Association was founded in 1979 to provide a forum and a focus for those involved in teaching and researching on modern France. From its creation, it has been an interdisciplinary association and draws its members from a wide range of academic disciplines and departments in higher education in the United Kingdom and around the world.

H2HGL

Series Standing Order

If you would like to receive future titles in this series as they are published, you can make use of our standing order facility. To place a standing order please contact your bookseller or, in case of difficulty, write to us at the address below with your name and address and the name of the series. Please state with which title you wish to begin your standing order. (If you live outside the UK we may not have the rights for your area, in which case we will forward your order to the publisher concerned.)

Standing Order Service, Macmillan Distribution Ltd,
Houndmills, Basingstoke, Hampshire, RG21 2XS, England.

MAY '68: COMING OF AGE

Edited by

D. L. Hanley

Reader in French Studies
University of Reading

and

A. P. Kerr

Lecturer in French Studies
University of Reading

M
MACMILLAN

in association with
THE GRADUATE SCHOOL OF EUROPEAN AND
INTERNATIONAL STUDIES
UNIVERSITY OF READING
and
THE ASSOCIATION FOR THE STUDY OF MODERN
AND CONTEMPORARY FRANCE

First published 1989

Published by
THE MACMILLAN PRESS LTD
Houndmills, Basingstoke, Hampshire RG21 2XS
and London
Companies and representatives
throughout the world

Printed in Great Britain by
Camelot Press, Southampton

British Library Cataloguing in Publication Data
May '68: coming of age. – (University of
Reading European and International Studies)
1. France. Left-wing political movements.
Political ideologies, 1968–1988   I. Hanley,
David, *1944*–   II. Kerr, A. P. (Anne Paterson),
1940–   III. University of Reading, Graduate
School of European and International Studies
IV. Association for the Study of Modern and
Contemporary France   V. Series
320.5'3'0944
ISBN 0–333–46697–7 (hardcover)
ISBN 0–333–46698–5 (paperback)

CONTENTS

List of Contributors

Laurence Bell,	Lecturer in French Studies, University of Surrey.
Jeff Bridgford,	Lecturer in Modern Languages, Heriot-Watt University, Edinburgh.
Celia Britton,	Lecturer in French Studies, University of Reading.
Jean Charlot,	Professor of Politics, Institut d'Etudes Politiques, Paris.
Roger Duclaud-Williams,	Lecturer in Politics, University of Warwick.
Vladimir Claude Fisera,	Professor of History, Université de Strasbourg.
Margaret Gibbon,	Lecturer in French Studies, N.I.H.E., Dublin.
Hervé Hamon,	Journalist and author of several books on contemporary French issues.
René Mouriaux,	Research Fellow Institut d'Etudes Politiques, Paris.
Pascal Ory,	Professor of History, Université de Paris X - Nanterre.
Antoine Prost,	Professor of History, Université de Paris I - Sorbonne.
Marie-Noelle Thibault,	Professor of History, Université de Paris VIII.
Ginette Vincendeau,	Lecturer in Film Studies, University of Warwick.

Editors

David Hanley,	Reader in French Studies, University of Reading.
Anne P. Kerr,	Lecturer in French Studies, University of Reading.

ASM & CF thanks the *Service Culturel de l'Ambassade de France à Londres* for its financial support.

ABBREVIATIONS

CCOMCEN	Comité de coordination des oeuvres mutualistes et coopératives de l'Education nationale
CD	Centre démocrate
CDI	Centre de documentation et d'information
CELF	Comité des étudiants libéraux de France
CERES	Centre d'études, de recherches et d'education socialistes
CFDT	Confédération française démocratique du travail
CFT	Confédération française du travail
CFTC	Confédération française des travailleurs chrétiens
CGC	Confédération générale des cadres
CGPME	Confédération générale des petites et moyennes enterprises
CGSI	Confédération générale des syndicats indépendants
CGT	Confédération générale du travail
CNC	Centre national de la cinématographie
CNPME	Confédération nationale des petites et moyennes entreprises
CNPF	Conseil national du patronat français
CPDM	Centre pour le progrés et la démocratie moderne
CPGE	Classes préparatoires aux grandes écoles
CSL	Confédération des syndicats libres
DEUG	Diplome d'études universitaire générales
EDF	Électricité de France
EGF	Électricité et Gaz de France
ENS	École Normale Supérieure
ESU	Étudiants socialistes unifiés
FEN	Fédération de l'éducation nationale
FGDS	Fédération de la gauche démocrate et socialiste
FLN	Front de libération nationale
FNSEA	Fédération nationale des syndicats d'exploitants agricoles
FO	Force ouvrière
IFOP	Institut français d'opinion publique
JEC	Jeunesse étudiante chrétienne
JCR	Jeunesses communistes révolutionnaires
MLF	Mouvement pour la libération des femmes
MRP	Mouvement républicain populaire
NWC	New working class

OAS	Organisation armée secrète
ORTF	Office de la radiodiffusion-télévision française
PCF	Parti communiste français
PCI	Partito communista italiano, also Parti communiste internationaliste
PEGC	Professeur d'enseignement général de collège
PDM	Progrès et démocratie moderne
PME	Petites et moyennes enterprises
PS	Parti socialiste
PSA	Parti socialiste autonome
PSU	Parti socialiste unifié
RATP	Réseau autonome des transports parisiens
RPR	Rassemblement pour la république
SFIO	Section française de l'internationale ouvrière
SLON	Société pour le lancement des oeuvres nouvelles
SMIG	Salaire minimum interprofessionnel garanti
SNCF	Société nationale des chemins de fer
SNESup	Syndicat national de l'enseignement supérieur
SNI	Synicat national des instituteurs
STS	Section des techniciens supérieurs
UDF	Union pour la démocratie française
UEC	Union des étudiants communistes
UFT	Union française des travailleurs
	Union de la gauche socialiste
UJCML	Union des jeunesses communistes marxistes-léninistes
UNEF	Union nationale des étudiants de France
UNR	Union pour la nouvelle république
VLR	Vive la Révolution

1. ELUSIVE MAY: THE PARADOX OF A MOMENT IN HISTORY

DAVID HANLEY AND ANNE P. KERR

In a country which boasts a history as turbulent as that of France, the fate of May was always, in the language of Althusser, the mentor of one particularly active group, 'overdetermined'. May could only be bracketed with the Commune, the Popular Front, the June days and the various *journées* of that revolutionary tradition which periodically shakes the established order. Indeed if one particularly influential interpretation is to be believed, such shocks are the only means by which French society has managed to accomplish even those moderate degrees of change which it has needed for its own development. On the face of it, such a view seems unexceptional; May was after all highly concrete and visible. Did not a student protest mushroom into a general strike involving nine million people? Was there not for a fortnight or more, to the delight and incredulity of those who lived through it, the almost total collapse of one of the strongest state apparatuses in the world? And did not there emerge during this period a myriad of initiatives and aspirations, new forms of organisation and participation, and most of all a new ease of communication, which still colour pleasantly the memories of activists who experienced these slightly unreal days? May even has something which classic historical moments share, namely a clearly defined ending; the Gaullist electoral wins of June pricked the bubble as decisively as the army dealt with the insurgents of 1848 or 1871. Thereafter the workers returned to work, the students went home and soon most who could afford it were spending their

1

wage rises on a holiday and buying the petrol which had mysteriously appeared once more; apparently the return to normal was overwhelming. Common sense and mankind's innate conservatism had, it seemed, prevailed.

Yet few at the time experienced things in this light, and today no one with close memories of 68 will accept that things have ever been 'normal' in quite the same way since then. Supporters of the spirit of 68, and indeed many adversaries, will point to the changes in lifestyle or political culture which have become more evident over the last twenty years and be tempted to ascribe these somehow to the influence of May. They will refer to manifestations as diverse as changing attitudes to the family or towards sexuality, the rise of the women's movement, the greater self-confidence shown by homosexuals, the growth of regional consciousness or local nationalisms or even the rise of a narcissistic type of modernity as exemplified by the 'yuppie',[1] seeing in all or any of these the benign or malign effect of the *évènements*. After all the events were so sharp and vivid, and they took place against what seemed to be a world-wide backdrop of revolution and social change.[2] The temptation to make May into a matrix of wholesale social and cultural change thus becomes very hard to resist.

There are of course and always have been rival theses which strive to reduce the importance of May or to exorcise symptoms that are felt to be dangerous. In their different ways the interpretations of Régis Debray or the PCF show a common fear of the events and the forces they threatened to unleash.[3] From the start the PCF sought to canalise the movement into a set of bread and butter demands; or if the way out had to be political then it involved passing through the 'advanced democracy' and the electoral victories to which the party

[1] G. Lipovetsky, ' "Changer la vie", ou l'irruption de l'individualisme transpolitique', *Pouvoirs* 30 (1986) 91-100.

[2] D. Caute, *Sixty-Eight: Year of the Barricades* (London: Hamish Hamilton, 1988); R. Fraser, *1968: A Student Generation in Revolt* (London: Chatto and Windus, 1988).

[3] R. Debray, *Les Rendez-vous manqués*, (Paris: Seuil, 1975); *Modeste Conrtibution aux discours et cérémonies du dixième anniversaire*, (Paris: Maspero, 1978). For PCF views, see R. Johnson, *The French Communist Party versus the Students*, (New Haven: Yale University Press, 1972) and for a more recent update C. Journès, 'Les interprétations communistes de mai 68', *Pouvoirs*, op. cit., 25-36.

was by then committed. Certainly fear of being *débordé à gauche* was strong. For the stern and vituperative Debray the students were, unlike the real guerilla heroes of the Latin American jungle, simply play-acting; the revolutionary games of today were but a prelude to the well-paid jobs of tomorrow to which higher education was a passport.

These hostile attitudes to May share one feature in common with the enthusiastic ones adumbrated above; both sides see May as a kind of whole, a historical moment in the grand sense with an integrity and completeness of its own, and as such accessible to total theoretical explanation. The essays in this volume offer a much more fragmentary and inchoate view, and not simply because they are by several hands.What emerges here is a view of May as a much more ambiguous and multi-faceted phenomenon than has often been believed. May cannot be apprehended as a single historical whole, any more than the Commune or the 1848 revolution; on the contrary it was a moment when on different levels changes proceeded at varying speeds and arguably not always in the same direction. While the surface events (student protest and mass strike) can be isolated with relative precision (although huge amounts of work remain to be done by way of local studies), their consequences, at least in the mid to long term, are a different matter. And it is even harder to pin down the deeper-lying, less visible sort of change, much of which was probably under way well before May and to which May might have acted as a catalyst (again differentially, according to the area concerned).

May will thus be seen as a sort of matrix of change, but through a necessarily fuzzy lens; historical change is never that precise, and indeed this is one of the lessons of May which one recognises with hindsight. The following remarks are intended simply to set a context for this multi- dimensional approach to understanding May; they address themselves briefly first to the causes of May and secondly to its broader consequences.

What are normally thought of as the causes of May are frightening in their banality. The student grievances of 1968 and before have, as Roger Duclaud-Williams shows, barely changed since then : overcrowding and underfunding, high failure rates, inadequate maintenance, lack of contacts between teachers and taught and above all fear of selection at entry to university. The higher education system may well have been, as Peyrefitte said, like organising a shipwreck to see who could swim; none the less every student wanted his chance to cling to a piece of driftwood, however small, rather than being forbidden entry to the vessel in the first place. Most of these features were still present in 1986, but the minor explosion of December hardly struck at the foundations of the state; and if groups of workers did follow the students into action, then they did so in a limited and very *ad hoc* fashion. One of the differences between the two movements may well have been, as Hervé Hamon suggests, the presence in 1968 of a generation of very high-class semi-professional political youth leaders, whose itinerary he has lovingly retraced. Yet it is hard to believe that these sophisticates, many of whom have moved on like their fellow revolutionaries elsewhere to successful entrepreneurial careers in the capitalist system they so detested,[4] were alone sufficient to catapult thousands of students into street protest. Even the widespread political indignation about the recent excesses of French colonialism and the considerable sympathy for the Vietnamese in their struggle against the USA would never have unleashed a major social movement on their own. Indeed as Celia Britton's chapter on the cinema suggests, the links between social change at home and revolution in a far-away underdeveloped country were far from evident anyway, and there was considerable ambiguity in the position of many French leftists, amounting in some cases perhaps to gesture-politics. We still know in fact comparatively little of the motives of many students, for it is at least arguable that many (perhaps the majority) were activated not by the passion for global social change of those who became, ephemerally, their leaders but by much more mundane concerns such as graduating and finding a job (however bright their prospects may seem when compared retrospectively with today's situation). Similar discrepancies probably existed within the working-class movement, where concern was rising at declining rates of pay and longer hours in the midst of

---

[4] In April-May 1988 Channel Four devoted a four-part documentary series, made by Daniel Cohn-Bendit and Steven de Winter, to following up the careers of activists from 68 in several countries. The films bring out quite a poignant contrast between Cohn-Bendit, still very much a libertarian, albeit more committed to working within a framework of representative democracy, and many of his former comrades from Amsterdam or New York, nowadays successful businessmen.

what was obviously a period of economic growth of unprecedented strength. Desire to get their share clearly fuelled the initial actions of many workers, even if in many cases the economistic first action rapidly led on to other forms of action and experiment (work-ins, attempts at workers' control, etc.) and the movement took on a generally more politicised character, albeit with highly variable characteristics according to sector and locality. But much work has still to be done on the motivations and more generally on the culture of the younger workers who often initiated strike movements, and we need in particular to know more of how they related to students and their culture. All too often film documentaries on 68 suggest superficial identifications between different kinds of youth (and indeed between youths of wildly assorted countries), usually by such devices as juxtaposing images of students and workers, to the accompaniment of a rock score and perhaps a fleeting image of Hendrix or Jagger on stage. Such techniques suggest a rebellious ambiance, which is true; but they also suggest a shared culture which may be misleading. The aspirations of Spanish or Brazilian students seeking to restore bourgeois democracy in the face of authoritarian régimes or of Czechs attempting to liberalise a Soviet-type system cannot be easily reduced to the same dimension as those of West German or Parisian activists aiming to transcend such a framework and to some extent thus taking it for granted.

But whatever the frustrations students and workers had to contend with, they had long been present and on their own could never have generated a protest like 68. A further catalyst was needed and here as Jean Charlot demonstrates, the reactions of government were a key variable. Hesitant and contradictory, unable to repress thoroughly yet not quick-witted enough to offer the right concessions early in the game (unlike the Jacques Chirac of 1986 who remembered his history lessons), the Gaullist government was strangely reminiscent of its July Monarchy predecessors on the eve of 1848. Undoubtedly its ineptitude helped create a movement that might well never have materialised otherwise. Often history turns on relatively minor factors such as this, and the dividing line between a significant moment and a non- event can depend on one such variable. Here is another lesson of 68 that is perhaps sometimes forgotten.

If May's causes were variable, so were its outcomes. In terms of party politics they were rich in paradox. On the right, the apparent triumph of Gaullism was in reality empty; Gaullism had had one last shot in its locker, enough to see off the 'events'. But soon the question of replacing the General and the whole generation of barons would be brutally raised; in particular the young Turks of the right awaited their chance to move into the forefront behind Giscard d'Estaing. May clearly sped the end of Gaullism and in so doing increased the tendency towards bipolarisation, forcing the centrists to line up with the right; one of the strangest and least remarked paradoxes of May was that it rendered even more difficult the existence of Christian democracy as an autonomous political current in the Fifth Republic. An even stranger consequence perhaps is that the ultimate beneficiary of this process was not the PCF or *a fortiori* the revolutionary left, but the great non-participant of May, reformist socialism, then incarnated by the dying SFIO and the stillborn FGDS. For the PCF May was a movement it could not control and was unable to exploit. May showed that a revolutionary scenario was no longer on the party's agenda (though few can have doubted that by 1968, surely) and hence can be seen as another step, and quite a big one, in the party's move towards irrelevance. For it was unable to convince revolutionaries, while reformists usually prefer the real thing to the imitation. The other great losers were of course the groups of the revolutionary left, Trotskyists, Maoists and to a lesser extent the PSU, whose moment of high visibility was not to last long. The *groupuscules* could help keep the movement going once it was launched, but once it ran out of impetus their limitations were cruelly exposed. Yet as Hamon shows they seem to have accepted these limitations and never to have plunged into violence or terrorism, then or later. It may be that they saw their function as essentially one of consciousness-raising. But it is still bitterly ironic that the main beneficiary of this effort should have been the revamped PS, both in terms of ideas and, as time went on, of activists with experience from 68. Perhaps there is another lesson here, namely that it is sometimes better to listen than to act. For the PS seems in many ways to have purloined and adapted some of the more popular and marketable ideas from the turmoil (as Laurence Bell shows with regard to *autogestion*) and to have fashioned them into a credible electoral mix at the expense of its more radical rivals. Alongside this phenomenon however, as René Mouriaux shows, the radical discourse of May does seem to have exerted a real influence on unions such as the CFDT, which have certainly continued to play a political role far beyond their normal pressure-group function.

The wider ideological or cultural effects of May are the hardest to assess, even after twenty years, and the following remarks are offered with some caution. May was not an event which somehow prefigured, as has been suggested, the ideological void which looms in the late eighties. On the contrary it was a huge ideological spasm. At the different levels of the movement old and new ideologies competed furiously for attention, as activists discussed intensely. At the most visible élite level it seems clear that Marxisms of various hues vied with libertarian and anarchist currents for control of a movement which largely escaped them anyway. Lower down, great masses of people became involved for the first time in some kind of ideological confrontation or debate. In many cases it may well not have been particularly well articulated or theorised, taking the form of a vague anti-capitalism or resistance to authority and hierarchy. How long these feelings persisted after May and in what ways they durably marked the 68 generation are practically impossible to say. But in terms of political behaviour, we do know that the generation of 68 has been the most faithful supporter of the left, in its various guises, since then;[5] here surely is one fairly measurable long-term ideological effect.

Another strange reading of May persists in seeing it as somehow prefiguring the possessive individualism which pervades the late eighties.[6] Such a view mistakes totally the character of May; to confuse the largely penniless activists with embryonic 'yuppies' is tantamount to confusing the radical rock music of the sixties with the neatly-packaged disco pop so prevalent today. May was indeed a time for self-expression, against authority, power and what Sartre would have called the practico-inert. Most activists saw no reason why such self-expression should not be pleasurable. What they did not do was to see that pleasure as an isolated, individualistic phenomenon. In its incoherent way the movement wanted all to have their say and to enjoy it, not just a few; it took its democracy seriously. The culture of the eighties with its élitisms and its exclusions, which heighten the pleasure of those who do manage to participate, is a different phenomenon, and logically so. For it is built on a capitalist system that has mutated out of all recognition from the low-tech, labour-intensive economy of the sixties.

---

[5] C. Ysmal, *Le Comportement électoral des Français* (Paris: Seuil, 1987).
[6] G. Lipovetsky, op. cit.

Other cultural phenomena are more problematical. The gay and women's movements probably owe something to 68 but it is not clear what. Both emerged more decisively in the early seventies rather than during the events; it would seem thus that May was a 'revealer' in Vladimir Fisera's phrase, bringing to the surface and amplifying subterranean developments within French society that were already well advanced. Both movements must have drawn confidence from the general ethos of self-expression and confidence in collective or group identities that were the real hallmarks of May. Yet paradoxically again, as Ginette Vincendeau shows, in terms of the women's movement, the relevance of such identities has by and large been ignored by one of the sharpest arms of that movement, namely women film makers.

No doubt consideration of the many other domains of human life which were affected by May would reveal similar paradoxes and inconsistencies. All of them would tend to make one aware of essaying general conclusions about May. Looked at in political retrospect it might be seen as a flash in the pan - several weeks of anarchy brusquely resolved by an election which the conservatives won. But seen over a longer term and from a more cultural angle, it could well be viewed as a sort of matrix which helped a number of attitudes to develop, some of which would have fairly measurable political or organisational consequences. In truth no overall explanation will fit, for May was untidy, as untidy as history itself. Rival actors pursued different strategies at different levels, with unforeseeable consequences. One senses the futility of trying to fit it all into some neat theoretical synthesis, the more so as so much of it has never been documented or analysed. Historians may feel that it is always thus and that one is always as it were cleaning up reality for the purpose of intellectual cosmetics. But May has a particular elusiveness beyond even that of the 'normal' historical moment and a refusal to be compressed into categories that accords well with the spirit of the *soixant'huitards*. It is our hope that the following pages will provide a guide to the labyrinth and a stimulus to further exploration.

Editors' Note. This book is based on the proceedings of the eighth annual conference of the Association for the Study of Modern and Contemporary France, held at the University of Reading in September 1987. Chapters 5 and 12 were translated by James Cutshall, chapter 13 by Debra Green, chapter 8 by David Hanley and chapter 3 by Anne P. Kerr. Chapter 2 was transcribed, translated and edited by the editors.

2. 68 - THE RISE AND FALL OF A GENERATION?

HERVÉ HAMON

Anyone wishing to address the issue of May 68 must first ask himself the question, much in use at the time: what's your angle, comrade? If I might refer to the work which I undertook with Patrick Rotman,[1] we both belong to the generation of 68 (on 3 May Patrick was actually in the courtyard of the Sorbonne, though I myself was on the beach). Being of this generation, we find it particularly difficult to view the events with any degree of detachment or objectivity. This is our initial handicap and we are very much marked by the May events, still present in our minds and in our relationships with our own children.

We wondered how to approach the writing of a book on 68 for a French public. It was something of a gamble, since the events have been as it were swept under the carpet. It is difficult to speak of them because they are a painful subject not just for the political class as such but also for many families. One good way of understanding 68 would be to retrace the events through the experience of the latter. The legacy of 68 can be perceived through the relationships now existing between men and women, parents and children, pupils and teachers. We are faced with a subject which people have banished from their thoughts since it arouses so much passion. Yet we were

---

[1] H.Hamon and P. Rotman, *Génération*, vol.1 *Les Années de rêve*, vol. 2 *Les Années de poudre* (Paris: Seuil, 1987 and 1988).

very keen to undertake this enquiry into an aspect of the life of the community which fits in with our previous work.[2]

Three or four years' work on this topic has convinced us that an understanding of the events can not be achieved simply by looking at the chronology of May 68. It is pointless to begin with 3 May, the day when a meeting was held in the Sorbonne courtyard to protest against police repression, particularly the measures taken against certain student activists from Nanterre. Although the meeting was a failure the irruption of the police into the courtyard unleashed a reaction beyond its control. But to give excessive weight to this meeting and to the cult figure of Cohn-Bendit, however likeable, is to misunderstand totally the May events. We therefore decided to go back ten years earlier. Rather than using academic analysis we decided to base our work on oral evidence and recollection which we believe has enabled us to give a reasonably rounded account but by no means a definitive one.

Our first task then was to gather a representative sample of this generation, that is people whose age-range today runs from the late thirties to the late forties. We chose some eighty people, half male half female. Some of the interviews stretched over 20 or 25 hours. We found the lapses of memory and the omissions as interesting as what was actually said. We deliberately avoided talking about chronology or using set questions. This material, together with evidence from biography, letters, film and press sources enabled us to write our account.

One salient point at once emerged. In April 1988 PCF candidate in the presidential election gained less than seven per cent of the vote. Twenty years ago this would have been unthinkable for our generation, for whom the PCF was the number one reality. A great effort of imagination is needed to place oneself in the context of, say, 1961 when communism was so significant domestically and internationally. It is very hard to reconstitute the political and cultural environment of this generation which would provide the leadership for 68. We claim no infallibility for our method which may well incur criticism from more academic analysts and from those whose experiences were different. We know only that there

---

[2] See for example H. Hamon and P. Rotman, *Tant qu'il y aura des Profs* (Paris: Seuil, 1984); *Les Porteurs de valises: la résistance française a la guerre d'Algérie* (Paris: Albin Michel, 1979).

were certain individuals with a symbolic stature, and certain key moments. What we have learned from our empirical and approximate research is that we need to go back about ten years, perhaps a little more. The first moment which seemed to us significant was 1957 when a group of young people were invited by the PCF to attend the World Youth Festival in Moscow. There were delegations from all over the world. In terms of content the festival was loosely structured. Besides communists the French delegation included Christians, secularists and even anti-communists.

This generation was marked by communism and revolution but also by war, or more exactly by three wars. It was born before or during World War II, experienced its childhood during the Cold War and its adolescence during the wars of decolonisation. This theme of war recurred constantly during conversations with our interviewees, irrespective of their social, family or ideological background, and always with a characteristic emphasis. They spoke of the Algerian War and of the horrors of nazism or fascism as if these could return unvanquished - an idea particularly strong among these erstwhile eighteen- or nineteen-year-olds. They read accounts of torture in Algeria which were available from 1957 onwards and knew about the army's behaviour during the battle of Algiers, from publications such as *Esprit* and *L'Express*. If such a comparatively small-scale colonial war could give rise to this type of conduct, then it followed that bestial instincts within mankind were far from dead and that there were still many battles to be fought. One particularly striking episode was the generals' *putsch* of 1961 when the Prime Minister Michel Debré urged the population to go *en masse* to Orly airport to forestall a possible landing by rebel parachutists. Such episodes reinforced our interviewees' forebodings about a re-emergence of Fascism, confirming what they had heard from their parents about World War II.

It was felt that the Allied victory in 1945 was incomplete and in some sense artificial. The students of the early sixties were not unaware of the fact that participation in the Resistance had been limited to a minority and that even among communist resisters the first to take action had been immigrant workers such as the Manouchian group. This led them to question their parents about their rôle and their attitudes during the war, and why it was that the Liberation had not brought about a social revolution. Those from families that had been either passive or outright collaborators felt that they had to make amends for their parents' shortcomings. Those from Resistance families, especially communists, felt that they had to complete the social revolution which had not materialised in 1946-7. These attitudes are of crucial significance for the whole generation.

That this generation was entering university in 1960 or 1961 was no coincidence so far as May 68 is concerned. For whatever the rôle played by other youth groups such as workers or peasants, which is in fact considerable, the fact remains that the principal ferment occurs among those engaged in academic study. Student numbers were increasing sharply as a result of the 'baby' boom' of the immediate post-war years and students saw in higher education a means of upward social mobility. The student population was highly concentrated in geographical terms, particularly in Paris, which drew in students from all over the country, creating networks which would play a rôle later. Whatever their political backgrounds, these students had to face one supreme factor: the dominance of the PCF, there being no viable socialist party at the time. There was the small but appealing PSU which many joined. But the whole intellectual and political climate was dominated by the PCF, whose influence affected even so prestigious an intellectual as Sartre (see his debate with Camus) and also Malraux. (When questioned about the authors whom they read most, our interviewees answered in order:1) Malraux 2) Sartre 3) Camus - the latter with some reservations, given his pro-settler sympathies during the Algerian War.)

At the end of the Algerian war activist students found it once again worthwhile to work within the PCF because it had put itself beyond the pale so far as the political establishment was concerned. It had behaved badly in 1956 over the Khrushchev report on Stalin's crimes, which it had covered up, and over the Budapest rising. During the Algerian war it had failed to give support to the independence movement, whereas in Indo-China it had done so because the movement was communist-led. Our generation of students was in contact with others who were assisting the FLN and who were able to show them the discrepancy between the PCF's public pronouncements of anti-colonialism and its 'prudent' tactics on the ground (though in fact these tactics never brought the electoral reward which the party hoped for).

Paradoxically in the early 1960s the PCF appeared both Stalinist and yet sufficiently lax for left-wing students to feel able to join it and try to de-Stalinise it from within, namely by joining the UEC. Student politics would henceforth revolve round two centres - that of the UEC in Place Paul Painlevé and of the catholic students at the Centre Richelieu. As a former catholic activist I can testify that the most significant developments took place on the communist side, not in terms of scientific analysis but in terms of myth-making. Students of various backgrounds flocked into the UEC - orthodox Stalinists, anti-Communist socialists and Christiáns, whether left-wing or no. It was the intelligent way at the time to be anti-communist. Marie-Noelle Thibault's recollections (see Chapter 13) will shed more light on this than I am able to do. She is a good example of the type of student from well-to-do and indeed religious backgrounds who joined the UEC at this time. Within the UEC they were active in two tendencies, first of which was the 'Italians'. These were close to the Italian communist party (PCI) and its theories of polycentrism as developed by Togliatti. They held that the PCF must abandon its Stalinism and publish the Khrushchev report. Although the PCI gave them no official recognition it did invite them to Rome where they participated in summer schools. The second tendency was the left, which felt that the 'Italians', although likeable, were merely elaborating a communist version of social democracy. The left sought to revive the revolutionary myth in all its purity. Intellectual life in the Latin Quarter was dominated by the struggle between these two tendencies, which was carried on in the UEC magazine *Clarté*, an unusually distinguished publication compared with the rest of the party-political press of the day. Many of today's leading journalists cut their teeth on *Clarté* - Michel-Antoine Burnier (founder of *Actuel*), Serge July (editor of *Libération*) and Jean Chalic (communications adviser to the Hachette group). *Clarté* raised issues beyond pure politics - new wave cinema, the films of Agnès Varda, relations between the sexes, non-establishment poets and playwrights. But when it did discuss politics, it did so from a deviationist standpoint, as in the interview with Togliatti which particularly enraged the PCF leadership.

The UEC challenged the structures of higher education, the PCF and the whole of the political class. It was not the only organisation to do so. It joined with the JEC in what was a veritable youth party, the UNEF. This union represented half the student body and could be said to have kicked off the May events on 27 October 1960, when it called for a demonstration against the Algerian war, not merely in favour of peace but as an open expression of solidarity with the opponents of colonialism, which represented a new departure. The demonstration was condemned by the PCF and CGT but was supported by the CFTC (soon to become CFDT), FEN and FO. It was a huge success and showed that it was possible to take action on the left without or even against the PCF; it also showed that the UNEF was indeed a youth party and thus more than a union. But this was to prove a weakening factor. These three forces - JEC, UEC and UNEF - thus constituted the locus of challenge to established authority.

What sort of problems exercised the minds of these students? First of all came the university which at this time seemed more and more like a railway station. Complaints centred initially on teachers who did not work or had not worked for years, on lecture rooms that were more and more crowded and on the non-existence of teacher-student relations, all of which engendered suspicion, hostility and frustration. It was in reaction to such conditions that students put so much effort into militant activity, which for them was a kind of 'alternative university' (to use an expression much in vogue in 1968). The headquarters of the UEC and JEC were their classrooms, rather than the Sorbonne.

These groups also helped students resist a particular state of mind, widespread at the time, which is well described in Georges Perec's *Les Choses* published in 1965. It was a kind of fear which involved a coming to terms with their origins, a promise to be kept, political and ideological depression resulting from the resolution of the Algerian problem, stemming from the idea that the old Europe was about to re-emerge. They felt that all truly significant events were taking place outside Europe. For a while - two years at most - they held out hopes for Algeria. Then there was the Cuban revolution which was seen as non-Stalinist and nothing to do with the USSR; *Clarté*-club, the UEC travel agency, organised trips to Cuba, which were taken up by students of all shades of opinion. Cuba stood for a revolution carried out by youth, by a minority whose legitimacy was almost indisputable in a country which had been an American playground. The Cuban leaders were deeply rooted in their people and anything but bureaucratic. Cuba gave the students the romance of the exotic, in an experience which had both a sensual and a political reality.

There was a fear of entering the adult world. Unlike today's youth, in 1963-4 young people were afraid of entering too soon and too easily into a world of infinite expansion and prosperity. They were more interested in dreams of generosity and solidarity, and adventure. They were profoundly moved by the thought that the revolution might be over and that there might be no more good causes to fight for. Such a view represented the high point of third-worldism.

The UEC continued to work inside the communist party, which it aimed to take over. It was after all the second-largest communist party in Europe. Far from being merely an amusing and deviant element of the party, the students were deadly serious in their aim of toppling its ageing leadership and turning it back into a revolutionary but democratic organisation, however mad and ambitious this objective might seem. They failed of course in their attempt, winning a first victory in 1963, suffering defeat in 1964 and expulsion in 1965. (The latter measure has been the PCF's standard procedure for dealing with internal opposition before and since.) The 'Italians' understood that revolution was neither possible nor desirable, whereas the left drew the opposite conclusion and formed *groupuscules*. Thus began the movement which would lead to the formation of the Trotskyist JCR under Alain Krivine, while at the École Normale Supérieure there began the pro-Chinese movement, later to be known as Maoist.

These youngsters were still on a voyage of discovery, searching for a different way of life and very strongly aware of a feeling of political bastardy. They felt that they were the only ones to be taking any initiatives but that they were not entitled to be doing so. In the congealed political landscape of 1965 only the working class stood out as a revolutionary force and even if it were to achieve anything, that in itself would be a miracle. From then on two pathways became clear. First was the pro-Chinese ideological movement centred around the École Normale Supérieure where Louis Althusser's lectures attracted the most brilliant students. These would provide the leadership of the future Maoist movement. Althusser's initial concern was to re-establish the dignity of Marxism, in contrast to the official PCF version as laid down by Garaudy. Even by 1965 young activists were already aware of the inconsistencies in the latter's writings. The more subtle Althusser took the line that it was possible to contradict official party positions via the use of theory without incurring expulsion. He attacked the party in a domain where it had never been previously challenged, namely dogma, suggesting that PCF ideology was in decay. He gave his élite pupils the unquestioned power which any avant-garde enjoys. They believed that they had a superiority and a legitimacy bestowed on them by their possession of knowledge and truth. This compensated for the feeling of illegitimacy or bastardy mentioned earlier. Althusser was thus no mere academic tutor but a highly subversive operator, aiming to influence the PCF and beyond that French public opinion at large. Althusser was a manipulator, who worked in the shadows, applying psychological pressure in the closed atmosphere of the École Normale Supérieure, manipulating his students and being manipulated by them. This is why he became a best seller, exerting enormous influence on the intelligentsia and the PCF. Even the JEC for all its Christian background felt obliged to study his writings.

From 1966-7 the pro-Chinese organised themselves seriously, as the Cultural Revolution gained momentum in China. This revolution was not at all understood, the main source of information on it being Robert Guillain's articles in *Le Monde*. From this source, which was in fact quite informative, the pro-Chinese concluded that it was a case of revolution within revolution. The Chinese had discovered what was lacking in France, that is a central power mobilising the masses to challenge its own self. This would have a marked effect on the small élite of the École Normale Supérieure and the intelligentsia in general and on other crucial areas of French society influenced by catholicism, namely some farmers' organisations and some unions. For a while this myth based on a false interpretation of what was happening in China was dominant.

Developments at Nanterre ran in parallel. If the UEC and the Maoists were two of the strands to be found in May 68 then the third was the anti-authoritarian strain to be found on that campus. Daniel Cohn-Bendit is a good representative of this. The influence of the Situationists on this movement prior to 1968 is less important in my view than has been suggested. They had grievances about their parents, about sex, about the university, about accommodation and about culture in general; their main weapon was mockery, all others having been exhausted. University reform had failed, the UNEF had run out of steam since the end of the Algerian war; all that was left was independent initiative and it was logical that this should take the form of provocative and insolent gestures.

There was nothing inevitable about May 68. Close analysis of day-to-day events suggests an extraordinary pattern of coincidence. To begin with the events were triggered off by a misunderstanding and it could be said that they were to a great extent caused by the then Gaullist government. If young people had not been so alienated by the low success rate in the universities, if they had been listened to by the government then I have no doubt that things might have turned out otherwise and the situation been defused. Even the world-wide anger which students shared over Vietnam, even the similarity of events at the Free University of Berlin and Nanterre need not necessarily have caused such an explosion. It was a complex affair of chance which only came about because certain random elements fused together.

There are several misunderstandings about 68, the first of which concerns youth. There were several varieties of youth in the streets in 68. The first was a species which none of the above-mentioned protagonists had taken into account - the youth of an apolitical pop culture. An example would be the 150 000 or so who attended the open air concert put on by Europe No. 1 in 1963 at Place de la Nation. These people shared none of the political preoccupations of the Latin Quarter students. The press also failed to pick up the significance of this phenomenon, simply referring to 'the over-excited atmosphere'. In an article in *Le Monde* Edgar Morin coined the phrase 'pop generation', pointing out that here was a force of youth with its own demands, here was a youth market with its own autonomy which we could not control and which would have an impact on us. Political ideology meant nothing to this relatively uncultured generation. It was not interested in anti-authoritarian demands *per se* but embarked on collective action purely as a means of furthering its own aspirations which were mainly individualistic; or this at least is what their behaviour in the street suggests.

But these uncultured youngsters would, as it were, infect the students. By their very freshness and violence they would reawaken long-forgotten capacities for rejection. Yet they needed leadership, for as the big demonstrations of the early days (5-6 May) showed, there was no one to give orders. There arose thus an *ad hoc* co-ordinating body, consisting mainly of veterans from the UEC and UNEF. These officers were four or five years older than their troops (a great age-gap at the time), and the relationship between the two was highly paradoxical. Here was my second paradox - a largely spontaneous mass movement, an authentic cultural or social movement being led by a revolutionary leadership that was frankly archaic. Most of the troops just wanted to smash the system or the parts of it that affected them; they hated university life, factory routine, sexual repression and the doctored news bulletins of the state broadcasting service in the France of the ageing de Gaulle. Yet they were led by quasi-professional revolutionaries from the time of the Algerian war.

Cohn-Bendit in some ways typifies this paradox, though he was only effective or indeed present during the first fortnight, having fled France thereafter to escape arrest. He could no longer bear the responsibility. He was acutely conscious of the contradiction between his own anti-authoritarian discourse and the authoritarian rôle which he was being asked to fulfil. He might well ask a 40,000-strong crowd of demonstrators which way they wanted to go, like a genuine libertarian; but he would still be expected to sort out the actual details of the procession in consultation with the police, along with other members of the co-ordinating committee. The leadership was, then, composed of men with an archaic political culture; their notions of representation owed much to 1848 and the Commune, and less to Lenin.

There were others more important than Cohn-Bendit, notably Krivine, whose JCR with its network of stewards played a key rôle in keeping order during demonstrations. Such leaders tried to give backbone to the movement, and some pattern can be discerned. It seems that they operated very much one day at a time. During the first week, the idea for a demonstration or other activity would emerge during the morning, and activity would peak around 7 or 8 p.m. At this moment someone would usually come up with another idea for the morrow. Thus the 'night of the barricades' came about as a result of an argument between Geismar (general secretary of the SNESup union, and a key figure in negotiations with the security forces), who did not want to escalate the protests for fear of violence, and others in the co-ordinating body who did, and whose views prevailed. In short this archaic avant-garde played a vital rôle which must be appreciated if we are to understand what happened after 1968, which was in fact a huge misunderstanding.

Another paradox is that the PCF was frightened. As pressure mounted in the streets, it tried to cut worker/student links and to slow down the spread of the general strike. This unrevolutionary behaviour helped make its leaders Marchais and Séguy among the most hated people in 1968. Marchais' failure to recognise that the 'German anarchist' Cohn-Bendit represented anything is typical. 1968 thus sped up a process which had been underway invisibly for a decade - the gradual divorce between the PCF and students and the intelligentsia.

Even more curious is the fact that despite all the strikes, the working class was nowhere to be found in May. The students only managed to link up with one sector of it, the *ouvriers spécialisés* (unskilled or semi-skilled workers). One good example is the penetration by the Maoists of the car factories at Flins. Among these young workers, many of them recently arrived from rural backgrounds, the students found a ready response, whereas the gates of Billancourt (the main Renault works in Paris) stayed closed to them. But there was no homogeneous working class *per se*, no bearer of an historic project of social transformation; this was another myth which began to crack visibly in 1968.

Finally 68 was a revolution which feared revolution, or at least its extreme forms. Despite the incredibly savage violence in the streets, there were virtually no deaths (perhaps five or six - a derisory number). On reflection this is no accident. The revolutionaries deliberately held back from taking life. Revolution may well have been a voyage of discovery, but it was not war, and they never felt that they were justified in killing for the sake of their ideas. Typical of this is the night when the Bourse was set on fire. The demonstrators had first resisted the temptation to attack the town hall, as was their original intention, because it was too well guarded and loss of life may have ensued. As the procession swung past the Ministry of Justice (which the minister and two aides hastily vacated by the rear exit), it was decided not to occupy the building - again because riot police and tanks would have been sent to clear it. Similar considerations deterred the protesters from invading the Elysée palace or, as they eventually returned to the Sorbonne, the Finance Ministry in the Rue de Rivoli; both objectives could easily have been taken with the numbers at the students' disposal, but the consequences in loss of life when the government hit back would have been too heavy.

So no attempt was made to 'seize the Winter Palace', to attempt the coup that would provoke civil war; although such had been the leaders' original intention, Leninists that they they were. Perhaps these highly politicised generals knew that their troops from a different generation would never follow. But at any rate this was when the generation that was a product of three wars finally renounced the temptation of war.

The last paradox is that May was neither reform nor revolution. Before the events debate had raged as to whether the system could be improved or whether it had to be replaced entirely. Yet in the heat of the events the question was never asked. Here is one lesson of May that perhaps deserves further reflection.

In many ways the leftist movements after 68 were profoundly regressive. They were obsessed with the idea that May had been a dress rehearsal for a new type of revolution, and they devoted themselves to preparing for this. The two main currents were equally archaic in their different ways, the Trotskyists with their classical Leninism and the Maoists with their parodies of warfare (liberating factories from the bosses, beating up foremen, etc.). These attitudes did have some effect on educated youth after 68, though the *lycéens* seem to have drawn from the events mainly anti-authoritarian and anti-hierarchical inspiration (as seen in the revolt by students at Louis-le-Grand against the system of preparatory classes for the *grandes écoles*). In contrast the PSU seems to have been a home for a less negative type of leftist.

So far as the women's movement goes, its development after 1968 has been misunderstood, for it was quite distinct from developments in the UK or Germany. For several years after 68 at least it was no mere corporatist movement, no vehicle for narrowly female demands. On the contrary its action had a more global dimension, running on to a wholesale critique of authority and women's relationship to politics and partisan activity. The women's assemblies at the Beaux-Arts in 1970-71 are typical of this wider approach to women's problems. The revolutionary homosexual movement began to emerge also after 68, seeking to construct a new politics based on an understanding of the relationship between politics and gender. Until about 1973 these movements practised decentralised grassroots politics without leaders; they had perhaps the best understanding of the mistakes made in 68 and more research could profitably be done on them.

It remains to ask when the spirit of May finally died. There are perhaps several moments along the way. The massacre at the 1972 Munich Olympics drew condemnation from all shades of French leftism, even from the Maoists who were not averse to violence. At bottom these activists were too politicised to follow their contemporaries in Germany and Italy into out and out terrorism. Present day terrorists like Action Directe are definitely not descended from 1968. In February 1973 when the Maoist militant Pierre Overney was shot at the Renault works when the Maoists were trying to raise the temperature of the class-war in the factory, the Gauche Proletarienne (the principal Maoist group) shrank from unleashing a violent riposte, much as the demonstrators had done on the night of the Bourse referred to above. When the Lip strike movement got under way in 1974 the leftists again backed away from violent confrontation, sensing that the Christian and new-left-influenced CFDT leadership of the movement was somehow more appropriate than they were. As the economic recession raged through 1974 and reformism progressed in the shape of the PS and even the beginning of the Giscardian septennate, the political and metaphysical universe of the 68 leftists was subject to increasing strain. Already such luminaries as André Glucksmann were taking their distance, and leftists moved variously towards religion, individual pleasure or the new right. The fall of Saigon and subsequent disappointment with the new régime simply completed a process that was already far advanced; the leftism of the 68 generation had breathed its last.

3. ÉCOLES, COLLÈGES AND LYCÉES[1] IN FRANCE SINCE 1968

ANTOINE PROST

Any account of the development of *écoles*, *collèges* and *lycées* since 1968 implies that 1968 is a watershed. Now if this is really the case for universities, it is very different for other levels of education. 1968 is not a genuine severance point and its influence cannot be ✳ determined unless it is put into a much wider context.

1968 IN PERSPECTIVE

In the sixties French education passed through a period of profound

---

[1] Translator's note: In the main French terms have been kept, with an equivalent indicated when the term first appears. An exception has been made for the names of schools and school-years, of which a brief explanation is given here.

École - primary; *collège* - lower secondary; *lycée* - upper secondary. The *école* has five successive levels: preparatory (*cours préparatoire*) for 6-7 year olds; elementary (*cours élémentaire*) 1 for 7-8 year olds; 2 for 8-9 year olds; middle (*cours moyen*) 1 for 9-10 year olds; 2 for 10-11 year olds.

Classes in secondary education are numbered, in ascending order from six to one, plus a final year (British equivalents are given in brackets): *6e* (1st), *5e* (2nd), *4e* (3rd),*3e* (4th), *seconde* (5th), *premiere* (6th), and *terminale* (6th II). The last three years are the province of the *lycée*, where preparation for the *baccalauréat* is carried out.

change.

A quantitative change first of all. Numbers rose substantially, as a consequence of three factors:

1. Growth of population, which resulted in school-age generations 30 per cent more numerous than those before the war. This factor is the only one relevant for primary education which has been compulsory for many years. This explains how from 3.3 million pupils in these classes (CP, CE1, CE2, CM1, CM2) in 1952-3, there was a rise to more than 4.8 million from 1963 to 1968 (these figures, like all those quoted in this chapter include state and private education together).

2. Pressure caused by social demand linked to the rise in the standard of living. Parents no longer needed their children to earn a living at the age of 14 or 15, and they wished them to prolong their education in order to gain better social positions. But the desire for advancement is not the only significant point. We must also bear in mind a change of habits which accounts in particular for the growth of nursery schools (1.3 million in 1959-60, 2 million in 1967-8, 2.6 million in 1976-7).

3. The deliberate policies of successive governments, obsessed by the lack of trained personnel. Around 1960, 5 to 6 000 engineers were trained annually whereas there was a need for double that number. And the same state of affairs existed at all levels of qualification. The development of education became a productive investment. Economic growth demanded a workforce with longer years of schooling - the ordinance of 6 January 1959 extended it to 16 years of age - in more general forms of training.

In consequence of these three factors, schooling was extended on average by three years and the numbers of *bacheliers* (those obtaining the *baccalauréat*) tripled, going, in general education alone, from under 50 000 in 1959 to 97 000 in 1965 and over 150 000 from 1973 onwards (see the appendix for further relevant statistics).

This growth took place in the midst of fundamental structural change. Before 1959, the organisation of French schools was characterised by the juxtaposition of two separate and competing networks: primary, primary/higher and primary/technical, on the one hand, and secondary on the other. The organisation which was introduced by the reforms of 1959 (Berthoin observation period at 6e and 5e) of 1963 (Fouchet, first cycle *collèges* 6e to 3e) and of 1965 (Fouchet, new organisation of the second cycle, *baccalauréats* A, B, C, D, E, technical *baccalauréats* F and G) were, in contrast, characterised by the superimposing of *écoles*, *collèges* and *lycées*: from age 6 to 11, all pupils attended the *écoles* (5 years): the *lycées* lost their primary classes. All pupils continued their education at the *collège* (4 years). After *collège*, they were orientated towards this or that course of study at *lycée* (3 years, except for shorter and earlier vocational courses) or towards 'working life'.

This reorganisation was carried out within a modified *carte scolaire* (school catchment area map) in the framework of mid-term planning. Single class primary schools were closed (14 000 schools abolished between 1960-61 and 1967-68). One vital reform which passed unnoticed was the ending of separation of boys and girls so as to group together numbers of pupils constituting classes. This allowed each class year to be entrusted, as far as possible to a different teacher. Primary schools lost their final year classes and their pupils aged twelve or more, who thereafter went to the *collèges*. 2 354 *collèges* were built between 1966 and 1975 (one *collège* for every working day!) for all first cycle pupils. Most *lycées* were thus deprived of their first cycle, and the space thus relieved allowed them to take many more pupils at *seconde, première* and *terminale*. Elsewhere new *lycées* were built, and former *lycées* became *collèges*. In short, a few years saw the complete restructuring of the French school system.

The unrest of the years before 1968 brought about a twofold questioning of education itself. On the one hand, its content seemed out of date, from the viewpoint of scientific advances, especially in linguistics and in mathematics, and an updating of these seemed essential. A beginning was made in 1963 with the forming of the Rouchette commission, for the teaching of French in primary schools, then of the Lichnérowicz commission for mathematics at all levels of education. Further, less radical updating, was carried out in physics and natural sciences. Besides, teaching methods seemed archaic. Schooling the mass of the population by pedagogical methods, thought proper at the turn of the century for middle-class children, seemed a futile endeavour. The democratisation of education, since this is at the heart of the matter, demanded new teaching methods which would appeal more to the pupils' own motivation, to their activities and to their own life.

This movement inspired experiments in *tiers-temps pédagogique* (three cluster curriculum) in some primary schools. It was a question of finding more flexible timetables than the very strict schedules (grids) of 20 or 30 minutes which were normally applied and of allowing more time for physical education and for the pupils' own activities. Affairs were not so far advanced in the *collèges* and *lycées* ; however the idea that thorough changes were essential was gaining ground. Broad sectors of public opinion supported this reforming tendency. It culminated in March 1968 with the Amiens conference. To hear so eminent a civil servant as Roger Grégoire state that pupils' lack of enthusiasm could be explained in three ways, gives a feeling of the 'mood of the time' a few weeks before the events.

> Attempts are made to pass on to them a cultural heritage to which they are indifferent, it is passed on via models which they reject...by means of an hierarchical system, intolerable both to their common sense and their dignity.[2]

THE IMMEDIATE IMPACT OF 1968

1968 was merely a rather long strike for the *écoles* and *collèges*. It was a different matter for the *lycées*. Lengthy discussions took place amongst pupils, and between teachers and pupils, where demands were made for new freedoms and a more open-ended educational contract. In all these general assemblies, authority was questioned, that of school heads by teachers, that of teachers by pupils. *Lycée* action committees were set up. Yet overall there was nothing to compare with the whirlwind that swept away the universities.

The first effect of 1968 was to make ridiculous, and hence impossible to maintain, the petty restrictions with a symbolic value: pupils began to smoke, girls were able to use cosmetics or wear trousers without being reprimanded; some teachers stopped wearing

---

[2] Association d'étude pour l'expansion de la recherche scientifique, *Pour une école nouvelle, Actes du colloque, Amiens 1968* (Paris: Dunod,1968) p. 76.

a tie, others started to *tutoyer*[3] their pupils. Outward signs of respect disappeared, where they had still existed: pupils ceased to wait for a sign from the teacher before sitting down and some experienced teachers were clearly so disconcerted by the *lycée* pupils' ease of manner that they asked for transfer to a *collège*.

Less obvious than this change in atmosphere, a more serious change affected discipline and the running of the *lycées* : the system of penalties and punishments disappeared without either formal decision or even discussion. It seemed thereafter unthinkable to punish the pupils by impositions or detentions. There was now one single though serious penalty - expulsion, temporary or permanent, and it could not be used for minor offences. Teachers could no longer rely on the administration: even more than in the past, each individual had to cope with classroom difficulties.

De Gaulle had called on Edgar Faure to become Education Minister, relying on his intelligence, flexibility and diplomacy to get the universities going again - a task in which even he seemed unlikely to succeed. Edgar Faure was probably the only politician to have analysed 1968 in terms such that many participants recognised themselves in his analysis. He explained the events as an absurd resistance by archaic principles and methods to the new aspirations of the young. Any attempt to return to the *status quo ante* would have anticipated further difficulties. On the contrary, it was vital to speed up reforms too long delayed. May 1968 thus proved the justice of the reformers' case. It did not bring to birth the idea of more reforms, save perhaps in the universities, but it hastened the fulfilment of reforms already in the pipeline.

In the primary schools this related to the *tiers-temps pédagogique* (order of 7 August 1969). The weekly timetable was reduced from 30 to 27 hours, with the abolition of Saturday afternoon classes.These 27 hours were sub-divided into large groups, thus avoiding a splitting up of subjects into sub-headings (reading, writing, grammar, etc.). 10 hours for French, 5 hours for arithmetic, 6 hours for sport and physical education, and 6 hours also for *activité d'éveil* (awakening activities), this term describing new teaching methods for history, geography, the natural sciences, drawing and singing.

---

[3] Translator's note: *Tutoyer* - meaning to use the second person singular 'tu', rather than the more formal plural 'vous'.

The plan was attractive. Yet unwilling primary school teachers could not be forced to devote one hour a day to physical education. Besides, they scarcely knew how to go about it, and had as a rule no facilities other than the school playground where it was better to make no noise, if other classes had to work. This part of *tiers-temps* was thus often cut out. *Activités d'éveil* for their part soon gave rise to resistance and sarcasm. Even the aim of arousing pupils' curiosity, of teaching them to think on the basis of their observations seemed suspect, if not subversive: many primary school teachers and a substantial part of public opinion were happier to see pupils still learning history and geography and writing out fair copies in their exercise books. A subject of dispute from the outset and on principle, the *activités d'éveil* were also difficult to undertake successfully. To have pupils learn résumés requires authority and continuity, but little imagination; routine will suffice. Innovation demands far more. The *activités d'éveil* required teachers who were imaginative but strict, capable of perceiving what could catch their pupils' interest, and sufficiently skilful and persistent to make them cover the whole progression leading from wonderment to knowledge. They were ill-prepared for it, and received little help. What is surprising in these conditions is not that weariness conquered in the long run, but that so many primary school teachers (one third? a half?) attempted the endeavour. It is not possible to say what the results were in the absence of serious enquiry. The widely held opinion which blames their failure has more to do with conviction than with objective information. No one knows exactly how the teachers used the one hour per day allotted to *activités d'éveil*.

In the *collèges* and *lycées*, Edgar Faure's first measure was to put the introduction to Latin back to 4ᵉ. At other times, this would have seemed like sacrilege, but it incurred no opposition in 1968. Secondly, a decree of 8 November 1968 reformed the schools' administration by creating administrative councils made up, one third of employees' representatives, one third parents' and pupils' representatives, one sixth providing for co-opted outside personalities, so that the administration had only one sixth of the votes. This same decree put two parents' and two pupils' representatives on the class councils. These teachers' meetings chaired by the school head, meet at the end of every term and give a judgement on each pupil, with a decision as to *orientation* (career guidance) at the year's end. This measure immediately gave rise to controversy. Those in favour made the case for openness and co-operation with parents, its enemies took the view that teachers should be able to discuss these matters only amongst colleagues, to allow for total frankness. At all events, these debates emphasised the power exerted in reality by the class councils. It was not surprising if the conflict between the will for change and resistance to it crystallised around their creation.

Other, more symbolic factors permitted further manifestations of conflict, for example, the arrangements of pupils' desks within the classroom. A teacher in favour of change would sometimes begin his hour's teaching by having them arranged in a circle or a square, at the beginning of the following hour a traditionalist colleague would have the desks put back in parallel lines. A circular of 6 January 1969 provided more grist to the mill, by suppressing termly compositions and rankings, and in its recommendation of the replacement of traditional marking for 0 to 20 by a more general form of marking, A, B, C, D, E. This made the calculation of averages very difficult and was a frontal attack on many teachers who were genuinely convinced of the absolute accuracy of their marking, sometimes even to half a mark. ('Sir, when I put 7½ this means that the work is worth 7½!') A vague guerilla war set teachers marking in letters and others still using numbers against each other in the same classes. Rankings still had an undercover existence: 'If there had been a ranking, this is the place you would have had,' the teacher would say.

The open division of the teaching body on these pedagogical questions is certainly one of 1968's major consequences. The previous consensus was only apparent: conflicts existed already, over Latin, for example. But they remained unclear, since every teacher defended him/herself from other people's criticisms, by themselves carefully avoiding criticisms which were too overt. May 68 caused these divisions to explode in the light of day. Traditionalists felt themselves to be aggressively treated by reformers and became aggressive in their turn. In some common rooms the atmosphere was tense, and long-term colleagues stopped greeting each other or shaking hands, because of opposing positions taken up during the strike. Furthermore, it was possible and logical to describe pedagogical differences in political terms: putting tables in a circle was done by 'leftists' and marking out of 20 by 'reactionaries'. Matters of professional choice which could have seemed infinitely unimportant thus symbolised a choice of society.

The wave of educational reform was permanently weakened by this assimilation. Before 1968, as was seen, it gained ground constantly: these were fashionable ideas, and those who did not share them began to feel outmoded. The events began by playing into the reformers' hands, and brought their ideas to power. But they gave them a subversive connotation which they had not had. Suddenly, they provided respectable arguments for the supporters of the *status quo;* opposition to reforms meant refusal of disorder, of the 'dog's dinner' of the revolution.

This became clear when it came to drawing conclusions from the work of the Rouchette commission on the teaching of French at primary school. New syllabuses had been drawn up and had been tried experimentally from 1967 onwards. In October 1970, a 'plan of renewal' was ready. It took account of modern linguistics, of the opinions of those involved and the results of the experiment. A decision had to be taken, and there was uproar. The plan introduced the idea of language registers, and adopted a descriptive viewpoint, not a purely normative one; there was no longer one sole 'proper usage' of the language by the 'educated adult', but several, according to environment, moments and situation of communication. The right took up arms against the scheme with political arguments. The necessary pedagogical and theoretical retraining would consist of ideological indoctrination. Quite seriously Pierre Gaxotte denounced in *Le Figaro* a systematic endeavour by the communists to destroy the French language.[4] The *Académie Française* came down against the scheme, and it was adjourned. This meant that questions such as whether the word *bagnole* (jalopy) can be used in class, whether there should be structural exercises in French or dictation were not technical questions, or questions of educational method, but indicated a choice of society.

EBB-TIDE

In such a situation, the political conjuncture made an ebb inevitable. De Gaulle left the Elysée, where he was replaced by Georges

---

[4] *Le Figaro* 30 November-1 December, 1970.

Pompidou. As a classics *agrégé* (holder of the competitive teaching exam, the *agrégation*), he was far more in sympathy with traditional forms of secondary education. Edgar Faure was replaced by Olivier Guichard (1969-1972) who limited the reaction with enlightened and unflappable liberalism; Joseph Fontanet (1972-74) endeavoured to reconcile order with dynamism. Lastly, René Haby (1974-8) bore down on the education system with a heavy coating of bureaucracy.

Each and all had of course to manage the heritage of 1968, and of previous years. For example, they completed the introduction of modern mathematics at all levels of education. The building of *collèges* was continued. J. Fontanet had put before public opinion an ambitious plan to reform the *collèges* when G. Pompidou died. R. Haby gave it up, and his own reform of 1975 was limited to the acceptance of 10 years development by merging the *collèges* and by making a definitive distinction between the three levels, *écoles*, *collèges* and *lycées*.

However, from his accession O. Guichard had had to abandon some of his predecessor's measures. He re-established the introduction of Latin at 5ᵉ. He allowed the school's administrative councils to decide that there would be neither parents nor pupils on the *conseils de classe*. He re-established marking out of 20, but only in examination classes. Clearly he did not regard a return to the *status quo ante* as a solution; he resisted this as much as he could and appointed a committee of wise men, chaired by a former minister, Louis Joxe, to suggest reforms to him. The measures it suggested took their inspiration from the pedagogical trends characteristic of the years before 1968. J. Fontanet who received them, retained only two, a relaxation in obligatory teaching (pedagogical) duties, which soon fell into disuse, and the creation in all schools of CDI where pupils could consult books and periodicals.

R. Haby was more authoritarian and less open than his predecessors. Yet his reputation is very different, owing to his reform of the history syllabuses. He in fact decided to include in the same educational basket, history, geography and an introduction to the social sciences, in first cycle classes. This reform which infuriated the specialists was given no chance: put into operation at 6ᵉ at the beginning of the school year in 1977, it was castigated as early as 1980 in a vast conference, under the auspices of media personalities such as Alain Decaux, as the cause of a reduction in the standard achieved by pupils at *seconde* who however had received

all their education from the old more specialised syllabuses. From
that moment public opinion placed R. Haby amongst the
'pedagogical' ministers. This was to consider only one part of his
activity, and the least important one at that. In all other areas, he was
the standard bearer of a return to orderliness, and of a retreat from
progress. He explained that pedagogical innovation had gone too
far.[5] He reformed the schools' councils to strengthen the weight of
the administration in them, he defined strictly the obligations of
service required of teachers, so as to have the means of imposing
sanctions on wildcat strikes. Above all, he stifled initiative by having
all decisions taken at ministerial level. His successor, the former
Chairman of Renault, Christian Beullac (1978-81), less sure of
himself, since he did not know the national education system, would
seem to have been more of a liberal and less of a centraliser. But
from R. Haby to C. Beullac, there was the same swing of the
pendulum from innovation to tradition: year after year, primary
school syllabuses were reviewed and corrected: *tiers-temps* was
abandoned, and the teaching of history as such was brought back
into the *activités d'éveil*.[6]

This ebb tide, at first tentative then more deliberate at ministerial
level, can basically be explained by the change in public opinion.
With the economic crisis, unemployment increased. It was no longer
the time for innovations, which worried parents who were on the
contrary anxious for reassurance about their children's future and
favourably disposed to old-style education. A change in the climate
of opinion, with the rise of economic liberalism in western countries
was accompanied by a restoration of law and order values, as well as
a sometimes cynical discourse on the virtues of competition and
selection.

More profoundly, the climate changed in the schools. After 1968
in the wake of the pedagogical current of the sixties, new types of
teaching had been developed: presentations by pupils, projects,
group work, independent work etc.These forms of teaching had
allowed some teachers to deal successfully with more argumentative

---

[5] See R. Haby interview, 'On est allé trop loin dans certaines reformes', *Le
Monde de l'Éducation* (May 1976).

[6] On history teaching in primary school,see Jean-Noël Luc, 'Une réforme
difficile: un siecle d'histoire a l'école élémentaire (1887-1985)', *Historiens
et géographes*, 306 (September - October 1985), 149-207.

pupils. But they became less effective, as the new generations were
not so much argumentative as disillusioned. Teaching difficulties
were increasing. The new syllabuses were more abstract and more
difficult. The new pupils had little desire to learn, coming as they did
from a milieu farther removed from scholastic culture, were growing
up in a media-powered society where scholastic knowledge had lost
its credit. Many other distractions, music, films, boyfriends,
girlfriends, appealed to them. Also they were less docile, as they had
been brought up in a less rigid and less restrictive fashion. Lastly,
the armoury of penalties and punishments had disappeared. The
problem of how to prevail upon and if necessary force pupils to
work became more crucial than ever for the *collèges*. It also reached
the *lycées*, long protected by selection.

The constraints of the school system provided one solution. The
only thing needed was the removal of the lazy and incompetent
pupils: the fear of the world outside was the beginning of wisdom.
Now it had been necessary to put in place in the sixties and then
more rigorously from 1977 onwards, *orientation* (career guidance)
procedures precisely to direct pupils towards the differing sections of
the second cycle, long or short. At the outset, this was a pedagogical
exercise since it was a matter of discovering the course of studies
most appropriate to the pupils' tastes, interests and abilities, not only
to their results. However the different sections did not have the same
outlets, and thus there was a hierarchy from section C to section A in
general education and from the electronic sections to those
concerned with panel beating, in vocational education. This
hierarchy, perfectly known by everyone, increased the demand for
'good' sections, and lessened that for 'bad' ones. Now the existence
of the 'bad' ones meant that they had to be filled, and all candidates
could not be put in the 'good' ones. Allowing free rein to the law of
supply and demand did not seem to allow the vast numbers of pupils
to be managed in the best way, given the existing possibilities of
taking them on: *orientation* therefore became a means of regulating
administratively the vast numbers of pupils.

At the end of *collège* (*3ᵉ*) families are asked which education
section they want for their children in the next year. The *conseil de
classe* gives an opinion on these wishes. Negotiation is then
undertaken. Once a decision is arrived at, families are allowed a
period of time within which they can appeal, as in law, to a higher
authority. Identical procedures exist for the end of *5ᵉ*, and since 1981

for *seconde*. Thus at the end of each year pupils in a class have three
possibilities: to go into the higher class, or the one which they have
asked for - the ideal solution; to do the same year again - the lesser
of two evils; lastly and to be avoided at all costs - *orientation* into a
class which they have not chosen. This is certainly an effective
mechanism - particularly so in a period of cut-throat competition for
employment.

Contrary to the views of ill-informed best-selling authors, far
from being weakened, selection has thus been massively
strengthened in French education. Two facts bear witness to this.
The first is pupil age, since this is one of the objective pieces of
information on which *orientation* can be based: given comparable
results a younger pupil in general receives more advantageous
advice than an older one. The growth of selection has thus brought
about a lowering in the age of the *lycée* pupil. The proportion of
pupils under 16 on the 1st of January of their 'seconde' year has
increased from about 45 per cent in 1965 to 62 per cent in 1981. The
second - a sign of the intensifying of scholastic competition - is the
dramatic increase in the numbers of those repeating a year -
especially in those classes which end in a choice made through
orientation. Between 1975-6 and 1985-6, the rate of repeating a year
has risen from 6.5 per cent to 16.6 per cent for *5e* from 7.3 per cent
to 14 per cent for *3e*, from 11.4 per cent to 17.7 per cent for *2e*, from
7 per cent to 12.7 per cent for *première*. The final year, crowned by
the *baccalauréat*, is now repeated by one pupil in five (19.6 per cent).

This intensified selection has a number of effects. Firstly, it
creates tension between families and schools. Parents in France are
not free in their choice of *collège*, which depends on the location of
the parents' home and the primary school attended. This is known as
sectorisation, the existence of geographical sectors which limit
recruitment. With the *collège*, then from *collège* to *lycée*, and at the
lycée, they are subject to *orientation*. Naturally they query
orientation decisions which they do not like, and obviously such a
vast bureaucratic machine is not perfect. For its decisions to be
accepted, the forecast of a pupil's future school career must have
minimal credibility. Now this is impossible, as too much depends on
the pupil, on his/her motivation, involvement in his/her studies, and
on the will to work. Parents, particularly those in the teaching
profession, who know their way around the school system, can find
ways of escaping from the limits of *sectorisation* and *orientation*. In

any case private education heedless of *orientation* decisions, provides a second chance for the latter's victims. This is the safety valve which makes it possible for people to bear the administrative management of pupils' fate in schools. Any alteration would be an attack on all those whose children run the risk of suffering from *orientation*.

It should now be easier to understand why there was such a large-scale attack on Savary's private education bill, whilst 84 per cent of the French no longer attend mass even once a month. Mobilisation against the Savary bill went far beyond Catholic circles and parents of pupils in private education (16 per cent of parents). 47 per cent of parents with pupils in the state system were opposed to the bill. They did not consider private education to be better than that of the state, since for the time being they were putting their faith in the latter. However they felt that it was important for private education to exist as a means of escaping from the constraints of the public sector.

In the second place, the maxim, 'work, or face *orientation*' is not completely effective. It is valid for those pupils who have something to lose, for those who manage to keep up with the leaders. Those who drop out, for one reason or another, who give up and are resigned to losing out, see no further point in working: in any case their doom, both scholastic and social, seems sealed. Dunces they are, dunces they will remain, until they are thrown out. In psychological terms, this is serious: how can we create a positive image of ourselves, in adolescence, when we have to regard ourselves as failed pupils, pushed towards types of training, which are poorly regarded and which have no outlets? In a situation where they feel themselves rejected, these pupils who have nothing to lose because they are losers already, bring into the classroom aggressive and disruptive behaviour, which upsets the work of the school to a greater degree the more numerous they are. The situation has become serious in some *collèges*. At the conclusion of their enquiry, Hamon and Rotman calculated that one third of *collège* classes have daily to contend with serious difficulties.[7]

Lastly, the very efficiency of the system is not beyond doubt. It makes a large number of pupils work but in what way? *Bachotage* (cramming for the *baccalauréat*), an age-old evil, is more rampant than ever. It is this very fact that explains the curious survival of one

---

[7] H. Hamon, P. Rotman, *Tant qu'il y aura des Profs* (Paris: Seuil, 1984).

of E. Faure's reforms: doing away with the composition. It might have been expected that this reform, appearing lax, would be repealed with the return to marking out of 20. Not so. Even before 1968, the headmaster's annual reports from the Jeanson de Sailly *lycée* made it clear that compositions were no longer enough to make the pupils work. Once per term was too little; it was better to increase supervision exercises and written questions. This is far better way of keeping *lycée* pupils up to scratch, because every mark counts in the average on which the *conseil de classe* gives an opinion. People certainly work in the French education system, but they work for marks, examinations and for *orientation*. Intellectual curiosity, imagination, creativity, thoughtfulness, in short, culture; do they come in as a bonus? It would perhaps be better to take this point into more serious consideration.

BETWEEN SAVARY AND CHEVENEMENT

The French left has always regarded state education as one of its great causes. It is thus surprising that it came to power without proper information on these problems. At all events it cannot be said that the actions of the socialist minister Alain Savary were dictated by his party political prejudices. Aware of having a particularly difficult domain to manage he spent a great deal of time in the study of its problems. His ministry is characterised by several reports, on the training of personnel, on *collèges*, on *lycées*, on school management. The effort put into such considerations cannot be denied.

In his day to day management A. Savary was guided by a very keen awareness of the limits of ministerial action. Paraphrasing one of his critics, the sociologist Michel Crozier, he might have said, 'education is not changed by decree'. Genuine in his wish to decentralise, he wished to give initiative back to the local levels of the education system, to the *recteurs*, but above all to the schools. If dealt with at the grass roots, problems would be better resolved, by those with the greatest knowledge of them. The ministry's task was to establish an outline framework to decide on the general direction to be followed, and to set things in motion. But it was typical of this management that one of his principal measures was to create in each *académie, missions* (delegations) concerned with the continuous

training of teachers, and that those officials entrusted with these
missions were left largely free to develop the training which seemed
to them best adapted to the needs of those for whom they were
intended. At ministerial level, these *missions* were co-ordinated in a
flexible manner, and not attached to a specific directorate.

The second great measure of A. Savary, in secondary education
was the modernisation of the *collèges*. Something certainly had to be
done, as the problems were serious. Louis Legrand was asked to
produce a report. As director of the research sector at the *Institut
pédagogique national*, he had in that capacity conducted unrivalled
research in about twenty *collèges*. J. Fontanet had taken his
inspiration from that research; R. Haby had ignored it and C. Beullac
had withdrawn L. Legrand from these tasks. Entrusting him with a
report was an indication of a specific approach. In fact the report
took up experimental ideas. There was a basic proposal to make
educational structures more flexible, particularly by the creation of
groupes de niveau (equal ability settings) in French, mathematics,
and modern languages. Controversy arose in a secondary proposal,
that of *tutorat* (form tutor). This term unhappily borrowed from
English indicated a teacher's individual responsibility for pupils to
guide them in their work. It seemed to be thought, because L.
Legrand proposed a choice of tutor by the pupils, that it was a moral
and emotional responsibility, and parents were stirred up against this
attempt to steal their children from them.

L. Legrand's plan was received as if it were a great new reform. It
was a 'revolutionary' plan. The way in which it was brought into
effect, and which annoyed its more radical originator, betrayed a
very different approach. It was not imposed; *collèges* were asked if
they were willing to undertake it, and what their own plans were
within the report's wider framework. Some assistance was reserved
for those *collèges* willing to undertake modernisation. A specific
effort as to training was made for these teachers despite the unions
who demanded this training for all. In short, there was no question of
forcing schools who did not feel the need to adopt new methods
which they would not have applied well. Rather, attempts were made
to arouse a wish for change at the grass roots and to help those who
were willing to try the venture.

The same spirit is to be found in the working party on the *lycées*
which I chaired. The method was even more explicit, as it began
with a public consultation whose transparency guaranteed its good

faith. The proposals of this group were numerous but modest and were not applied. In this sense, there was no Savary reform for the *lycées*. They aimed essentially to give more initiative to the schools in the definition of pedagogical duties and the organisation of pupils' work.

A vast surge of opinion arose against this policy. Whilst selection had never been as strong, laxity was thought to hold sway in education. It was claimed that primary school teachers no longer taught anything, indeed that they were forbidden to teach anything. A dishonest book, *Le Poisson rouge dans le Perrier,* sold 60 000 copies.It mentioned nursery school exercises as being done at primary level, and school book prefaces as being official instructions, whilst in passing it treated Piaget as an ayatollah. It was claimed that the standard was going down catastrophically. Since the only existing scale of measurement, the tests used by the army for all young Frenchmen, show that it is in fact going up, proof to the contrary was not and could not be offered. In short it was felt that there had to be a reaction against the educational theorists whose innovations were hastening education to its doom.

The right was in the van of this campaigning. This included the political right and *Le Figaro*, also *Le Point* and *L'Express*, the educational right, with the autonomous unions, and the *société des agrégés*, still led by Guy Bayet. Extra help, probably decisive, came from the extreme left wing intellectual circles in Paris. Those who had been Maoists and Trotskyists on the eve of 1968, given their doctrinaire and authoritarian mentality, could not accept such a degree of self-government and consequent margins of error surrendered to lowly agents in decentralising measures. French academics have besides always tended to think that the purpose of education was the reproduction of their own kind, and to be alarmed if they did not find enough of these in the classrooms. To counteract such a campaign, a systematic campaign would have been necessary. Now A.Savary was not a man of the media and his relations with the press were not of the best. Opinion was won over, preoccupied as it was by the recession and unemployment.

This campaign reached its climax at the same time as the rising against the Savary bill on private education. Denigration of state education threw into relief the necessity of private education. People did not see that, paradoxically, A. Savary's policy, and in particular his insistence on individual attention for pupils, aimed to remedy the usual reproaches levelled by parents at state education. A. Savary's successor, Jean-Pierre Chevènement made no attempt to resist this movement. He put himself at its head, to turn it round. From conviction as well as from opportunism, he took on the role of defender of high standards, tradition and the authority of the teacher. His press conference of September 1984 at the beginning of the school year won him the applause of the entire right. For G. Bayet, he was the first minister for 16 years to have used the language of reason. This meant that he appeared to public opinion as the minister who was bringing to a close the period opened by 1968. He had blown the whistle on playtime.

It is however necessary to distinguish J-P. Chevènement's rhetoric from his action. The rhetoric was resolutely old-fashioned, especially in his early days. Glorifying the myth of the school of J. Ferry, he was much closer to the authoritarian Empire.As a Jacobin and a centraliser, J-P. Chevènement genuinely did not perceive the need for pedagogical initiatives. For him, difficulties originated only from the withdrawal of those teachers who had lost faith and had given up teaching the entire syllabus, with all its demands. All the pressure of the SNI-PEGC was needed before the new instructions for primary school explicitly acknowledged freedom of teaching methods. New syllabuses and instructions were fashioned for *écoles, collèges*, and *lycées*, and with a happy and well-received initiative they were published in paperback. The learning of the *Marseillaise* was re-established in schools, as was the examination of *brevet des collèges* certificate.

Heightened by symbolic measures, this rhetoric of normality, of the return to authority, of competition in 'republican élitism' was immediately understood by many *lycée* heads or inspectors and many initiatives were stifled as early as September 1984. But this rhetoric which denied the left's pedagogical traditions, from F. Buisson to Langevin-Wallon, via P. Lapie, or E. Herriot, not forgetting J. Zay, was what public opinion was waiting for. It has raised the image of state education and won for its author real popularity.

J-P. Chevènement's action was much more subtle. He gave to the general inspectorate a weight which C. Beullac would have thought excessive. He buried the long-maturing plans of his predecessor which would have culminated in, for example, the training of *lycée* teachers. He was however forced to continue the modernisation of the *collèges*, in default of any other solution. He merely generalised it administratively, thus departing from the originality of the earlier approach. *Collège* teachers gained from this a reduction in hours of service independently of their commitment to any modernisation. On the ground, some officials, *recteurs*, heads of schools, *chefs de mission académique à la formation* (area professional training officers) had acquired habits which they did not lose. Overall, the most significant of J-P. Chevènement's measures were on the one hand the creation of a vocational *baccalauréat* which modified profoundly the purpose of that education, with relatively new methods, and on the other hand, the announcement of the objective of 80 per cent *bacheliers* by the year 2 000, an unrealistic proposal which was not based on any serious study and would seem surprising on the part of so enthusiastic a defender of standards, but which had an irreversible effect on public opinion.

Between A. Savary and J-P. Chevènement the most fundamental difference concerns the means of ensuring the coherence and efficiency of the school system. With J-P. Chevènement, as with his right-wing successor René Monory, its regulation is dominated by a system of explicit pedagogical and administrative norms. The minister's task is to dictate these norms and to have them respected, thanks to the assistance of the hierarchy. With A. Savary a new form of regulation was sketched out based on interaction between the participants, on information and on training. Perhaps for the first time, those working in education were not treated like a regiment. Underlying this novel mode of administering the educative system lay the conviction that it is impossible to have entirely appropriate norms, and even more so to have them abided by. Teachers have an indomitable desire for freedom and their rôle will - fortunately - never be reduced to the mere carrying out of instructions: it is much better to take note of this in order to seek out how national cohesion may be arrived at.

Put in this way, the management of A. Savary was the more modern, but it is against him that opinion has given its verdict. Certainly he was not successful with the media, but this explanation is inadequate; more numerous and more skilful press attachés would probably have changed nothing. We are not here in the domain of reason, but of passion. School education is not only a world of intellectual apprenticeship for the French, but one of national identity. In underlining the need for change whilst leaving initiative to those involved A. Savary upset the school's image; in this way he caused disquiet not only on the subject of its efficiency but also on the perpetuation of a 'French identity'. By the strong affirmation of his authority and presenting to the French the image, albeit sometimes caricatural of their most traditional education, J-P. Chevènement has reassured them about their school and about themselves. There lies probably the crux of the education problem in France, as suggested by the excessive importance it gives to national history. Nor does this assist in the adaptation of an educational system to the problems of a profoundly changing society.

APPENDIX

Table 3.1. NUMBER OF PUPILS/STUDENTS
(Figures given in thousands)

	1958/9	1960/1	1975/6	1984/5
Primary				
State	869.5		2,591.2	2,527.1
State and private	1,174.4		3,165.6	3,180.2
Secondary (long)				
State	326.3		735.2	887.1
State and private	421.9		960.8	1,160.3
Secondary (short)				
State	256.2		576.9	623.1
State and private	383.2		746.3	817.3
CPGE and STS		29.1	81.5	151.4
École de commerce et d'ingenieurs		26.1	44.7	69.8
Universities		214.7	805.4	942.7

Table 3.2. PERCENTAGES OF SCHOOL AGE
POPULATION RECEIVING EDUCATION

Age	1958/9	1975/6	1984/5
14	68.4	97.2	97.7
15	53.0	91.7	95.3
16	43.5	69.5	86.8
17	27.7	49.9	75.9
18	16.9	25.2	51.5

4. STUDENT PROTEST: 1968 AND 1986 COMPARED

ROGER DUCLAUD-WILLIAMS

INTRODUCTION

In the last days of November and the early days of December 1986 the world witnessed a reawakening of student protest in Paris. Suddenly and unexpectedly hundreds of thousands of normally politically apathetic students were galvanised into action. The immediate cause of their discontent was a bill being prepared by the minister with responsibility for the universities, Alain Devaquet.

The bill was primarily intended to repeal the Savary law on the universities of January 1984. Many politicians, students, and trade-unionists on the right had campaigned in 1983 and 1984 against the adoption of this socialist legislation but had not been able finally to obstruct the bill's passage. It was clear, as soon as a right wing majority in the national assembly had been elected under the leadership of Jacques Chirac in the spring of 1986 that a bill of some sort on university questions was in preparation.

There was considerable disagreement within the government as to the form which the new legislation should take. The more radical right wing faction within the majority hoped to make a substantial move in the direction of a more selective approach by universities to the recruitment of their students, higher fees, and a dismantling of the system of nationally guaranteed university qualifications in favour of the system in which each university would be responsible for awarding its own degrees. These radical critics of the existing

43

French university system were also hoping for a reform of the internal arrangements for university self-government with a view to considerable simplification and a reduced role for students and junior staff and an increased and preponderant role for teachers of professorial rank. Devaquet himself, although a member of the RPR, generally considered to be the most right wing of the three elements making up the majority coalition, was in fact a moderate on university questions. He agreed that the arrangements for university self-government needed considerable simplification and was also ready to go some way towards satisfying the demands of the radicals on student selection but he set his face firmly against any substantial rise in university fees and was not in favour of any move away from national towards university qualifications.

Student protest culminated in three massively supported demonstrations on 27 November and the 4 and 10 December. During the weekend following the demonstration of 4 December it was first announced that all those clauses in the bill to which the students objected would be withdrawn and that Devaquet was handing in his resignation; finally it was reported that the bill would be withdrawn in its entirety and also that the government would not be proceeding for the time being with its proposed reforms of the nationality code and the plan to privatise some prisons. Spokesmen for the student protestors had objected to both of these measures, particularly the former. Students could reasonably claim total victory with respect to the proposed university reforms and could also reasonably argue that they had inflicted a serious blow to the prestige of Jacques Chirac and his government.

This chapter does not seek to trace the history of those organisations which have sought to represent students in the period between 1968 and 1986; instead, without ignoring some of the more important events of the intervening years, it seeks to use a comparison of the movements of 68 and 86 to throw light on the changing character of student politics. There might seem to be some danger of distortion involved in concentrating attention on two clearly exceptional periods eighteen years apart. The justification for proceeding in this manner is that the routine of student politics is less important than the exceptional and unpredictable outbursts of student anger which occur from time to time. In the long periods of relative calm which lie between these outbursts the political activity of the small minority of active students is concentrated in factional infighting within the two major student unions. During these periods of calm, governments and public opinion pay little attention to the organised expression of student views. The student movement acquires real political importance when these contending groups of student activists are linked to the normally inactive mass of students. It would seem that such a link can only be established when students feel that their academic future is threatened by some shift in government policy. This was certainly the case in 1973, 1976, 1983 and 1986.

The comparison undertaken here will be organised under four headings. We shall first consider the organisation and character of the student movement at the moment of maximum mobilisation. Secondly we shall examine the links, or lack of links, between students and the organised or unorganised working class. Thirdly we shall examine the impact of student protest on government and regime and finally we shall seek briefly to place student protest in the general context of political protest in France. It is clear that any proper understanding of the importance of students as political actors leads one well beyond the realm of higher education and throws considerable light on the changing character of the French political system as a whole.

STUDENT AIMS AND ORGANISATION

It is possible to point to a number of striking parallels in the student politics of 1968 and 86. At both periods in time the student movement, if we may use this expression, was highly fragmented and characterised by an extremely sharp division between the activist élite and the much less active majority. With respect to the separation mentioned above we may note that the claimed membership of the two largest student organisations, UNEF(ID) and UNEF(SE), makes a total of nearer 5 than 10 per cent of the student body.[1] (None of the three right wing student organisations claims any significant membership.)

---

[1] For UNEF-ID see *Le Monde*, 16 February 1982. For UNEF-SE see *Le Monde*, 31 May-1 June, 1981. *Le Monde*, 2-3 March 1986 reports a vote of UNEF-ID 37 per cent and UNEF-SE 23 per cent but these figures are incomplete.

The student turnout in university elections during the 1970s and early 1980s was invariably between 25 and 30 per cent. The following figures on the distribution of the student vote present a sorry picture of fragmentation along ideological and disciplinary lines. These figures refer to elections taking place in December of 1982, (later election results give an incomplete picture because many of those universities with more right wing students and staff fail to organise elections under the 1984 Savary law): independent candidates, 37 per cent; candidates standing in the defence of particular local or disciplinary interests, 10 per cent; UNEF(SE) (communist controlled), 21 per cent; UNEF(ID) (control shared between Trotskyists and socialists), 19 per cent; CELF (Giscardian), 3 per cent.[2] These results are based on a 25 per cent student turnout. If we compare this picture with poll data for 1986 on the partisan distribution of student preferences, we can see that the sharp separation between organised and unorganised opinion referred to above emerges clearly: close to the socialist party 43 per cent, communist party 3 per cent, RPR 12 per cent, UDF 12 per cent, Front National 2 per cent.[3] These figures suggest that the centre of gravity of student opinion is left of centre, that the communists and the extreme left receive very little support, but that there is substantial support for the major political parties of the right. This rather moderate body of students finds itself represented, at least at the national level, principally by two organisations, one of which is controlled by communist students and the other of which was controlled by a majority of Trotskyist students until 1986 when many of these left the Trotskyist PCI to join the socialist party. The fragmentation of student organisation and the mismatch between student opinion and organised student representation could hardly be more striking.

What we know of student attitudes and organisations in 1968 suggests that, although the organisational picture was one of greater unity with the picture being dominated by a single UNEF, the reality was one of intense conflict between, at the élite level, communist students and their anarchist and Trotskyist enemies, and at the mass level, a majority of students much more concerned about educational than social and political problems, and much more moderate in their

---

[2] *Le Monde*, 1 March, 1983
[3] *Le Monde*, *Campus*, no.1, March, 1986.

political views than those who sought to act and speak on their behalf.[4]

⋆⌈ The question naturally arises at this point as to how it is possible for leaders and followers to come together in such circumstances in order to unite in large demonstrations behind slogans which seem to genuinely represent the views of a great many students. The answer seems to lie in the intense anxiety of many students about their academic future and possible careers. In this connection we should remember that the majority of those French sixth formers who are successful in obtaining the *baccalauréat* would certainly prefer, wherever possible, to gain entry to one of the variety of institutions who select their students either through setting a further exam, or using *baccalauréat* marks, or by examining individual pupils' school records. For many students therefore the university is a second or third choice and acts essentially as a safety net. Therefore any legislation which is likely to tighten university entrance requirements seems to be depriving the student of an important insurance policy against possible failure to gain entrance to those institutions of higher education which have the most to offer him.

Of course, in the period between 1968 and 1986 educational policymakers had attempted to reduce wastage and anxiety arising from the situation described above. Their efforts had taken essentially two forms.[5] The first was the creation of a two-year university qualification, the DEUG. The intention here was to provide some students with an honourable and useful exit route from higher education at an earlier point in their studies and in this way to reduce the numbers of students leaving the university without any qualification at all. Secondly the governments of the 1970s sought to expand the provision of short vocational courses, entry to which required more than a mere *baccalauréat* pass with the aim of reducing pressure on the universities and giving some students at least a form of higher education in which the link between their studies and their future career would be more evident. ⌉⋆

---

[4] R. Boudon, 'Sources of Student Protest in France', *Annals of the American Academy of Political and Social Sciences*, 395 (May 1971).
[5] A. Prost, *L'école et la famille dans une société en mutation 1931-1981* (Paris: Nouvelle Librarie de France,1981); L. Schwartz, *Bilan de la France en 1981* (Paris: La Documentation Française, 1981); H. D. Lewis, *The French Education System* (London: Croom Helm, 1985), Ch. 4.

With student numbers continuing to rise during the 1970s and 1980s these solutions were simply not capable of being applied on a scale appropriate to the size of the problem. Hundreds of thousands of students were still unable to find places on the more selective and vocational courses and were therefore obliged to enrol in the university where failure and drop-out rates, even where a two-year qualification was concerned, remained wastefully and frighteningly high.

A further crucial parallel between 68 and 86 lies in the way in which, on both occasions, police brutality, widely reported in all the media, immensely strengthened the determination of the students and weakened the moral and political position of those in authority. It was the brutality of the police in 1968 which ensured so much initial public sympathy for the student movement, a degree of sympathy which only began to evaporate when, later in May and June, it became evident that there was a systematic resort to violence on the part of some elements at least on the student side of the barricades. The student leadership of 1986 had clearly learnt this lesson and the restraining efforts of those stewards appointed by student organisations were widely commented on. The police, however, were either slower to learn or found the application of the lessons of 1968 more difficult to apply. The death of Malik Usekin, as a result of wounds inflicted by the police whilst he was taking part in one of the student demonstrations, made it practically impossible for the government to reject student demands.

Our comparative study of two movements of student protest has so far concentrated on some important similarities. Before reaching any general conclusions under this heading, however, we must turn to the consideration of some equally important contrasts. One of the most important of these can be located at the level of ideology. Marxism provided the student leaders of 1968 with their key concepts and their insistence on the need for a revolution. This Marxism might take any number of forms but was ever present in May 68. Whilst the language of the student spokesmen of 1986 was still clearly the language of the left, it was no longer necessarily Marxist. The cry was now for an end to discrimination, for a more active solidarity, of opposition to selection, and the values which were espoused were those of democracy and of the Republic. Whereas the students of 1968 were in rebellion against the university, the police, the government, the Fifth Republic, and even the capitalist organisation of society, the movement of 1986 focused on a much more narrow target. On this later occasion the immediate cause of the movement of protest was a very particular piece of educational legislation and although, in their campaign to have the bill withdrawn, student organisations and spokesmen were at times willing to raise other issues, most energy was concentrated on the Devaquet bill. Once the government had agreed to withdraw this bill and once the students had organised a demonstration to mourn the death of Usekin, the movement came abruptly to an end and the national student co-ordinating committee which had organised the major demonstrations disbanded. At no point does there ever seem to have been an attempt to prolong the battle or to widen the objectives of the movement, although we can safely assume that many of the more radical elements on the extreme left of student politics would have tried to move in this direction, had they believed that there was any possibility of success. As it was, almost everyone seems to have been agreed that the chances of student success were increased by keeping objectives precise and by avoiding revolutionary and utopian language.

There is another sense in which the movement of 1986 can be described as more narrow than that of 68. The 86 movement was above all a political movement with precise objectives. Demonstrations seem to have been organised as instruments for the defence of student interests. In 68 political activity was often expressive as well as instrumental. Another way of stating the same contrast would be to say that May 1968 was at one and the same time an important political and cultural event, whereas in 86 the cultural dimension was hardly present. Joffrin has tried to argue, on the contrary, that we can only fully understand the movement of 86 if we take full account of the cultural dimension.[6] Although he is able to illustrate his argument at great length it does not finally seem convincing. The circumstances in which the movement arose, its explicitly formulated objective, namely the blocking of the Devaquet bill, and its duration, all seem to suggest a political rather than a cultural phenomenon. Although undoubtedly many secondary school pupils and young people who had left education took part in the 86 demonstrations, those arguments emphasising the cultural identity of the movement seem to depend too much on a non-existent

---

[6] L. Joffrin, *Un Coup de jeune* (Paris: Arléa, 1987).

coincidence of the categories of adolescent, youth, and student.

The movement of 86 can be distinguished from its predecessors in a number of other ways. Whereas debate and organisation in 68 had frequently been chaotic and far from democratic, in 86 there was great respect for democratic forms. The practice of general assemblies in the universities and delegates mandated to a national co-ordinating committee had grown up in the movement of 76 and that of 83 and was continued in 86. Another contrast with many earlier movements was the way in which the students in 86 stood very much alone. There was no attempt, for example, to draw academic staff into the movement. Many junior lecturers had been prominently involved in the events of 68.

One of the most important themes in the student protest of 68 and 76 had been that of hostility to outside, and particularly business, involvement in the management of universities. The spectre of capitalist control had haunted the lecture rooms in which students met for discussion in those years. Rather surprisingly, this theme was entirely absent from the 86 campaign. Perhaps the impact of the post-1973 economic crisis and the socialist government's advocacy of economically appropriate courses in higher education had helped to bring about this change of heart.

There is also a contrast between the predominantly defensive and, to that extent, conservative character of the 86 movement and the demands for change of all kinds made in 68. It is true, of course, that on both occasions there was an element of the defence of established student interests in access to higher education but, whereas in 86 this dominated the student protest, in 68 it was only one amongst many other themes, many of which were more radical. This point is well illustrated if we contrast the attitude of students on these two occasions to participation in the self-government of the university. In 68 students wished to emphasise that they were citizens and adults and therefore had a right to express political opinions and to take part in the democratic government of their cwn universities. In 86 there was relatively little attention paid by student spokesmen to the issues of political expression and participation. This is all the more surprising because the draft bill contained clauses which abolished the *conseil d'études et de la vie universitaire*. This body was one of the three university councils created by the 1984 Savary law and it was the council in which student representation was the greatest. Its abolition was therefore, in principle, a serious blow to student participation in university affairs and the lack of student response is all the more surprising given that student representation in other governing bodies was also to be reduced by the bill. We see illustrated here once again the more defensive, narrow, and specifically educational aims of the 86 movement contrasted with the broader aims of 68. The students of 86 reacted as consumers of education whereas those of 68 appeared to wish to assume the role of citizens in the academic community. How can we best explain the particular mixture of continuity and change which has just been described?

If we were to sum up the pattern of continuity and change which has been described in this section, we could do so by saying that continuity is most marked in areas of student concern with educational policy and student organisation, whereas change is most evident with respect to the broader ideological and political concerns of the two movements. As to the first of these points, continuity, the explanation to be invoked has been hinted at earlier. The anxiety of students and their opposition to any reform, of which increased selectivity of recruitment is a part, grows out of the character of the institutions in which they study. The Faure orientation law of 1968, the aim of which was to reform the universities with a view to improving the students' lot, had much more impact on the distribution of power within the university than it did on the degree of university autonomy or the problem of student selection and drop-out rate. Since, therefore, the French university was unchanged, at least with respect to those of its features which were most crucial to the students' plight, student anxieties and student attitudes towards educational reform were also unchanged.

But with respect to the broader political picture things were very different. The electoral appeal and political influence of the PCF had declined after 68 but much more noticeably from 1979 onwards. Quite separately from this political decline, and perhaps more important for our purposes, was the much diminished appeal of Marxism to those on the left, particularly to those close to the PS. The student leaders of 1968 and some of their followers, whether anarchists, communists or some variety of socialists, were invariably Marxists. After five years in power as managers of the mixed French economy, and with a much diminished need to compete with the PCF for votes, the PS in 1986 was much less interested in fundamental social criticism than had once been the case and the same was true for many of the leaders of the 1986 student movement, many of whom felt themselves to be close to the socialists. Aware of its weakness and vulnerability, the left in 1986 was more concerned with defence than attack.

STUDENTS AND THE WORKING CLASS

The peculiarly acute character of the 1968 crisis arose from the way in which student protest spilled over into the factories and combined with a near general strike. But there was no successfully concerted action or set of shared objectives between these two movements in 1968. Attempts were made by some student leaders to create links with the organised and unorganised working class but these failed. In 1986 no significant moves in this direction were made. The National Student Co-ordinating Committee did ask for support from the major trade union confederations but the only support which was expected and which was forthcoming was attendance at demonstrations.

But, as already pointed out, the combined impact of students and workers in 68 had never depended upon the existence of active solidarity and therefore the absence in 86 of such solidarity was no guarantee that the Chirac government would not run into difficulties of the same kind as those experienced by de Gaulle and Pompidou in 1968. In fact, however, history was not to repeat itself. There were substantial strike movements, beginning in December and running on until the middle of January 1987, in SNCF, the Paris Transport Authority, the Merchant Navy, and EGF. Many observers were surprised at the intensity and duration of these strike movements, particularly the train drivers' strike and it is difficult not to recognise some causal connection between the movement of student protest and these phenomena. But the two movements did not overlap in time in 86 as they had in 1968 and the numbers of workers involved and the degree of disruption achieved was very much less at the later date.

Whilst these differences in scale and timing must be acknowledged as important, it is still nevertheless the case that we can see at work in 1986 exactly the same process which, in 1968, had allowed the movement to spread from the students to the workers. The process was one of the weakening of state authority and the consequent tendency of aggrieved interests to exploit this moment of weakness to press home their demands. But overspill was clearly much less significant in 86 than in 68 and this for the simple reason that Chirac decided to give way to the students almost as soon as their movement had gained any momentum and in this way their grievances were dealt with and their protest had come to an end before industrial action began. We must therefore ask ourselves why a government, which had been elected on a platform promising university reform of the kind contained in the Devaquet bill, was so quick to beat a retreat once challenged by the students.

The first reason for retreat was the government's intense embarrassment at the death of Malik Usekin as a result of the ill-treatment he received from the police. Secondly, and unsurprisingly, Prime Minister Chirac was concerned with possibly adverse electoral reaction which might damage his chances in the presidential elections of 1988. The image which Chirac was intent on cultivating was one of moderation and reasonableness. He was concerned to live down a reputation for hot-headedness and ruthlessness which he had once possessed. He must have believed that the success of his government and therefore his own chances of being successfully elected president depended much more on economic policy and the government's record on inflation and unemployment than on any hypothetical reform of the universities. However desirable such reform might be, it was bound to arouse student and teacher hostility, and could only bear fruit, and this of a rather intangible character, in the long term.

Finally, what were the lessons to be learnt from the management by de Gaulle and Pompidou of the crisis in 1968? Superficially, their refusal to retreat immediately before student and worker demands and the consequently protracted character of the crisis, paid handsome dividends. Public opinion had proved unsympathetic to students and strikers with the result that the Gaullist party was returned in unprecedented strength in the parliamentary elections of June 1968, but Chirac was not in a position to exploit the foolhardiness of his opponents in the same way in 1986. He was Prime Minister and not President, and, as such, was not in a position to dissolve the assembly. This power lay with his political enemy, François Mitterrand. In these circumstances the best policy appeared to be to cut one's losses and to minimise risk by withdrawing the bill and accepting the Minister's resignation.

POLITICAL STABILITY: THE GOVERNMENT AND THE REGIME

We have already said something about the reasons for the Prime Minister's decision to cut the crisis short by giving way to student demands. In so doing we have begun an examination of the broader political context but much more needs to be said under this heading. Whatever changes may have occurred in the character of the student movement and its links with the working class, we need also to ask ourselves whether the constitutional regime of the Fifth Republic and, more narrowly, whether the right wing majority led by Jacques Chirac, was more solidly established than their predecessors in 1968. After all, although the students and workers of 1968 were unable to shake the Fifth Republic, they were able to bring about the premature retirement from politics of General de Gaulle and this was no mean achievement.

The students of 1986 were neither anti-Chirac nor, in any sense, hostile to the institutions of the FifthRepublic. The politically conscious leadership of the movement felt, no doubt quite correctly, that the students would lose much support if they appeared to wish to ignore the results of the 1986 parliamentary elections. There was a short period, immediately after the moment at which the government had conceded on the Devaquet bill, when some voices within the student movement could be heard calling for a continuation of the protest movement - a continuation which would only be possible if new and broader aims of a more political character were adopted. With a realism which their predecessors of eighteen years earlier had not possessed, the members of the National Student Co-ordinating Committee decided to resist the temptation to re-enact May 1968 and instead dissolved themselves.

But we should not imagine that the students' success was entirely without wider political significance. Some of their spokesmen had called for the government to renounce its intention to introduce a new nationality code, regarded by many as discriminatory against the French-born children of immigrant parents. Some student spokesmen had also attacked the government's announced intention to privatise some prisons. The government announced that it would not be proceeding immediately with either of these measures and that the pace of reform generally must slow down, but no more than this can be claimed for the student movement.

The student movement of 1986 was led with more moderation than that of 1968. Even the Trotskyists among student leaders made no explicit attack in their public statements on the constitutional principles embodied in the Fifth Republic. They clearly, and correctly, perceived that popular and élite support for the Fifth Republic had grown very strong over the years and that any attack on their part on the supposedly undemocratic character of parliamentary and presidential institutions would rapidly backfire. It is worth reminding ourselves, however briefly, of just how this had come about.

Whilst those socialists and others on the left close to Guy Mollet had helped to establish the Fifth Republic and defended its institutions against their critics, other socialists, including Mitterrand, and the communists, had made the defence of parliamentary institutions against the presidentialism of De Gaulle an important political theme in the years between 1958 and 1965. The success and even more the popularity of these institutions meant, however, that by the time the left came to power in 1981, no one in either the socialist or communist parties was any longer very interested in constitutional reform. The steady rise of unemployment from the mid-1970s onwards also provided politicians with an apparently much more relevant theme for debate. More immediately, once Prime Minister Chirac was installed in office as a leader of a right wing coalition and a period of cohabitation between him and the left wing President, François Mitterrand, had begun, their supporters in the established parties of left and right shared an interest in showing that the institutions of the Fifth Republic could work effectively in these novel circumstances. These trends, some of them long term and others more short term, reinforced moderation and consensus in 1986 and prevented the left-right polarisation of 1968 and the equally acute internal divisions within the left and right wing camps. Had the crisis of 1986 lasted longer and become more serious then perhaps the divisions within the right and between moderate socialist and Trotskyist groups on the left would have emerged. But, for reasons already explained, this was not to be.

PROTEST

The term 'protest' has been used to describe a variety of political
phenomena and there is a considerable literature on the place of
protest in French political life. The term has been used to describe a
range of phenomena extending from merely unconventional and
extra-parliamentary activity at one end of the spectrum to forms of
political protest which are both violent and illegal at the other. The
students of 1986 were involved in massive but peaceful and orderly
demonstrations, and stewards were active throughout in seeking to
restrain those intent on taking on the police. Without pretending to
review exhaustively the contending explanations of protest which
exist in the literature, it is useful for our purposes to distinguish
between two to some degree contending interpretations of this
phenomenon. Hoffmann stresses above all the way in which French
protest constitutes an obstacle to the normal workings of a modern
democracy.[7] He points to the failure of many protest movements to
formulate clear objectives and their tendency to move from the
voicing of a particular grievance to a global critique of the society of
which they are a part. Many of the characteristics attributed by
Hoffmann to French protest can be illustrated from the history of the
Poujadist movement of the 1950s. One of the points which
Hoffmann particularly wishes to underline is that, whilst a
movement which globalises its demands may attract more attention
and stimulate wider debate and at least appear to constitute more of a
threat to established institutions, this globalisation distracts attention
from what may be perfectly legitimate particular grievances. What
ought to be a rational and calm discussion of the needs of a
particular group turns into impassioned ideological confrontation.

Hayward's discussion of the phenomenon of protest in relation to
the working of democracy shows a more sympathetic attitude to
those involved in the protest.[8] He emphasises the ways in which the
centralisation of government and the fragmentation of interest group
structures constitute obstacles to the effective communication of

---

[7] S. Hoffmann, 'Protest in Modern France', in M. A. Kaplan (ed.), *The
Revolution in World Politics* (John Wiley & Sons, 1962).
S. Hoffmann, *In Search of France* (New York, Harper & Rowe, 1963).
[8] J. Hayward, 'Dissentient France: the Counter Political Culture', *Western
European Politics*, I, 1 (1978).

demands for government action. In such circumstances the resort to protest may overcome these obstacles. Existing structures, it is argued, were developed for the effective communication of the grievances and demands of the past and, when new issues emerge and new groups form to champion new causes, they may often, at least initially, need to resort to some form of protest in order to get a foot in the political door. Hayward's examples tend to be drawn from environmentalist and anti-nuclear groups who wish to oppose some aspects of government policy but cannot find the allies they need within the more established and more conventional left. What light does the case of student protest throw on these general descriptions and explanations?

Our case does not seem to fit either the destructive or constructive mould. The movement took great care to avoid the development of the kind of radical social criticism so often associated with movements of protest, including that of the students of 1968. Student demands were perfectly clear - the maintenance of national, as distinct from university diplomas, no increase in university fees, no limits on the rights of students with a *baccalauréat* pass to attend the university of their choice.[9]

It is no easier to fit the student case to the description offered by Hayward. By no stretch of the imagination can students be described as a newly emerging or previously unrecognised group. The demands which student spokesmen voiced were not new but on the contrary extremely conservative - consisting entirely of a defence of the *status quo* against what was perceived as a threat from the right. One of the key questions raised by the Devaquet bill and by earlier attempts to reform French university provision concerned the proper balance to be struck between quantity and quality of provision. This is, of course, exactly the kind of question which, though perfectly genuine, can never be addressed by a movement intending to defend the interests of a particular category of public service consumer. Any student organisation which establishes a clear policy on the appropriate balance between quantity and quality of university provision will, by so doing, divide its supporters and thus undermine its own political strength. Nor were the issues raised by the students in any sense novel or unfamiliar. The issues of university finance,

---

[9] D. Assouline and S. Zappi, *Notre Printemps en hiver* (Paris: Ed. de la Découverte, 1987).

autonomy and student selection had been debated in very similar terms throughout the 1970s and 1980s.

If then this movement of protest cannot be characterised as either particularly constructive or destructive, how should it be described? With respect to its aims and impact the movement seems to correspond very closely to the conventional operations or organised interests in advanced liberal democracies. Much received wisdom about the activities of organised interests stresses the extent to which they are reactive, conservative, defensive of established interests and much more often an obstacle than a spur to reform.[10] All of this seems true of the case under study here but with respect to the means employed, namely the massive demonstration, and the pattern of organisation, namely weak and fragmented, the student movement was far from typical of organised interests in Western Europe. How can we explain this deviation from a pattern of organisation and behaviour so frequently found in France and other West European states? Another way of putting the same question is to ask why the organisations which represent students are not integrated into the central decision-making process in such a way as to produce a more regulated and predictable environment for all concerned?

A complete answer to this question would involve us in an extended discussion of the specificity of the French state and the forms of relationship which exist between it and organised interests. There is insufficient space here to do this but it is appropriate to offer some remarks on the subject. Two approaches to this kind of problem can be found in the literature. The first, which is more common, stresses the nationally distinctive pattern of relationships between interests, organised and unorganised, and the state. As applied to the case of student interests this explanation would take the following form. Student organisations are often led by leaders with either communist or extreme left views. This prevents the operation of the process of mutual accommodation which can normally be observed in government/interest group relations. This minority of activists holds views which are not representative of the student body as a whole but their positions of elected responsibility cannot be successfully challenged by moderates because of the apathy and lack of participation in union affairs of the majority of students. This lack of student involvement is itself reinforced by a

---

[10] E. Schattschneider, *The Semisovereign People* (Dryden Press, 1957).

feeling of remoteness and alienation from factional conflict of a highly ideological character which seems to have no connection with day-to-day student problems except at moments of crisis when established expectations seem threatened. Thus a vicious circle establishes itself which links contending and poorly supported but highly politicised organisations on the one hand with a largely apathetic and ineffectively represented clientele on the other.[11] Those who support this first type of explanation believe it to be nationally specific because ideologies of the radical left and right play a more important part in French politics than in the politics of most other West European states. Confirmation that this pattern of relationship between organisations and those whom they seek to represent is nationally rather than sectorally specific derives from the observation that the vicious circle described above applies as much in the case of workers and trade-unions as it does in the case of students and their representative organisations.

The second form of explanation relies not on what is nationally specific but on what is particular to the sector or policy arena in question. The obstacles to effective organisation highlighted in this explanation are of rather a different character - students' natural anxiety about their own future as individuals, the constantly changing composition of the student body, consequent difficulties in achieving any degree of continuity in student organisation, the manner in which student concerns vary widely by course of study and institution.[12] The strength of this second approach is that it can more easily cater for variations in the forms taken by government/interest group relations from one sector to another. The limits of this approach become apparent when one concedes what seems difficult to deny, namely, that there is something nationally distinctive about the French consultative system. The trick lies therefore in somehow combining these two approaches in order to allow for both sectoral and national distinctiveness. Neither approach can be judged satisfactory and we must await a convincing synthesis of the two.

The particular combination of these two approaches which has been adopted here distinguishes between the substance and the style

---

[11] D. Gallie, *In Search of a New Working-Class* (Cambridge: Cambridge University Press, 1978).

[12] S. M. Lipset (ed.), *Student Politics* (Basic Books, 1967).

of representation. It has been argued that, with respect to aims and outcomes, the student movement can be fitted without difficulty into the conventional framework of much pressure group analysis. Here there is no deviation from the standard pattern which needs to be explained by reference to either national or sectoral specificity. With respect to the means of expression and organisation employed by the student movement the picture is quite different. Here we have suggested that the explanation requires us to take account of characteristically French patterns of organisation but also to bear in mind certain difficulties of organisations inherent in the status of students.

CONCLUSION

A sharp contrast between the educational and the political emerges clearly from our analysis. With respect to what is educational we find that certain problems which were acute before 1968 still remain essentially unresolved despite the legislation of 1968 and 1984. As regards what is political, however, we find that important changes have occurred. Constitutional arrangements which were still relatively new and controversial in 1968 had, by 1986, won general acceptance. Relatively cohesive coalitions on left and right (the communists after 1984 excepted) have grown in strength and moderation. The trade-union movement, never strong, has, particularly since 1979, seemed weaker still.[13] These changes mean that an explosion in the realm of education is no longer likely to spill over into the wider world of politics and shake the foundations of the State. Of course, we must not forget that May 68 did produce the orientation law for the universities later in the year but the solutions contained within this law did not resolve fundamental difficulties.[14]

---

[13] E. Lange et al (ed.), *Unions: Change and Crisis* (London: Allen and Unwin, 1982); M. Kesselman (ed.), *The French Workers' Movement* (London: Allen and Unwin, 1984); W. Rand-Smith, *Crisis in the French Labor Movement*, (London: Macmillan, 1987); M. Noblecourt, 'Le Pouvoir syndical en France depuis Mai 1981', *Pouvoirs*, 26 (1983).

[14] E. Shils and H. Daalder (eds), *Universities, Politicians and Bureaucracies* (Cambridge: Cambridge University Press, 1982) Chs 2 and 3.; J. Chevalier, *L'Enseignement supérieur* (Paris: Presses Universitaires de France, 1971). See also note 5.

Subsequent movements of student protest have only served to make the task of would-be reforming ministers more difficult. Viewed educationally, May 68 was the first of many. It was a full-scale dress rehearsal for a number of subsequent educational crises. It therefore looked forward and signalled the difficulties still to be overcome. Politically, however, May 1968, at least for the moment, seems the last of many revolutionary crises. It was the last performance of a spectacle which had enjoyed a long run and in no sense a rehearsal.

FURTHER READING

P. Boumard et al., *L'Université en trance* (Paris: Syros, 1987).

D. Gluckstein, *Qui dirige? Personne. On s'en charge nous-mêmes*, (Paris: Ed. Selio, 1987).

Le Monde de l'education, special issue, (January 1987).

Raison présente, special issue, 82, (March 1987).

5. THE AFTERMATH OF MAY 68 FOR GAULLISM, THE RIGHT AND THE CENTRE

JEAN CHARLOT

In order to assess the political impact of the crisis of May 1968 on the right and, in particular, on Gaullism, it is first necessary to ask a question: who emerged victorious from the May ordeal, General de Gaulle or Georges Pompidou? In the historiography of 1968, this question invariably brings us back to how we should interpret the celebrated day of 29 May and General de Gaulle's disappearance to Baden-Baden.

For the General's supporters - Alain de Boissieu[1] his son-in-law, François Flohic[2] (1979) his aide-de-camp, François Goguel[3] (1984) and the principal organisers of the Institut Charles de Gaulle - there can be no doubt: subjectively as well as objectively, 29 May was one of the tactical triumphs so typical of General de Gaulle. For the Pompidou camp - Georges Pompidou himself [4] (1982), Jacques Massu[5] (1983), the sole first-hand witness of the Baden-Baden

---

[1] A. de Boissieu, *Pour servir le Général, 1946-1970* (Paris: Plon, 1982)

[2] F. Flohic, *Souvenirs d'outre-Gaulle* (Paris: Plon,1979).

[3] F. Goguel, 'Charles de Gaulle, du 24 au 29 mai 1968' *Espoir*, XLVI, (March 1984) pp. 3-14.

[4] G. Pompidou, *Pour rétablir une Verité* (Paris: Flammarion, 1982).

[5] J. Massu, *Baden 68* (Paris: Plon, 1983).

discussions, and the journalist Philippe Alexandre[6] (1969) - on 29 May de Gaulle wavered and Massu, the old soldier, had to exert all his powers of persuasion to bring him back to the straight and narrow. Pompidou is therefore the only one to have 'stood firm' from beginning to end of the May crisis.

François Goguel defends the theory of the clever tactical ploy with great subtlety: of course de Gaulle was 'tempted to go', but there is a difference between *'being tempted* to give up and *having decided* to give up'. What is more, none of the General's acts from 25 May to 29 May can be taken to mean that he had given way to temptation, nor yet that he was on the verge of giving way.[7] Massu was taken in by the General's apocalyptic pronouncements and believed in all good faith that it was he who had managed to dissuade him, but de Gaulle had decided to stay and continue the fight the day before, and had indeed said as much to Michel Debatisse.[8] On 29 May, 'the day of dupes', Massu was, all things considered, no more than a pawn, as was Pompidou, while the General was in complete control of the game.

Jean Lacouture notes with some finesse that the theories of both schools, tactics on one hand and pandemonium on the other, are brought together and merged in the heated letter written by General de Boissieu to Georges Pompidou on 26 July 1968. Lacouture therefore opts for a synthesis of the interpretation of the de Gaulle and Pompidou camps:

Why bend over backwards to formulate contradictory hypotheses when everything is said the day after by a totally reinvigorated de Gaulle in a phrase from his address to the French people, whom he claims once more to unite: 'For the last twenty-four hours I have considered all the possibilities. Every one of them. And perhaps all at once'.

And Lacouture makes of the General 'in these fraught hours, a seething mass of contradictions'[9]

---

[6] P. Alexandre and R. Tubianal, *L'Elysée en péril 2-30 Mai* (Paris: Fayard,1969).

[7] F. Goguel, op. cit., p. 5.

[8] F. Goguel, op. cit., pp. 10-11.

[9] J. Lacouture, *De Gaulle vol. III, Le Souverain* (Paris: Seuil,1986).

We will not add yet another interpretation to these three readings of 29 May but, perhaps, another way of presenting the problem. The difficulty with the three theories that are offered to us is that they all aim to find the historical truth, not on the basis of the inadequate, mostly undisputed facts themselves, but by interpreting these facts in the light of the supposed psychology of the protagonists. For the hard-line Gaullists, de Gaulle - on 29 May - remains what he had always been: consumed by the futility of everything, tempted by submission, apocalyptic and provocative towards his entourage, but also sufficient unto himself, strong enough to pull himself together, lucid and a past-master of the art of tactical dissimulation and surprise. Fair enough. But who can swear that, faced with an intellectual and cultural crisis which, unlike Pompidou, he was unable to understand, at a time when old age was adding to his fatigue, de Gaulle did not react to May 1968 other than in his usual way? Does the 'suicidal' referendum of April 1969 not suggest that the attraction of resignation and retirement was irresistible? This is what most Pompidou-orientated analysts of 1968 believe. This might equally be accepted. But de Gaulle did not resign on 29 May 1968, and he left his fate to the verdict of the nation before resigning on 28 April 1969. Who can swear that the Gaullist view of a de Gaulle who was always in control of himself is false? In this psychologically based debate, Jean Lacouture's notion of synthesis does not go to the heart of the matter and ends up by overlooking an interpretative difficulty that remains untouched. Hence the necessity of approaching the problem in a different way, not as a historian attempting to grasp *the* truth about 29 May 1968, but rather as a political scientist who more modestly accepts the idea that there are *several* truths - the General's, Pompidou's, together with those of Giscard and Duhamel, plus that of the French people. These change with time, contradicting and influencing each other, and their complex and conflictual interaction dictates and explains the aftermath of May 1968 - for Gaullism first and foremost, but also for the non-Gaullist right and the centrist opposition.

THE IMPACT ON GAULLISM: THE END OF A SORT OF GAULLISM

In the last analysis, things are simple when viewed objectively: neither de Gaulle nor Pompidou was able to put a stop to the May crisis alone - it was the combination of their instincts and initiatives that brought about the shift of opinion at the end of May and permitted the electoral triumph of June. Pompidou, on his return from Afghanistan on 11 May, took the university situation in hand, reopened the Sorbonne and played the appeasement card. He failed. From 25 May to 27 May he attempted to defuse the social crisis first by negotiation and then with the Grenelle agreement. He failed once more. His tactics - play for time, avoid a showdown with the students and disarm the communist party and the CGT with social concessions in the classic manner - bore fruit in the long-term but revealed themselves inadequate to overcome the crisis. As for de Gaulle, he procrastinated from 2 May to 11 May, tempted by repression, but not sufficiently sure of himself to force it upon Louis Joxe, Christian Fouchet, Alain Peyrefitte and Maurice Grimaud. After Pompidou's return to France, de Gaulle gave him a free hand and went to Romania from 14 May to 18 May. His first attempt at dealing with the crisis, the speech of 24 May and the proposal of a referendum, failed completely. The second, the speech of 30 May after his disappearance on 29 May - succeeded. But would it have worked if he had settled for announcing a threefold *non-decision*: no retirement, no change of Prime Minister, no referendum on 16 June? This must be open to serious doubt. It was the announcement of the dissolution of the National Assembly which showed a way out of the crisis. Now, the dissolution was added at the last minute under pressure from Georges Pompidou, who made it a condition of his remaining at the head of the government.[10] If one accepts that the decisive shift of opinion dates from 29 May and the announcement of legislative elections on 30 May, then the crisis of May 68 was indeed settled thanks to a joint initiative on the part of General de Gaulle and Georges Pompidou.

MAY - JUNE 1968: THE REPRIEVE

Whatever men's natural bad faith and their desire to embellish their own actions, both de Gaulle and Pompidou were aware of their own limitations during the May crisis; in their respective accounts, one

---

[10] G. Pompidou, op.cit., p. 197. This is confirmed by Tricot in G. Pilleul et al., *'L'Entourage' et de Gaulle* (Paris: Plon, 1979). pp. 320-321.

would seek in vain instances of either man neglecting what the other did. But in the end it was Pompidou who came out of the May ordeal psychologically untarnished.[11]

The Alternative

Pompidou admits that he did not foresee events and 'still less their gravity'.[12] Upon his return to Paris on 11 May he felt that he knew 'how to proceed' with the university situation, at a time and in an area where 'the General, no doubt, failed to understand what was going on'.[13] Neither did he hesitate when faced with the social crisis. He assumed full responsibility without fear or hesitation, and accepted the immediate, double failure of his initiatives with some surprise but without becoming dispirited or, more importantly, disconcerted. When the university crisis and the social crisis turned into a crisis of power, Pompidou showed that, for him, openness and dialogue were not synonymous with weakness: he followed the procedures that would have allowed tanks from the Satory barracks to intervene in Paris had it become necessary.[14] During the few hours in which de Gaulle was missing on 29 May, Pompidou faced up to the situation: he directed the search, did not, in order to allay suspicion, alter his itinerary, but did take precautionary measures - alerting the television stations for that very evening and announcing a statement to the Assembly for the day after.[15] To those members of 'the majority' who urged him to go, he replied without the slightest contrariness that his position was not at stake, but that of 'General de Gaulle, the Fifth Republic and, to a very large extent, the Republic plain and simple'.[16] If he accepted setbacks, it was immediately to shrug them off, certain of the line he had followed from the very start. 'You're an optimist [de Gaulle said to him on the evening of 28 May]. What is more, you've been too optimistic from

---

[11] See the nuanced analysis of E. Balladur, *L'Arbre de mai* (Paris: Atelier Marcel Jullian, 1979).

[12] G. Pompidou, op. cit., p. 191.

[13] Ibid., p. 183.

[14] Ibid., pp. 190-191.

[15] Ibid., p. 195.

[16] Ibid., p. 196.

the outset.' 'When have I been wrong?' [he objects]. 'You told me
an agreement would be reached with the CGT.' 'It was - it was the
CGT who couldn't get it accepted [...] It will be a bit more
expensive, but we'll get there in the end'.[17] In spite of everything, he
was still aware of his inability to resolve the crisis on his own. The
General's hypothetical resignation on the morning of 29 May seemed
to him 'a catastrophe. Not only was the General's prestige still an
essential element of power, but legally speaking his retirement
would have put me in an impossible situation. Should we ask M.
Monnerville to act as caretaker?'[18] When de Gaulle reappeared at
Colombey on the evening of that same day and telephoned him to
confirm both his return and the Cabinet meeting the day after,
Georges Pompidou's 'first reaction' was 'immense relief'.[19] Next
day before the Cabinet meeting, he saw 'de Gaulle in all his
greatness'.[20] The vital fact remains. For Pompidou, taking stock of
the situation, de Gaulle - unlike himself - could not stand the test of
May. He writes as much, hiding behind the supposed verdict of
public opinion:

It was I again who, during the May days, negotiated, talked to
the country, to the Assembly, to the unions, to the politicians.
In the eyes of the masses, it was me who held out. The General
had been 'absent'.[21]

Writing to François Mauriac in a letter dated 23 July 1968, Georges
Pompidou showed that he had become, psychologically, because of
the May ordeal, *the alternative*, no longer the General's devoted
disciple and faithful lieutenant:

It's like this. The General can leave his stamp and his stamp
alone on his last years in power. Couve will be a faithful,
intelligent, skilled and worthy lieutenant. For my part, I will try

---

[17] Ibid., p. 191.
[18] Ibid., p. 192.
[19] Ibid., p. 196.
[20] Ibid., p. 197.
[21] Ibid., p. 203.

[...] to devise methods of action and objectives that might satisfy the young people who are at once avid and alienated.[22]

Doubts

Compared with such certainties on the part of Pompidou, the doubts which overtook General de Gaulle in May are all the more startling. If he criticised the decisions made by Pompidou and stressed his defeats during the crisis, he also recognised his constancy and firmness under pressure. Receiving the Pompidous for dinner on Tuesday 2 July, two days after the last round of legislative elections, de Gaulle said to Mme. Pompidou: 'I can tell you that your husband stood firm'.[23] On 10 July, with Pompidou stepping down as head of government, de Gaulle wrote to urge him to hold himself 'ready to fulfil any commission and take up any mandate that might one day be offered [to him] by the Nation'. And on 9 September 1968, having made his point that it was for the Head of State to relieve the Prime Minister of office and having done so, he affirmed publicly to Pompidou that he had 'shown, during the unrest of May and June, an exemplary and praiseworthy firmness and contributed to nationwide success in the elections' and that 'it was only right that he should be held in reserve by the Republic and not exhausted'.[24] Alain de Boissieu, remembering that Pompidou's son Alain had been married on 30 May 1968, had written to him on 23 July: 'We are full of admiration for your calmness and serenity in the midst of the storm'.[25] Now, at the same time de Gaulle was not trying to hide - even in public - his own uncertainties during the crisis: he 'hesitated' when due to leave for Romania on 14 May, France's condition seeming 'unmanageable' to him.[26] On 29 May he was indeed 'tempted' to retire, then, once more, he 'became resolved'.[27] On 1 June he admitted to Georges Pompidou himself, perhaps in a reference to 29 May: 'For the first time in my life I dithered. I am

---

[22] Ibid., p. 247.

[23] Ibid., p. 203.

[24] Press Conference, Elysée, 9 September 1968.

[25] G. Pompidou, op. cit., p. 248.

[26] Televised interview with Michel Droit, 7 June 1968.

[27] Ibid.

not proud of myself'.[28] With the passage of time, the General erased the memory of his hesitations and proceeded to reconstruct events in what was, from his point of view, a more satisfactory form. On 9 September 1968 in his first post-May press conference, he said it was not he who had hesitated over which path to follow, but his government, which 'found no immediate solution'. As for himself, 'all the while shoring up the resolve of those in positions of responsibility and stressing the necessity of reforms when the return of public order made it possible to implement them', he waited 'for the situation to become clearer in the eyes of the nation before acting on a large scale, knowing full well that, up to a point, the affair had been amorphous and hence unmanageable'.[29] This was putting a different gloss on the word 'unmanageable' and was an avoidance of accepting where the real power lay until 29 May. But Charles de Gaulle was not a man to content himself with mere show, nor yet with a reprieve given him by a victory in the legislative elections which, to put it bluntly, he doubted was his at all.

APRIL-MAY 1969: THE TRANSFER OF POWER

'I am old and you are young, you are the future,' de Gaulle had said to Pompidou on the telephone on the morning of 29 May 1968 - before 'embracing him'.[30] Having taken a grip on himself and regained the initiative a day later, on 30 May, de Gaulle was now no longer in a mood to give up and hand over power. On 10 July 1968 he had Pompidou replaced, although the latter had, after initially expressing a wish to go, finally asked to stay on at Matignon. François Mauriac asks in his *Bloc-Notes*: 'The statesman who was virtually alone in keeping his head on every front during the May crisis, and who was responsible for the greatest electoral victory any party has ever won in France, is standing down? [...] has been sacked?'.[31] Pompidou later personally confirmed to him that he felt himself to have been dismissed. De Gaulle, for his part, said that he had acted according to Pompidou's expressed wish to take a break.

---

[28] G. Pompidou, op. cit., p. 201.
[29] Press conference, Elysée, 9 September 1968.
[30] G. Pompidou, op. cit., p. 193.
[31] *Le Figaro* 12 July 1968.

At the time, the French people did not clearly see the growing rift between General de Gaulle and Georges Pompidou. According to the IFOP, in July 1968, 27 per cent of the French people were in favour of Georges Pompidou's departure, 25 per cent against, and 48 per cent expressed no opinion. On the other hand, 48 per cent were happy with the choice of Maurice Couve de Murville as Prime Minister and 12 per cent unhappy, while 40 per cent expressed no opinion. Most importantly, more than two-thirds of the people (67 per cent) thought that by replacing Pompidou with Couve de Murville the General had sought to establish the former as his successor, as opposed to a mere 12 per cent who had thought he had simply chosen to get rid of him.[32] While it is true that the events of May had slightly dented the General's popularity - 61 per cent in favour, 31 per cent against (+30) immediately *before* 22-29 April 1968, 53 per cent in favour, 27 per cent against (+26) immediately *after* 19-26 June 1968 - contrary to what is often claimed, they did not really increase that of Georges Pompidou: 48 per cent in favour, 34 per cent against on 9-16 April (+14), 46 per cent in favour, 34 per cent against on 12-18 June (+14).[33] At a deeper level, however, the General's image had been damaged and Pompidou's reinforced. One of the IFOP's questions, put to a representative sample of Parisians only on 27 May, that is immediately *before* the decisive turn of events of 29 May to 30 May 1968, and on 31 May, that is immediately *afterwards*, provided illuminating results. Those questioned were asked whether in the last three weeks [in the last few days' in the case of the poll of 31 May], their opinion was better or worse concerning General De Gaulle and Georges Pompidou. Table 5.1 presents the findings. It is obvious that Georges Pompidou's *potential* popularity, if not his immediate popularity itself, was better strengthened by the May ordeals than was the potential popularity of General de Gaulle, in spite of his eventual revival of 29-30 May.

---

[32] *Sondages* 1969, nos. 1 and 2.
[33] *Sondages* 1969, nos. 1 and 2.

Table 5.1. POPULARITY RATINGS, DE GAULLE AND POMPIDOU.

	27 May			31 May		
	Better	Worse	(Difference)	Better	Worse	(Difference)
de Gaulle	15%	55%	(-40)	41%	36%	(+5)
Pompidou	40%	34%	(+6)	47%	29%	(+18)

Source: *Sondages*, 2, 1968

According to a confidential and unpublished IFOP poll commissioned by the interministerial liaison service of the Ministry of Information and conducted on 16-17 June 1968, between the two rounds of legislative elections (nationwide sample of only 305 individuals), it seems that 89 per cent of the French people demanded above else the maintenance of law and order - which Pompidou and de Gaulle alike could provide - and that an overwhelming majority doubted the General's reforming zeal. 77 per cent of those questioned thought that 'if the General had wanted to enact social reforms he could have done it long ago...'. In the minds of the French people, everything was ready for the handover of power.

At the end of 1968 and the beginning of 1969, relations between de Gaulle and Pompidou declined irreparably. From Pompidou's point of view, firstly, this was due to the Markovitch affair that lasted from 4 November 1968 to 9 January 1969: although the General showed belatedly, but publicly, that in the end the affair had nothing whatever to do with the Pompidou family by inviting him to dinner at the Elysée in January, his former Prime Minister would never forgive his not having confided in him in the first place and having allowed certain of his ministers to carry on regardless when he and his wife were the victims of political intrigue.[34] On the General's side, it was the declaration in Rome of Georges Pompidou's candidacy and its repercussions that brought the rift about. The affair was very probably a complete fabrication on the part of the press, but de Gaulle would have none of it and reacted

[34] G. Pompidou, op. cit., pp. 260 et. seq.

brutally by letting it be known that he had been re-elected President
of the Republic on 19 December 1965 for a term of seven years, and
intended to carry out his mandate until the very end. Straight away,
Pompidou lashed out once more in Geneva:

> I will perhaps have, God willing, a destiny on the national
> stage... As time goes by and as my thoughts return to the matter
> once more, I tell myself that whatever the act of bad faith that
> started the affair and furthermore, however clumsy and
> excessive official reaction was, it was not just chance that
> caused my words to receive such attention. Indeed, since the
> jolt he had suffered in the presidential elections, the General
> had been in decline. Since May 1968, France had known
> unconsciously that the end was near. Naturally people were
> beginning to think about what would come after.[35]

At the time of the announcement of Pompidou's candidacy, in his
reply to the message that informed him of it at Colombey, de Gaulle,
although he expressed approval of a candidacy which in his opinion
was eminently natural and, under the circumstances, on the cards
anyway, added: 'It would undoubtedly have been better not to
announce it several weeks in advance, for this has lost hundreds of
'yes' votes, lost you some yourself and most important of all might
prove a bit of a personal embarrassment to you if you are elected'.[36]
Had Pompidou committed *patricide* in order to inherit? The trial
would be conducted by his most implacable enemies within the
Gaullist camp.[37] Let us merely say on this score that it is a fact of
life that the son should break free of the father, especially when
asked to give up the whole idea of succeeding him. Did not
Alexandre Sanguinetti and Jean Charbonnel - without de Gaulle's
objecting - go so far as to ask Georges Pompidou on the eve of the
negative referendum of 27 April 1969 to promise publicly not to put

---

[35] G. Pompidou, op. cit., p. 269.

[36] Letter from General de Gaulle to Georges Pompidou, 30 April 1969,
quoted in G. Pompidou, op. cit., p. 287.

[37] See L. Vallon, *L'Anti de Gaulle* (Paris: Seuil, 1969) and A. and P.
Rouanet, *Les trois derniers Chagrins du général de Gaulle* (Paris: Grasset,
1980) for a popularised version.

himself forward as the General's eventual successor?[38] Did not the General himself declare to his brother-in-law Jacques Vendroux on the evening of Monday 28 April 1969 when speaking of his political heirs and Pompidou in particular: 'I no longer have anything to do with them, they're strangers to me'?[39] Was the referendum of 27 April 1969 which exiled de Gaulle to Colombey and opened the way for Pompidou's succession really *suicidal*? Malraux was sure of the fact: 'He wanted to be beaten! He wanted proof of - what shall we call it? ingratitude'.[40] Jean-Marcel Jeanneney, who drafted the referendum, spoke out against this view: ' It's fair to say that de Gaulle knew that he was taking the risk of being beaten, but it is not true that he wanted to be beaten'.[41] The Institut Charles de Gaulle organised a meeting/debate on this subject between witnesses and academics, during the course of which all the witnesses - Maurice Couve de Murville, Jean-Marcel Jeanneney, Bernard Tricot, Bernard Ducamin, Admiral François Flohic and François Goguel - opposed the notion of political suicide on the part of General de Gaulle.[42] The arguments advanced were not, however, entirely to the point. According to the witnesses, the decision to call a referendum had been taken in May 1968, that is to say at a time when the result of 27 April 1969 was impossible to predict. This is as may be, but as soon as the project was shelved *sine die*, General de Gaulle had the option of burying it or reviving it at the most opportune moment. Maurice Couve de Murville implicitly recognises this when he draws a distinction between the period during which the referendum was postponed 30 May 1968 - 1 February 1969) and the period which began with the Quimper address (2 February 1969) in which the General announced the purpose of the referendum and its approximate date, the spring (the precise date of 27 April was fixed on 11 March). During the first period, Couve de Murville urged de Gaulle to give up the idea of a referendum: as soon as the announcement was made, Couve de Murville was of the opinion that

---

[38] J. Charbonnel, *L'Aventure de la fidélité* (Paris: Seuil, 1976), p.167.

[39] J. Charbonnel, *L'Aventure de la fidélité* (Paris: Seuil, 1976), p.167.

[40] *L'Express*, 7-13 August 1972.

[41] *L'Express*, 14-20 August 1972

[42] Institut Charles de Gaulle, 'Le référendum de 27 avril 1969 fut-il un référendum suicidaire?', *Espoir*, XVI (September 1976), 4-30.

the General had burnt his boats.[43] A fortnight after the Quimper address, on 15 February, the General asked Jean-Marcel Jeanneney if the referendum had to go ahead. He replied, like Couve de Murville, that there was no turning back, but that it was still possible not to turn it into a popular vote of confidence. De Gaulle refused.[44] On 17 February he questioned Roger Frey, the best electoral specialist in his entourage.

> 'Can we win this referendum?' 'I don't think so, General.' 'Then can we put it off?'

Having asked for and been given a few minutes to think about it, Roger Frey gave his opinion.

> 'General, I don't think it's possible to delay. There's your reputation as a democrat to consider.'[45]

In about the same period - 'after 19 February' - the General mused aloud in front of Bernard Tricot: 'When all is said and done, my options are still open; what has actually happened is that the government has suggested a date for the referendum to me, but I can still say no.' The general secretary of the Elysée, like Couve de Murville, Jeanneney and Frey, immediately convinced him that such an attitude was 'impossible'.[46] At the end of February and the beginning of March, before the date of the ballot was finally fixed for 27 April, Michel Debré and Raymond Marcellin tried one last time to convince de Gaulle to extricate himself. It seems that they even believed they had succeeded in convincing him. It was an illusion.[47] From this mass of testimony, it is fairly clear that:

1. General de Gaulle publicly launched the postponed referendum of May 1968 at the beginning of February 1969 against the cautionary advice of his entourage and especially of Maurice Couve de Murville.

---

[43] Ibid., p. 16.
[44] Ibid., p. 23.
[45] J. Lacouture, op. cit., p. 752.
[46] Institut Charles de Gaulle, op. cit., p. 26.
[47] Ibid., pp. 23-26.

2. As soon as he was committed by his own action, he was seized by doubts, but since the most influential members of his entourage were of the opinion that the referendum could not be delayed a second time, he refused the compromises put to him - split the question of reforming the Senate (unpopular) from that of decentralisation (popular); not let his own fate ride on the result of the ballot - because such compromises all seemed unacceptable in his eyes.

Was it political suicide? Not really, at least to the extent that General de Gaulle sought a lifeline as soon as he felt the whole affair to have been a mistake. But it was a trap into which he fell, imprisoned like his entourage by his own image; a trap, moreover, that he had built for himself. He had the political instinct to forget the abortive referendum of May-June 1968; he did not have the *psychological* capacity to do so. May had to be erased at all costs; the victory of June was not of his making; in short, he had personally to regain the support of the people or go. The strongest proof of this attitude is found in the very subject of the referendum of 27 April 1969. Unlike the projected referendum of May-June 1968, it does not concern the universities. Neither does it concern - in spite of the General's constant references to the meaning of the crisis and how it should be healed - the reform of co-operative enterprises. To be brief, it concerns none of the great battlegrounds of May 68. 'He wanted to bring regionalisation into it because he wanted to be beaten!' was the conclusion drawn by Malraux.[48] It would be more accurate to say that the pretext for the referendum was not of the slightest importance to de Gaulle because his sole reason for existence, at that time more than ever before, was his personal right to say 'yes' or 'no'. It is hard to doubt that de Gaulle hoped, in spite of all evidence to the contrary, that 'yes' would prevail. But to him bitterness and retirement were better than uncertainty...

Less than a year after the May crisis, its most important consequence for Gaullism and for France was therefore 'the end of a sort of Gaullism', that of General de Gaulle himself. But against all contemporary indicators, it was not 'the end of Gaullism' but, on the contrary, its 'routinisation', its institutionalisation.[49]

---

[48] *L'Express*, 7-13 August 1972
[49] J. Charlot, *Le Gaullisme* (Paris: A. Colin, 1970) pp. 148-50.

THE IMPACT ON THE RIGHT AND THE CENTRE: THE 'ROUTINISATION' OF GAULLISM AND THE SCHISM OF THE CENTRIST OPPOSITION

Compared with the de Gaulle/Pompidou duel, the non-Gaullist right of Valéry Giscard d'Estaing and the centrist opposition of Jacques Duhamel, Alain Poher and Jean Lecanuet appeared rather lacklustre during the May crisis and the aftermath of May 68. Their role was still important: they contributed to de Gaulle's overthrow but also showed themselves to be incapable of filling the Gaullist 'parenthesis' by offering an alternative which was acceptable to the French people.

THE WRONG DECISIONS OF MAY 68

The Giscardians and the opposition centrists made the wrong political decision in May 68: they gambled on de Gaulle rather than on Pompidou, and this through misplaced opportunism rather than conviction.

The Giscardians

Since his 'Yes, but...' campaign in the legislative elections of March 1967, Valéry Giscard d'Estaing had not stopped criticising General de Gaulle's 'solitary exercise of power'. The reasons were the decrees of 1967, the General's stands against Israel, the Middle Eastern conflict and his attitude towards a free Quebec on the occasion of his visit to Canada. But Giscard took care to soften the effect of his criticism by appealing to the General himself to make the necessary changes, by inviting him - all things considered - to reform himself. To which de Gaulle simply riposted that you cannot govern with 'buts...'.

Giscard's tactics did not change during the 1968 crisis. In the censure debate in the National Assembly on 22 May he refused to condemn the government so as to avoid adding 'adventurism to disorder' and unambiguously continued to align himself with 'the majority'. But he did add that 'the first reform that must be carried out consists of changing the way in which France is governed'. He upbraided the Prime Minister, Georges Pompidou, whom he accused of leading the 'party of fear', the 'tribe of those who prefer injustice to disorder'. However he cultivated the Presidency of the Republic and General de Gaulle: 'if this office did not exist, and if it had not been occupied by the present incumbent, everything would have been swept away by now'. On the morning of 30 May, before the intentions of General de Gaulle, now back from Baden-Baden and Colombey, were known, Giscard called for legislative elections and expressed the hope that the President of the Republic would continue in office. But, going one step further than on 22 May, he demanded the sacking of Pompidou and the formation of a government swelled by opposition centrists, composed of 'men of renewal'. Giscard, to recap, pressed General de Gaulle to act on his own behalf in order to replace Gaullists with Giscardians and centrists. Not having been successful on 30 May, he went on to demand it, along with the independent republicans, all through the legislative election campaign in June, putting exactly the same arguments in exactly the same terms. Except, that is, for 'overlooking' the now inopportune criticism of Georges Pompidou.

The Opposition Centrists

Throughout the May crisis, the centrist opposition - with its party the CD led by Jean Lecanuet and especially with its parliamentary group PDM whose figurehead was Jacques Duhamel - naturally went further than the Giscardians in its criticism of those in power. As early as 11 May, the day of Georges Pompidou's return from Afghanistan, Jean Lecanuet demanded the immediate dismissal 'of those ministers who, since they are incapable of tackling the problems to which they are assigned, resort to repression', while Pierre Abelin floated the idea of a new government led by Pierre Mendès-France. In a statement on 19 May, the political council of the CD urged the government's dismissal and the 'lawful' formation of a new government 'uniting democratic and republican forces', charged with the formulation of a new policy of reform and dialogue to be submitted to the country in a general election. Ten years on, the opposition centre turned to its own ends the process of gaining power used by General de Gaulle in May 1958. On the evening of 29 May, in similar mood, Jean Lecanuet related to the press the unanimous decision of the steering committee of the CD to call for the formation of a 'government of public salvation, with nobody left out and no jobs for the boys', stipulating that Pierre Mendès-France seemed in its eyes particularly well qualified to lead such a government. In the meantime, on 22 May, 34 PDM deputies out of 42 had voted for the censure of the Pompidou government; and on 26 May, the CD had attacked the referendum proposed by de Gaulle two days earlier, judging that 'referendums kill dialogue'.[50]

So, while being more critical of the government and the current majority, the centrist opposition, just like the Giscardians, supported General de Gaulle. In the statement of principles which it offered as a model to its candidates in the legislative elections, the PDM called for 'a change of policy without a change of Republic' and for a change of majority brought about by a vote for the centre, but paid homage to General de Gaulle while suggesting that he might resign: 'If France continues to be divided into two factions, the civil war which we avoided yesterday will break out tomorrow... and General de Gaulle will no longer be there.' In reality, given a hypothetical victory in the legislative elections, the centrists were ready to accept, if necessary, *cohabitation* between a new parliamentary majority, of which they would be the axis, and General de Gaulle in the Elysée. In the 'model speech' offered to PDM candidates it was indeed possible to read: 'We demand, and are the only ones who can guarantee it, a new majority and new methods. The President of the Republic is not in question: he was elected for seven years in 1965.' An anonymous June interview, from the same set of notes for PDM candidates, is still more explicit:

> Given his methods, his isolation and his style, the Head of State, at his age and after what has happened, no longer seems the man capable of embodying the new beginning that the nation hopes for [...] If the left comes to power, I think that the General will go. If we make it, the men who want to transform the majority from within, the General will only go if he wants to start another crisis by imposing his will upon us in spite of the popular verdict.[51]

---

[50] See the résumé of these attitudes in *Democratie Moderne*, 19 June 1968.

[51] PDM, *Dossier du candidat* (unpublished), June 1968.

The results of the June 1968 legislative elections sounded the death-knell for Giscardian and centrist aspirations. Admittedly the Giscardians gained 21 seats, but the Gaullists, with 97 seats gained, had for the first time in the history of the Fifth Republic an *absolute* majority of seats in the National Assembly. As for the centre opposition, it lost 15 seats and remained a tiny group in Parliament. Instead of learning the lessons of May, they had now to learn those of their defeat in June.

April-May 1969: A Painful Change of Sides

When, a year later, the question of the change-over between de Gaulle and Pompidou came to be settled in the Gaullist camp, Giscard changed his bets. He came out against de Gaulle on 27 April and for Pompidou in the presidential election, while the centrists, united in their 'no' to de Gaulle, were divided between support for Alain Poher (Jean Lecanuet) and regrouping around Georges Pompidou (Jacques Duhamel, Joseph Fontanet, René Pleven). The double defection of Giscard and Duhamel to Pompidou was far from being a certainty from the outset. Georges Pompidou had first of all to want it, and impose it on the Gaullists, some of whom, on the contrary, dreamed of having done with Giscard and the centrists who had contributed to the General's downfall by advocating a 'no' vote on 27 April. Pompidou simply gave them to understand that, in order to win, a 47 per cent ' yes' vote in the referendum had to become a vote of more than 50 per cent in the second round of the presidential election. The Gaullists could only hang on to power by accepting 'change with continuity' and on the further condition that Giscard fail to find an alternative to supporting Pompidou, thus keeping the Gaullists in power. What if he were to become a candidate himself? He thought this premature, not wishing to try his luck at the Presidency without a serious chance of winning. What about backing another candidate against Pompidou, someone from the majority and old enough for Giscard to be able to step into his shoes next time around? Giscard proposed this to Pinay, who declined. In the context of the post-June 1968 balance of political power, good sense finally dictated that he ally himself with Pompidou and against his own direct rivals, the opposition centrists who, like himself, hoped one day to take over from the Gaullists. His very real attachment to the institutions of the Fifth Republic and his political affiliations woven, in spite of everything, by eleven years of electoral, parliamentary and governmental alliance with the Gaullists meant furthermore that Giscard's own inclinations lay in this direction. In fact, his support for Pompidou allowed his own return to government, to the Finance Ministry which he had unwillingly left after the presidential election of 1965. Most important of all, it kept alive his presidential chances for the future. Obtaining the co-operation of Jacques Duhamel, Joseph Fontanet, René Pleven and several other opposition centrists with Georges Pompidou and the majority was even more problematic, for it presupposed a split within the CD. However, the end of de Gaulle's Gaullism made things easier; Pompidou was not de Gaulle. Had he not publicly declared himself willing to negotiate for the support of any opposition centrists who were ready to leave the opposition? The resounding failure of June 1958 had destroyed more illusions about overturning a regime by way of the centre than anything else. Seeing that Pompidou had opened himself up to the centre, Jean Lecanuet and, what is more, the bulk of the CD played the Poher card against Pompidou. And most observers believed, in the light of opinion polls, that the former would defeat the latter. This was to underestimate the French people's attachment to an idea which had been new in 1958 but eleven years on had become ingrained: that of a President of the Republic who was strong, competent and desirous of fully assuming supreme power at the head of the executive. The decision to vote for censure in May 1968 had earned the opposition centrists, much against their own expectations, a comprehensive defeat at the polls in June 1968. The choice of Alain Poher - at best an identikit candidate of the Third Republic and at worst, of the Fourth - as their champion to take on Georges Pompidou in the presidential election made their failure complete. All that was left for them to do was to rally to Giscard in 1974. There was the satisfaction of playing a part in the defeat of the Gaullist candidate, Jacques Chaban-Delmas, but also the painful obligation of confirming left/right bipolarisation, accepting the Fifth Republic's semi-presidential system and governing with a more broadly based majority in which the Gaullists, though admittedly no longer dominant, were the major party in terms of votes and seats. In 1969 the Gaullists had been forced to accept certain changes - like the entry of Great Britain unto the European Economic Community - in order to ensure the preservation of the Fifth Republic and of Gaullist power. In 1974, the centrists, by supporting Giscard, were forced to resign themselves to sacrificing their constitutional, European and Atlanticist ideas. All in all, 1968, by leading to the downfall of General de Gaulle, ensured through Georges Pompidou that the Fifth Republic's institutions, once they had shown themselves able to survive de Gaulle, became generally accepted, just like the Gaullist party itself which, contrary to what had been the case in 1956 under the Fourth Republic, had proved its electoral autonomy from the figure of its illustrious founder. Some said that Pompidolism was not Gaullism at all. But inquisitions over a stolen inheritance left the overwhelming majority of the Gaullist political leadership and its electorate completely indifferent.

6. MAY 68: PARENTHESIS OR STAGING POST IN THE DEVELOPMENT OF THE SOCIALIST LEFT?

LAURENCE BELL

It is generally accepted that the events of May 1968 were a left wing - and some would say anti-capitalist - happening. Yet in the elections that followed in June 1968 and in the presidential election the following year the left was badly defeated and when the fortunes of the socialist left did begin to pick up again this was largely due to a return to the pre-1968 strategy of unity among socialists and union with the *Parti Communiste Français* (PCF). In examining the place of May 68 in the development of the socialist left in France we shall look firstly at the origins and development of the strategy of *union de la gauche* and then at the origins of the ideology of the tendency in the *Parti Socialiste* (PS) which claimed to be closest to the legacy of May 68.

The strategy of the *union de la gauche* under the Fifth Republic can be traced back to 1965 and arguably to 1962. The collapse of the Fourth Republic and the return to power of de Gaulle in 1958 had greatly weakened the left. The PCF, still entrenched in its Cold War isolationism lost over one million votes and all but ten of its seats in Parliament. The socialist party (SFIO), whose leader, Guy Mollet, at first supported de Gaulle's return, lost all but forty-four of its seats. A substantial minority of its leaders and activists broke away to form the *Parti Socialiste Autonome*, which shortly afterwards formed the rump of the *Parti Socialiste Unifié*. The *Parti Radical* lost its *mendésiste* wing and adopted an ambiguous position with regard to de Gaulle.

Attempts failed to unite all the disparate forces on the left opposed to de Gaulle by converting the electoral alliance *union des forces démocratiques*, constructed to fight the 1958 elections, into a new, broad party given the task of regenerating the non-communist left. Attempts to regroup the socialist left outside the SFIO led to the creation in 1960 of the PSU, a small party which was destined to remain small. The PSU, which attracted much attention owing to its outspoken opposition to the Algerian War, thought it could play a key role in forging a new strategy of unity on the left in preparation for *l'après gaullisme,* but its own internal cohesion, which had been sealed by its opposition to the Algerian War, crumbled once the war had been brought to a close.

The SFIO with its network of local councillors and mayors still intact therefore remained the key to any regeneration of the non-communist left. However in the early 1960s the SFIO leadership thought that with the end of the Algerian War de Gaulle could be dispensed with and that it could return to its former role as lynchpin and power broker in the party system.It therefore hesitated between centrist alliances and the siren call of a PCF eager to end its isolation and reintegrate itself within national politics by courting its 'natural' ally, 'social democratic' reformism.

The November 1962 parliamentary elections saw a minor although historic shift in alliances with a small number of second ballot agreements between the SFIO and the PCF. However, these elections, in which the SFIO engaged in all sorts of alliances in different parts of the country, saw the Gaullist UNR sweep the board and reinforce its position. With the second bombshell of 1962 - the introduction by referendum of the direct election of the president - the logic of the new political system began slowly to unfold. Neither the PCF nor the SFIO yet knew how to approach such an election, the first of which was to take place in 1965.

The first response on the left to the challenge of presidentialism came from the political clubs which had sprung up in the wake of May 1968. These clubs, along with a number of trade union leaders and the news magazine *L'Express* (then the mouthpiece of the 'modern left'), launched the idea of a broad centre-left candidacy which would rally public opinion *en masse* and force the parties of the left to follow. The candidate chosen for this daunting task was Gaston Defferre, whose hostility to the PCF was an open secret. The Defferre campaign, which occupied the stage from 1963 until June 1965, foundered because public opinion did not rally massively, because the trade unions distanced themselves and because it therefore became dependent on a coalition of parties not eager to enter into an alliance. Defferre's candidacy was deftly killed off by Fontanet for the MRP and Mollet who viewed it as a threat to his leadership of the SFIO.[1]

Mitterrand, who had supported Defferre throughout, then stepped into this vacant space and, without committing himself to any party, made it known that he would not refuse the support of the PCF. After a brief but dynamic campaign Mitterrand's 45.5 per cent in the second ballot against de Gaulle in December 1965 dented the General's image of being untouchably above the political *mêlée* and modified the political ball game overnight. The *Fedération de la Gauche Démocratique et Socialiste* (FGDS), constituted in September 1965 by the SFIO, the *Parti Radical* and the political clubs grouped in the *Convention des Institutions Républicaines* and led by Mitterrand gained in strength from the near miss of the presidential election. The PCF in supporting Mitterrand had had its eye firmly fixed on the 1967 parliamentary elections and edged the FGDS towards an electoral agreement and a common platform. Mitterrand, before any other major politician, had realised that under the new political ground rules of the Fifth Republic, the only way ahead for the non-communist left was to find a formula which would first allow unity among non-communists and then collaboration with the PCF. This collaboration would at first turn to the advantage of the PCF but would, calculated Mitterrand, eventually undermine its position to the advantage of the non-communist left if the latter were able to present itself as a credible left-wing alternative and woo the communist electorate.

While the FGDS-PCF agreement for the March 1967 elections was limited to second ballot *désistement* (standing down in favour of the best-placed candidate of the two formations), this policy of unity was a paying one and the FGDS won 19.3 per cent of the vote and 116 seats while the PCF won 22.5 per cent of the vote and 77 seats. When the 44 seats of the centre groupings were added to this,

---

[1] G. Suffert, *De Defferre à Mitterrand* (Paris: Seuil, 1966), pp. 106-111.

the Gaullists came within a hair's breadth of losing their parliamentary majority. In February 1968 the FGDS and the PCF attempted to produce a common platform, which, if nothing else, clarified their differences. Time, however, seemed to be on the side of this alliance, since the parties, now in possession of the formula for success, would have had four more years to overcome their differences. May 1968, however, was to derail these expectations.

The wave of protest which burst forth in the student world and spread throughout French industry, paralysing the country in the space of a few weeks, seemed light-years away from the parliamentary and electoral concerns of the parties. After initially condemning the student movement the PCF began to realise that the tide of the strike movement was unstoppable and sought to control it and orientate it in a direction favourable to a *union de la gauche* strategy. This was not an easy task and when it appeared that the Gaullist state might crumble only to be replaced by some version of a broad *union nationale* with the FGDS at the helm, the PCF attempted to block this by campaigning for a democratic government of the people which would include the PCF.

Mitterrand for his part jumped the gun. A parliamentary vote of censure had failed but, following de Gaulle's announcement (24 May) of a new plebiscite disguised as a referendum on 'participation', which he looked sure to lose, thus precipitating a presidential election, Mitterrand called a press conference. Here (28 May) mimicking the illegality he had accused de Gaulle of ten years earlier, he called for the formation of a provisional government offering himself and Pierre Mendès-France as leaders. He announced that in the event of a presidential election he would be a candidate. But Mitterrand was caught out of step by the turn of events and neither the electorate nor the FGDS, in whose name he had nevertheless spoken, forgave his apparent opportunism and readiness to flout legality. With greater ease than expected de Gaulle was able to turn the situation around completely on 30 May by returning from his consultation with the army and announcing a general election.

State-controlled television and radio stations offered a highly censored version of the events. The government was able to play on the widespread fear caused by the chaos into which the country had been plunged and insinuated that the events had been engineered by a communist plot. A significant proportion of the working class wanted a return to stability which would enable it to enjoy the benefits of the pay rises negotiated in the Grenelle agreements.[2]

In the June 'elections de la peur' the supporters of de Gaulle and Pompidou won a resounding victory. The FGDS and the PCF both lost out heavily, falling to 16.5 per cent and 20 per cent of the vote respectively. Of the 16 *conventionnels* who had entered parliament in 1967 all but Mitterrand lost their seats. The June defeat signalled the break-up of the FGDS, most of whose members blamed Mitterrand for the débâcle. The *Parti Radical* withdrew and the SFIO turned its back on Mitterrand. When he finally resigned from the presidency of the FGDS in November, the federation collapsed completely.

However, if we are to believe Mitterrand's own account of things,[3] it was from this third 'journey through the wilderness' in his political career that he emerged as a convert to socialism. Furthermore from his 1965 and May 1968 experiences he had learned firstly, that, whatever their differences, the parties of the left were forced to live together by the bipolarisation of the party system brought about by the direct election of the President and secondly, that the political struggle facing any *présidentiable* required him to have the backing of a solid political party which he could control tightly in all circumstances.

The road to the *congrès d'Épinay*, which was to relaunch the process of reunifying the socialist left, was not yet clear however and it took the complete débâcle of Defferre in the 1969 presidential election (5 per cent of the vote), from which Mitterrand stood well clear, to rule out yet again the possibility of a SFIO centre-left strategy which turned its back on union with the PCF. Even after this demonstration and after a swing back to a *union de la gauche* strategy within the SFIO, (renamed the *Parti Socialiste* in 1969), it took the careful collusion of those socialists eager to free the PS from the dead hand of Mollet to bring Mitterrand to the leadership of the party at Epinay (1971). Mitterrand's narrow victory at Epinay was built on an unlikely alliance of Mauroyists, Defferrists and the

---

[2] In these negotiations, which took place at the Ministry of Labour in the rue de Grenelle, the government and *patronat* were obliged to concede a 35 per cent increase in the national minimum wage.

[3] F. Mitterrand, *Ma Part de vérité* (Paris: Fayard, 1969), p. 152; pp. 163-84.

CERES, the extreme left of the party. Because of this dependence on the support of the extreme left and because the party needed to regain some left-wing credibility (a credibility tarnished by the Molletist SFIO since 1956), the CERES was able to play an important role in formulating PS policy. Left-wing credibility was of vital importance if the PS was to be able to rival the PCF within the *union de la gauche* sealed by the signing of the *programme commun* in June 1972.

Observers have noted the increased polarisation of party politics along class lines following 1968 and particularly the increased prominence given to economic class issues.[4] However this would seem to have resulted as much from purely political factors as from a faithful translation of socio-economic realities into political discourses. While it would be foolish to claim that the political parties could ignore the negative aspects of the rigid economic growth of the 1960s or France's highly unequal distribution of incomes, the polarisation of party positions along *class* lines seems to have been at least equally affected by the elimination of centre parties and of major non-economic issues such as *laïcité* versus clericalism and by the creation of a block on the left dominated, in its early years at any rate, by 'the party of the working class'.

The radicalisation of the non-communist left therefore appears not to have been directly connected to May 1968, but to have been a function of its rivalry with the PCF in a strategy which was interrupted by the events. However, the PS in the 1970s adopted the notion of *autogestion* as the central plank in its new ideological identity and *autogestion* is often thought to have been an original product of May 1968. This view is reinforced by the fact that the PS's identification with *autogestion* seemed to be strengthened when those elements which held themselves to be the guardians of the positive legacy of May 1968, notably the Rocardians from the PSU and the followers of Edmond Maire from the CFDT, joined the PS. Their *Quinze Thèses sur l'autogestion* were taken up by the PS in 1975.

The beauty of the term *autogestion* was, of course, that it meant all things to all men: the CERES (the nearest thing to a Leninist tendency within the PS) had its own version; Mitterrand occasionally

---

[4] R.W. Johnson, *The Long March of the French Left* (London: Macmillan, 1981), pp. 116-20.

used the term; the centrist Gaston Defferre, for long the mayor of Marseille and the very un-*autogestionnaire* director of the newspaper *Le Provençal*, eventually declared himself in favour of *autogestion;* and by the end of the 1970s even the PCF had its version of *autogestion*.[5] However, it was the *courant des assises*, later to become the Rocardian tendency in the PS, which most closely identified the essence of democratic socialism with *autogestion*, since for this tendency *autogestion* summed up not only the ends to be achieved, but also the means of achieving them. It will therefore be useful to examine the ideas of the so-called 'modernist' or Rocardian left before and after 1968. This is a less partial and specialised approach than it might first appear in so far as many of the PS's policy orientations in the 1970s, (decentralisation, participation or *autogestion*, democratic planning and so on), were first launched by the modernist tendency in the PSU in the 1960s. This focus is equally interesting in the light of the Rocardians' apparent itinerary from the heat of the May barricades and the leadership of a revolutionary PSU to the 'right wing' of the PS.

The major tenets of the doctrine of the modernist left did not in fact stem from 1968 but were formulated in the early 1960s by such theorists as Serge Mallet, André Gorz, Pierre Belleville and Alain Touraine.[6] Broadly speaking the 'modernist' left arose out of an amalgam between part of the *mendésiste* 'modern' left and the former *nouvelle gauche*, whose most prominent leader was Gilles Martinet of *L'Observateur*. The term 'modernist' derives, one must assume, from an analogy with the modernist, anti-orthodox, intellectual movement in the catholic church in the early years of the twentieth century. The modernist left in attacking 'orthodox' Marxist assumptions claimed to be defining a form of socialism adapted to the conditions of modern industrial society or organisational capitalism and differed from the largely pragmatic and non-

---

[5] B. Brown, *Socialism of a Different Kind* (Westport, Connecticut: Greenwood Press, 1982), Chs. 4 and 5; J. Rollet, *Le PS et l'autogestion* (Doctoral thesis, IEP, Paris, 1982), p. 602.

[6] S. Mallet, *La nouvelle Classe ouvrière* (Paris: Seuil, 1963), p. 269; A. Gorz, *Stratégie ouvrier et néo-capitalisme* (Paris: Seuil, 1964), p. 174; P. Belleville, *Une nouvelle Classe ouvrière* (Paris: Julliard, 1963), p. 317. For an example of A. Touraine's early work, see 'Problèmes actuels du mouvement ouvrière', *Cahiers de la République*, 21 (1959), 22-36.

ideological 'modern' left in its self-conscious assertion of itself as the bringer of ideas and practices which would complete and fulfil the rationalising, progressive, universalist and humanist aspirations of Marxism while discarding the historically redundant aspects of economistic Marxist dogma. Touraine and Mallet started out from sociological analyses of industrial organisation rather than from analyses of the movement of capital or of differential rates of profit. While it would be an exaggeration to say that they espoused a simple convergence theory,[7] like Aron or Dahrendorf, they seem to have taken Industrial Society to be a form of universal reality in itself and often drew examples of advanced organisation from the USA. Touraine was later to write that capitalism was not a mode of production but merely a development soon to be superceded.[8] Rocard in 1959 entitled a quasi-theoretical pamphlet not *Socialisme ou Capitalisme* but *Socialisme et Civilisation Industrielle*.[9]

With this focus on Industrial Society the modernists concentrated, on the one hand, on plans for the realistic socialist management of an advanced industrial economy (this was the *mendésiste* input in which Rocard, the *inspecteur des finances*, excelled) and on the other hand on a critique of the dehumanising and alienating aspects

---

[7] Broadly speaking convergence theory, which was popular in the late 1950s and 1960s, held that Western and Eastern bloc countries were following similar, converging paths of development. There was therefore less difference between Western democracies and Eastern communist countries than had traditionally been supposed since both types shared characteristics common to all advanced industrial societies. These characteristics were: a high degree of socialisation in the organisation of production; the increased role of organisation and of State regulation in economic and social activity; the coexistence (in Western societies at any rate), of a private sector; the prominent role played by experts and managers, who were not owners of the means of production. This outlook gained particular credence in France where the collapse of the Fourth Republic had shown the weakness of parliamentary democracy and where a state élite had played an important role in post-war economic development, especially through planning.

[8] A. Touraine, *L'Après Socialisme* (Paris: Grasset, 1980), p. 34.

[9] This paper, originally circulated within the sixth Parisian section of the PSA was later published in two parts under Rocard's pseudonym, Georges Servet, in *Les Cahiers de la République*, 25 (May-June 1960) and 26 (July-August 1960).

of modern industrialism (this stemmed from a personalist stance which was not hard to reconcile with the writings of the young Marx). This dual concern led Jean Poperen to characterise them as representing 'la social-technocratie'.[10]

The modernists who took control of the majority in the PSU in 1963, had read and meditated on James Burnham's 'managerial revolution' thesis. Although they rejected Burnham's revamped historicism which recast managers as the new agents of historical change, they concluded that in modern capitalism the domination of property-owning capitalists was being replaced by that of technocracy. If not blocked, the new technocrats would form a new ruling class and develop authoritarian, bureaucratic forms of political domination. Controlling technocratic decision-making therefore became a much more important goal for socialists than expropriating capitalists; that is, the defence of liberty through the development of democratic participation became more important than the collectivisation of the means of production. From these first assumptions, they drew two major conclusions. Firstly, the 'old' working class in the archaic sectors of the economy was incapable of combating the domination of technocracy. Close to this was Serge Mallet's assertion that the labour movement, in its stance of 'conflictual participation' in capitalism, had forgone both the possibility of attacking capitalism from without and the possibility of achieving significant leverage within the system. Trade union action could no longer be revolutionary and the trade unions had themselves become bureaucracies which blocked the class energy of workers.[11] Secondly, the rise of the technocracy and of the bureaucratic political forms which accompanied it had brought about the effective eclipse of parliamentary democracy. The domination of techno-bureaucracy would therefore only be countered by those equal to the task - the new skilled workers, the *nouvelles couches* of advanced industries. Some 'moderate' modernists, such as the members of the *Club Jean Moulin*, conceded that although in modern industrial societies real power and indeed real legitimacy lay with the executive branch of the State, which communicated directly with interest groups and public opinion, Parliament could play an

---

[10] J. Poperen, *La Gauche française 1958-1965* (Paris; Fayard, 1972), p. 27.
[11] S. Mallet, *La nouvelle Classe ouvrière*, 5th edn (Paris: Seuil, 1969), pp. 67-72.

important role in expressing *contestation*.[12] All were agreed however that complex modern industrial economies needed to be regulated by a technically competent State and that the authoritarian threat inherent in such a State could only be countered by new forces which were, so to speak, born of the same generation of development.

The left should therefore encourage co-operation between the *salariat* and technocrats whenever retrograde interests needed to be liquidated and new productive forces developed. On the other hand, it should organise the struggle of the *salariat* against technocrats whenever the latter threatened to become authoritarian. The left therefore had to abandon its old conceptions and develop a new ideology. The old parties of the left, because they clung to *archaïsmes idéologiques* and were either bureaucratic machines or corresponded to a now defunct parliamentarianism, had to be jettisoned and give way to a new form of political society, of which the political clubs and *sociétés de pensées* which flourished in the early 1960s were only a first manifestation.[13] The PCF in particular was tainted by its totalitarian ideology, its bureaucratic functioning, its political absolution and its social paternalism. For Mallet the PCF had become retrograde because it defended the backward sectors of the economy in the face of the positive aspects of modernisation.[14] Indeed the relationship between the non-communist left and the PCF constituted such an obstacle to the renovation or regeneration of the left that such a regeneration would require the triumph of an intellectually and morally superior ideology over communist ideology.

But if the organised labour movement as a whole was no longer revolutionary and had no real institutional clout, how could even the *nouvelles couches* put up anything but a defensive struggle against encroaching technocracy? Here Mallet's New Working Class (NWC) thesis came to the rescue. This is interesting in that it shares certain characteristics with the notion of *autogestion* prevalent in France in the 1970s. Broadly speaking the NWC thesis ran as follows. The operatives and technicians of the new automated industries were in a

---

[12] Le Club Jean Moulin, *L'Etat et le citoyen* (Paris: Seuil, 1961), p. 323.

[13] P. Fougeyrollas, 'La gauche est morte, vive la gauche!', *Les Cahiers de la République*, 21 (1959), 86-96.

[14] S. Mallet, *Le Gaullisme et la gauche* (Paris, Seuil, 1966).

qualitatively different position from the old working class which was dominated by technics and by the mechanical division of labour. Through the repeated division of tasks in 'Taylorised' or 'Fordist' production the labour power of the old working class had become abstract, devoid of any individual content and divorced from the individual who became merely a 'carrier' of a fragmented function. In the end workers were reduced to being pure labour power which could be distributed quantitatively through a labour market between interchangeable functions. Human labour power became pure commodity without its own autonomy and characteristics and its remuneration was unrelated to production.

By contrast the labour power of the new highly qualified workers took on a specific meaning and content owing to the education they had received and their assignment to specific complex tasks. Their work therefore regained its autonomy and qualitative contents. Labour power became the concrete possession of an individual again and could thus no longer be subjected to the impersonal quantification process of capitalism or organised in an authoritarian hierarchy. The worker's effort was therefore to be considered as an active and 'organic' participation in the life of his firm and one which tied workers and firm together in a relationship of mutual dependence. Thus, on the one hand (and here the theory made a leap), the greater sense of responsibility which the worker derived from his situation in production led him to an awareness of the economic realities of the firm and to a desire to control them. On the other hand, the firm's reliance on its workers as qualified and specialised individuals who were difficult to replace, placed the workers in a strong bargaining position in their pursuit of self-management demands. Mallet and Gorz argued that the way ahead towards a 'free society of producers' lay in the expansion of such demands. However such a possibility was predicated, we should note, on workers' being able to control or negotiate the *exchange value* of their labour. In what sort of economic system, we might ask, could the labour power actively possessed by the individual, autonomous worker take on its full economic and social significance? The answer must be: in a *market economy*. However this was to be a sort of 'natural' economy freed from the aberrant constraints of capitalism. This is reminiscent of the utopian socialism of Fourier and Robert Owen.

Despite the fact that it was based on a narrow definition of capitalism and accepted a socialism based on exchange value, this theory had considerable political success in the 1960s. There were many reasons for this. Firstly, in positing the control orientation of the new working class, the theory seemed to close the gap between the everyday economic demands of workers in particular local situations and the overall political action of the labour movement. It would therefore claim to do away with the distinction between reform and revolution, and this was a major revisionist achievement. Secondly, one of the major concerns of revisionist theorists was the bureaucratisation of working class parties and trade unions. According to the NWC thesis the development of unionism centred in the workplace and the new 'autonomy' of the individual worker meant that trade union structures would no longer be detached from their membership and the risk of bureaucratic deviation would be reduced. The new forms of workplace unionism could thus be viewed as heralding the new democratic relations between producers in future socialist society.

Finally, the appeal of the NWC thesis lay in its affirmation of cultural and individual autonomy, that is in its affirmation of the irreducible value of the *person* in the face of the dehumanising aspects of industrial society. However the overall claim of the theory that the NWC had a revolutionary anti-capitalist potential seems to have been based largely on the idea of capitalism as a mode of organisation of labour and production, whereas in reality, capitalism is primarily a system of production regulated by *profit* which brings different modes of organisation into being when they are the best way to maximise profit, and dispenses with them when they cease to be so.

After May 1968 Mallet argued that the May-June strike movement had borne out his thesis.[15] It is certainly true, contrary to the expectations of those who saw the integration of workers in modern production as leading to a new social consensus, that the new categories of skilled worker, technicians and even some executive staff played an active role in the massive strike movement. However in May 1968 the new working class behaved much the same as the old and in the following years the forms of militancy which developed were not especially governed by control issues. As

---

[15] See the foreword to *La nouvelle Classe ouvrière* (Paris: Seuil, 1969).

time went on and as the working conditions of modern industry became more prevalent, the 'new' working class lost its specificity and its advantageous position of scarcity in the labour market.

However, the idea of a 'natural' economy based on exchange value, regulated by contractual relations and positing a form of immanent socialism (which broke with the seizure-of-power conception of the break with capitalism) continued in the *socialisme autogestionnaire* theories of the 1970s developed by the PSU and the CFDT. There were some significant differences however. Modernist thinking prior to May 1968 was coupled to a productivist doctrine of industrial society or, more precisely, to a doctrine which saw the organisation of production as the principal mode of control in industrial societies. One of the salient - and modernist - aspects of the NWC thesis was that the autonomy it posited lay not in a revolt against the industrial order but in a logical development of that order. This disappeared from the themes of *autogestion* and *autonomie* in the 1970s and the revolt of May 1968 with its anti-productivism and radical critique of 'consumer society' which reflected a dawning awareness of key changes in capitalism, is a pointer to why this occurred. Before considering this point, however, we shall look briefly at the position of the PSU in May 1968.

The PSU, which in 1968 was under the dual leadership of Rocard and Heurgon is usually presented as the political party closest to the May movement. This is to a large extent true: among the political parties only the PSU had its ear to the ground in the student world and had the ear of the student movement. Marc Heurgon, the indefatigable membership secretary, whose microscopic knowledge of the party machine and membership throughout the country enabled him to keep a tighter rein on the party than Rocard, also paid attention to anything and everything that happened in left-wing circles. He was one of the few political leaders fully conversant with the student political groups which had been forming on the left of the PCF.[16] Throughout the 1960s the student branch of the PSU, the ESU, had controlled the UNEF, the students union, and since 1965 had shared this leadership with the dissident communist students whose *groupuscules* were to play a key role in the student phase of the events. Furthermore the modernist intellectuals in the PSU were delicately poised in their leadership position since their rank and file

---

[16] J. Poperen, *L'Unité de la gauche* (Paris, Fayard, 1975), pp. 106-8.

support within the party came largely from the ex-UGS tendency, which with a high proportion of catholic workers was easily swayed towards populism and *basisme*. These different elements welcomed the events as a *divine surprise* and, spurred on by Heurgon, involved the PSU, which then acted as a sort of relay between the student movement and the 'adult' world of the authorities and the trade unions.

While the party's modernist tendency with its gradualist notion of the conquest of the nodal points of decision-making in a productivist society was not particularly in tune with either the revolutionary violence of the *groupuscules* or the anarcho-surrealism of, for example, the Situationists, it obviously could not ignore a mass movement which, after the onset of the strikes, began to convince Rocard that power was for the taking.[17] The dilemma of the PSU's leadership was epitomised by the resolution to the crisis which it sought. Rocard drafted a programme which, while it recommended monetary and financial safeguards against the effects of wage increases on the franc and the balance of payments, also called for France's withdrawal from NATO and for the creation throughout the country of *comités populaires* which would replace official institutions and relaunch the economy and public life.[18] After the failure of de Gaulle's speech announcing a referendum (24 May), the PSU leadership tried to persuade Pierre Mendès-France to form a transitional government on the basis of this programme. Although he had been arguing for ten years that the Gaullist regime would end as it had begun (that is, in the street), Mendès, who was a man imbued with a strong sense of republican legality and order, refused. Four days later de Gaulle imposed his solution.

On the question of the long-term effects of May 1968 Michel Rocard has commented recently, 'Mai 1968 nous a retardé de dix ans.' Asked if he now held a negative view of May 1968, he replied, 'Pas de jugements de valeur, pas de jugements de valeur. Il y a eu Mai 1968 et on fait avec!'[19] In short the PSU was short of the troops it needed to weigh in against the rest of the non-communist left in a likely future merger. Rocard had refused a merger with the FGDS

---

[17] K. Evin, *Michel Rocard ou l'art du possible* (Paris: Eds. J-C. Simoën, 1979), pp. 82-6.

[18] For an abridged version of this programme, see ibid., pp. 225-8.

[19] Interview with the author, 2 July, 1986.

after its relative electoral recovery in 1967 because the PSU was not large enough and did not represent enough electoral capital to weigh significantly in the balance, and because he felt that the FGDS had not sufficiently renewed its doctrine to be able to wrest the ideological high ground from the PCF. While he knew just as well as the *unitaires* of the PSU that the path forward lay in the unification of the left, Rocard had a different idea of how to approach this and hoped to be able to build up the political strength of the PSU so that its ideological message would have more impact within a merged non-communist left. May 1968 threw this strategy into confusion.

Rocard now claims to have become actively involved in the May events in order to prevent the loss of life and prides himself on having organised PSU seminars on violence in history in order to prevent the development of revolutionary terrorism in France.[20] He doubtless hoped that after the dust had settled on the violent and 'archaic' revolutionary aspects of the May revolt, a whole generation would be won over to his 'socialism of a different kind'. The reverse happened, however and from 1968 until 1971 the PSU was assailed by the revolutionary leftism of the new membership which May 1968 had brought it, and its modernist leadership had to perform an ambiguous ideological balancing act to stay in control of the party.

All the parties of the left tried to appropriate one aspect or another of the May events in order to 'salvage' (*récupérer*) some of the aura attaching to them. An important example of this was the left-wing critique of the PCF which May 1968 made possible and which the proponents of *autogestion* then sought to exploit. May 1968 did, however, leave its mark on the 'political culture' which Rocard and friends took with them to the PS when they abandoned the PSU in 1974.[21] In the 'modernist' theory of the 1970s - continued by ideologues such as Alain Touraine, Patrick Viveret and Pierre Rosanvallon - the combative role of the *nouvelles couches* or the new working class was replaced by that of the anti-bureaucratic

---

[20] Ibid. See also 'Une Méthode en politique: entretien avec Michel Rocard', *Le Débat*, 38 (1986), p. 12.

[21] For Rocard's more positive evaluation of the legacy of May 1968 see 'L'Avenir de Mai 1968', in Michel Rocard, *Parler Vrai* (Paris: Seuil, 1979), pp. 97-101. Rocard abandoned the leadership of the PSU in 1973 following the PSU's poor showing in the elections of that year and the loss of his own seat in Parliament.

social movements (the regionalist, ecology, anti-nuclear and feminist movements), which had developed in the wake of May 1968 and which reflected the anti-statist and pluralist notion of social change which had also been an element of the events. As the French economy continued to restructure and particularly after the onset of the recession in 1974, the technical aspect of the NWC thesis gave way to its ethical/political aspect. *Autogestion*, which had begun as an ideology of the labour movement (and one which was consonant with the post 1968 rehabilitation of the anarcho-syndicalist tradition), became less and less the affirmation of a 'natural' community of producers and more that of a political collectivity recognising the 'autonomy' of the individual and regulated by contractual relations rather than by the State.

In short *autogestion* shifted from being about the control of productive forces to being a new theory of political democracy.[22] Why was this so and in what way does it relate to the May 1968 critique of the commodification of culture and daily life? The answer has to be sought in a fairly long-term development. In a capitalist society whose members were primarily engaged in labour and which was organised around the task of replenishing the labour supply, the goal of the left was to ensure that the latter was carried out more rationally by removing capital from the administration of productive forces and replacing it with the self-management of producers. However, the development of capitalism has led not to the emancipation of labour from capital but to the increasing independence of capital from labour:

> Instead of engaging the rest of society as producers or servants of the productive process, capital today engages society as consumers or servants of consumption. The most obvious consequence of the changed mechanism of the reproduction of capital, and of the new form of systemic domination is the obsolescence of the self-management of producers as a valid alternative to the present system.[23]

---

[22] See for example, P. Rosanvallon and P. Viveret, *Pour une nouvelle Culture politique* (Paris: Seuil, 1977).

[23] Z. Bauman, 'The Counter-Culture of Modernity', *Telos*, 70 (Winter 1986-7), p. 87.

On the other hand, since capital is less dependent on labour, it no longer needs to be and indeed can no longer be the major force in the reproduction of the social system, the major part of which was formerly the reproduction of labour-capital relations. 'The reproduction of the structure of domination becomes directly the matter of law and order, rather than indirectly the matter of the 'work ethic'. Systemic reproduction, in other words, has become more than ever before the responsibility of the political State.' [24]

In this situation the demand for autonomy is channelled into the market where it seeks satisfaction in the commodity preferences of the consumer, whereas, on the other hand, the expansion of the State's functions leads to the expansion of unaccountable State bureaucracies and a shrinkage of the domain of political debate. Thus the critique of the commodification of individual identity on the one hand and the defence of political democracy through the expansion of citizenship right and the demand for new forms of political intervention applying to a broad spectrum of everyday issues on the other, are closely linked in what Zygmunt Bauman has recently referred to as a 'counter-culture of modernism'.

Despite the apparent paradox of terms, the post 1968 'modernist' left was well placed to voice this 'counter-culture of modernism', owing to its long-standing critique of bureaucratic centralism and statism, to its championing of civil society, social movements and a politics based on ethics, and to its willingness, in its contest with the 'orthodox' left, to pose the question of State power and thus create a bridge between libertarianism and political liberalism.

However, in the late seventies Rocard seemed ambiguously poised between modernism and a counter-culture of modernism, and the 'two political cultures' debate[25] which racked the PS at that time was both the irruption into the party and media arena of the 'counter-culture' as an organised tendency and a restatement of the *neo-mendésiste* critique of the left's lack of economic 'rigour' and of its lack of realism regarding the constraints facing socialist change. All things considered, we should perhaps not expect too much ideological purity from a politician who, as a *présidentiable*, is caught in the three-sided situation of trying to be faithful to his ideological identity, trying to rally support within his party and

---

[24] Ibid., p. 89.
[25] M. Rocard, *Parler Vrai* (Paris: Seuil, 1979), pp. 76-84.

preparing to run the gauntlet of a presidential election which, with a 50 per cent pass mark, requires the successful candidate to have broad appeal.

To summarise then: if we consider the development of the mainstream of the non-communist left, then May 1968 appears to have constituted an interruption rather than a direct contribution, and *autogestion* in the PS of the 1970s appears to a large extent to have been an ideological identity with which to rival the PCF. Even if we take those elements on the socialist left which thought themselves closest to the spirit of 1968, we see that by the mid-1970s they were in part looking to their pre-1968 themes. However, with its explosion of political subjectivity and anti-consumerism, May 1968 doubtless contributed to a more pluralistic, less statist and more decentralised conception of social change which, with some delay, has played a role in questioning anew the agenda of the left in France.

7. THE EVENTS OF MAY - CONSEQUENCES FOR INDUSTRIAL RELATIONS IN FRANCE

JEFF BRIDGFORD

INTRODUCTION

The events of May were to provide the greatest wave of strike activity ever seen in modern France. On the 14 May the Sud Aviation factory in Bougennais was occupied and within two days so were the Renault factories in Cléon, Flins, Le Mans and Boulogne-Billancourt too. By 17 and 18 May there were strikes at the SNCF, Air France and the ORTF, and subsequently at thousands of other workplaces such that by the end of the following week the country was almost completely paralysed. According to Seale and McConville in their contemporary account: 'At no time did a general strike call go out from the Paris headquarters of the union federations; and yet all over the country a calm irresistible wave of working-class power engulfed the commanding heights of the French economy. In thousands of plants the workers not only struck, but locked themselves in with their silent machines, turning the factories into fortified camps.'[1]

The tide began to turn some days later, particularly after the

---

[1] P. Seale and M. McConville, *French Revolution 1968* (London: Penguin Special, 1968), pp. 152-153.

demonstration organised by the Gaullists on the 31 May, and by the beginning of the following week the drift back to work started to gather pace. Some sectors, particularly the metalworking industries, stayed out longer and indeed in the Renault and Citroën plants the strikes were to last 33 and 36 days respectively.[2] So great was the strike wave and the ensuing confusion that in its official statistics the Ministry of Labour was unable to provide a total figure for the number of strikes in 1968 and was only able to provide an estimate - 150 million - for the number of days lost through strike activity.[3] Caire offered the following figure off the cuff - between 8 and 10 million employees on strike.[4] Henri Krasucki, on behalf of the CGT, the major trade union confederation then as now, estimated that there were nine million men and women on strike.[5] These claims were disputed later on by Adam who estimated that between 6 and 7.5 million employees were on strike at some time during that period.[6]

It is not the aim of this chapter however to chronicle the different stages of this particular strike wave,[7] nor to provide an explanation of its causes, which have ranged from the economic to the meteorological. It will however assess the impact of the events of May on certain major features of industrial relations in France. Clearly this chapter as others in this collective work will encounter major methodological problems of causality. Is it possible to identify one specific catalyst for social change - important though the events of May undoubtedly were? Moreover is it possible to claim that the events of May led directly to change or did they merely speed up a process that was in train anyway? It is proposed to consider the period immediately following the events of May, thus reducing the

---

[2] G. Caire, 'La situation sociale', *Droit Social*, (July-August, 1968),.451-468.

[3] Ministry of Employment figures quoted in J-D. Reynaud, *Les Syndicats en France*, Vol II, (Paris: Seuil, 1975), p. 221.

[4] op. cit., p. 452.

[5] *Le Bilan Social de l'Année 1968* (Confédération Générale du Travail, 1968), p. 5.

[6] G. Adam, 'Etude statistique des grèves de mai et juin 1968', *Revue Française de Science Politique* (February 1970), 105-119.

[7] For details, see in English, P. Seale and M. McConville op. cit. In French, see L. Rioux and M. Backmann, *L'Explosion de Mai* (Paris: R. Laffont, 1968).

potential for interference from other factors - the increasing politicisation of industrial relations in response to the development of the union of the left, the repercussions of the oil crisis and the introduction of the government's response to this, the Barre plan. The chapter will be divided into two parts. The former will concentrate on the direct response to the crisis, the *constat de Grenelle* which was initially reached but not signed by the representatives of the employers' associations and of the trade union confederations. The latter will focus on the turn of the decade and highlight two major areas of industrial relations, industrial conflict and attempts to institutionalise this conflict through collective bargaining.

THE CONSTAT DE GRENELLE

Negotiations in direct response to the events of May were held in the Rue de Grenelle, a part of the Ministry of Social Affairs (hence the name) between the representatives of the major trade union confederations and of the employers' associations and were presided over by the Prime Minister Georges Pompidou accompanied by the Minister for Social Affairs Jean-Marcel Jeanneney and the Secretary of State for Employment Jacques Chirac. After thirty hours of negotiations a provisional agreement, the *constat de Grenelle*, was reached.[8]

Given the effervescence of the period and the claims for *l'imagination au pouvoir*, it is interesting to note the prosaic nature of the proposals. There was no mention of the control of the process of work, nor of any infringement of management's 'right to manage'. The emphasis was very much on traditional demands and the central issue was wages. It was agreed that the minimum legal wage, the SMIG as it was then, would be increased to 3 francs per hour (from 2.20 francs), thus providing an improvement of 35 per cent, a significant increase relatively and a major factor in the erosion of wage differentials. However, this latter element should not be overstressed unduly since the number of *smigards* was relatively restricted - just over half a million were being paid the minimum

---

[8] *Droit Social* (July-August 1968), 448-450.

legal wage in December 1968.[9] In the private sector wages were to increase by 7 per cent on 1 June 1968 and by a further 3 per cent on 1 October. In the public sector although there was no specific figure quoted as such there was a commitment to enter into negotiations sector by sector. In fact real wages rose quite significantly in 1968 in comparison with previous years,[10] and, according to Mathieu, these wage settlements would lead to a 15 billion francs increase in the national wage bill, once all the effects had worked through the economy.[11]

A number of other significant elements were discussed. An objective of a 40-hour week was set. Those working more than 48 hours per week would have their hours reduced by two hours and those on between 45 and 48 hours would have their hours reduced by one. The negotiators agreed to meet at a later date to discuss the issues of job security and vocational training. The government agreed to consider certain improvements in the system of health insurance and in family benefits and pensions. There would be an arrangement by which strikers would be reimbursed for the wages lost during the strike. Of more potential significance for industrial relations in France, the representatives of the employers agreed to take part in negotiations at a later date which would bring bargaining agreements up to date; revise wage scales so that negotiated wages would come into line with real wages; reduce the importance of bonuses and incorporate them into basic wages; study the feasibility of reducing sex and age discrimination; and finally revise and simplify wage structures.

Another feature of significance to French industrial relations was the commitment made by the government to the introduction of a law on trade union rights at the workplace, which in fact was voted for in December of that year. For the first time it would be legally possible to establish a trade union presence in firms with more than fifty employees, to appoint trade union delegates with protection against being fired, to set up premises and to collect union dues. However it must not be forgotten that the demand for trade union

---

[9] J. Bron, *Histoire du Mouvement Ouvrier* Vol. III (Paris: Editions Ouvrières, 1982), p. 159.

[10] R. Flanagan, D. Soskice and L. Ulman, *Unions, Economic Stabilisation and Economic Policies* (Washington: Brookings Institute, 1983), p. 578.

[11] quoted in G. Caire op. cit., p. 456.

representation in the workplace was not new and indeed the text of
the law did not differ greatly from one proposed by René Mathevet
to the Conseil Economique et Social four years earlier.[12] This law
was to give considerable impetus to plant level organisation, and as
Table 7.1 shows, there was a two-fold increase in the number of
trade union branches and delegates from 1970 to 1974.

Table 7.1 - TRADE UNION BRANCHES AND DELEGATES

Year	1970	1971	1972	1973	1974
% of firms with trade union branches	27.5	31.3	35.3	40.0	43.0
number of trade union branches	11,775	13,991	17,242	20,721	23,882
number of trade union delegates	13,199	15,875	20,151	23,828	26,818

Source: A. Beaufils.[13]

It could be argued that greater workplace presence was one, but only
one, of the reasons for the more or less steady increase in
membership in all major trade union confederations during this
period, as Table 7.2 shows.

The *constat* granted undeniable improvements for employees and
necessitated concessions from employers, and yet 'it was rejected on
the 27 May by Renault workers at 8 a.m...but greeted with approval
at 11 am at a special meeting of the executive commission of the
CNPF'.[15] The former thought that they could obtain more in these

---

[12] J-D. Reynaud, S. Dassa, J. Dassa and P. Maclouf, 'Les évènements de
mai et juin 1968 et le système français de relations professionnelles (1)',
Sociologie du Travail (January-March 1971) p. 77.
[13] A. Beaufils, 'Les sections syndicales', *Revue Française des Affaires
Sociales*, 3 (1979), 167-186.
[15] H. Weber, *Le Parti des Patrons* (Paris: Seuil, 1986), p. 167.

particular circumstances, whilst the latter were pathetically grateful for being let off so lightly. Further negotiations ensued in each industrial sector and this basic provisional agreement was improved. In the private sector, the 210,000 employees in the clothing industry obtained an 18 per cent wage increase. The 225,000 employees in road transport obtained a wage increase of between 10-26 per cent and a one hour reduction in the length of the working week. The 162,000 employees in the banking industry obtained a 12.5 per cent wage increase and a reduction of one and a quarter hours in 1968 and a further one and a quarter hours for 1969. In other industries the wage increase was in fact less than that offered by the *constat*, but there were other compensating features. The chemical workers, for example, were only going to receive a 7 per cent wage increase, but on the other hand their working week was to be reduced by two hours in 1968 and a further two in 1969. In the public sector there was a greater commitment to a reduction in wage differentials. The 1,612,000 employees in the civil service only received 7.56 per cent for the better-paid, but the low-paid received 16.63 per cent. Moreover there was a commitment to a gradual reduction in the working week, for those working 48 hours to 46.5 and for those working 45 hours to 44. In the postal service and in the electrical and gas supply industries the low-paid received a relatively higher wage increase and there was also a differential reduction in the length of the working week.[16]

Table 7.2 - TRADE UNION MEMBERSHIP

Year	C G T members	F O membership cards sold	C F D T (100 in 1948)
1968	2,301,543	798,948	144.8
1970	2,333,056	810,886	156.5
1972	2,318,120	843,552	171.5
1974	2,342,811	874,427	180.1

Source: R. Mouriaux, A. Bergounioux, M. Branciard.[14]

[16] G. Caire. op. cit., pp. 458-460.
[14] These figures are provided by the trade union confederations

The events of May demonstrated the advantages of mass industrial action for obtaining certain immediate benefits. In the second part of the chapter it is proposed to study the succeeding period to consider what further impact the events of May may have had on industrial relations in France and more specifically in terms of industrial conflict and collective bargaining.

INDUSTRIAL CONFLICT

The events of May led to an improvement in wages, certain working conditions and trade union rights, but, according to Jean-Louis Moynot, one of the leaders of the CGT, there were political benefits too. He concluded that May 68 had made strikers aware of the way in which they were exploited and had encouraged them to question the capitalist ownership of the means of production.[17] Would the strikes of May 68 encourage employees to continue to strike whether for economic or political reasons?

If the five-year period preceding 1968 is compared with a similar succeeding period it can be seen from Table 7.3 that there was indeed a clear increase in the number of strikes (3 292 400 per year on average for 1969-1973 but only 1 944 600 for 1963-1967).

Indeed the early seventies too witnessed a relatively turbulent period of industrial unrest with 1971 having a particularly high level of strike activity. However there was actually a slight decrease in the number of days lost through strike action per year over each five-year period (3 210 700 compared with 3 239 000). The figures for the number of strike participants show that there was a significant overall increase. Overall strike activity increased considerably in the period after 1968 and it would be tempting to conclude that these changes occurred specifically as a result of the experiences and successes associated with the events of May. This was no doubt the case, but it is worth noting that the increase in industrial conflict did not in fact begin in 1968; it was in some ways prepared for in 1967, a year of significant *conflictualité*. There were other changes. Erbès-

---

themselves. R. Mouriaux, *La CGT* (Paris: Seuil, 1982), Annexe 1; A. Bergounioux, *Force Ouvrière* (Paris: PUF, 1982), p. 46; M. Branciard, *La CFDT* (Paris: PUF, 1986), p. 113.
[17] *Projet* (November 1970), 1048.

Seguin, Casassus and Kourchid undertook a major study of industrial conflict in France during the period of the late 1960s and early 1970s, choosing 1966-7, 1972 and 1974-5 as milestones. On the whole comparatively more strikes were of longer duration in the latter two periods,[18] thus demonstrating a greater level of militancy and commitment, perhaps as a result of experiences gained in 1968. The authors also noted a change in the outcome of strikes. In the latter two periods comparatively more strikes had a favourable outcome and less were described as a failure.[19]

Table 7.3 - INDUSTRIAL CONFLICT (1963-1973)

Year	Number of strikes	Number of days lost (thousands)	Number of strike participants (thousands)
1963	2,382	5,991.5	1,147.8
1964	2,281	2,496.8	1,047.3
1965	1,674	979.9	688.0
1966	1,711	2,523.5	1,028.6
1967	1,675	4,203.6	2,823.6
1968	nf	150,000.0	nf
1969	2,207	2,213.6	1,443.6
1970	2,742	1,782.1	1,079.8
1971	4,318	4,387.8	3,235.0
1972	3,464	3,755.3	2,721.3
1973	3,731	3,914.5	2,246.0

nf=no figure
Source: Ministère du Travail

---

[18] S. Erbès-Seguin, C. Casassus and O. Kourchid, *Les Conditions de développement du conflit industriel* (CNRS, Université de Paris VII, 1977), p. 185.
[19] Ibid.,p. 187.

For some, May 1968 was an inspiration and indeed set the tone for major industrial conflicts in the early 1970s, particularly in terms of the type of strike action and strike organisation. Indeed Charles Piaget, the leading figure in the strike and subsequent work-in at the Lip watch factory, claimed that Lip was only made possible because the events of May had shown the way. He noted that:

> En Mai 68 nous avons redécouvert pours certains, découvert pour d'autres, dont je fais partie, les formes de combat qui n'étaient plus utilisées depuis longtemps: la grève avec occupation d'usine, la grève active, avec la participation effective d'un grand nombre de travailleurs, l'élaboration des revendications faites par les travailleurs eux-mêmes. Nous avons découvert ou redécouvert les assemblées générales quotidiennes, souveraines sur les prises de décision, le comité de grève actif. Mai 68 ce fut une bonne école.[20]

In the opening paragraph of this chapter Seale and McConville also alluded to the fact that many strikers in 1968 occupied their places of work and although only a minority of strikes (5 per cent) in 1971 were described by Durand and Harff as 'violent',[21] there appears to have been a greater readiness to occupy plants. According to Durand, in one single day in the autumn of 1969, which he describes as not being particularly more turbulent than any others, *Le Monde* noted that seven plants were occupied; Manufrance, la Compagnie des Ateliers et Forges de la Loire and la Société de Constructions electromécaniques in St-Étienne, Thomson-CSF in Brest, Bréguet-Dassault in Anglet, Saviem in Limoges, Alsthom in Tarbes.[22] There perhaps was also a greater readiness to take senior managers hostage. Commenting on his 1971 survey, Dubois noted that this practice, although not a new phenomenon, had become more widespread and that employees had had increasing recourse to this

---

[20] C. Piaget, *LIP* (Paris: Stock, 1973), p. 19.

[21] M. Durand and Y. Harff, 'Panorama statistique des grèves', *Sociologie du Travail* (October-December 1977), p. 364.

[22] C. Durand, 'Ouvriers et techniciens en mai 1968' in P. Dubois et al., *Grèves revendicatives ou grèves politiques?* (Paris: Anthropos, 1971). p. 11.

type of action.[23] The figures show an increase in this form of strike activity but from a low base. However, in spite of these well-publicised examples, it still remained very much a minority form of strike activity.

As to Piaget's second point concerning strike organisation, Reynaud too was of the opinion that the increase in the number of strikes in France since 1968 was accompanied by a transfer of decision-making concerning strike action to the firm and even towards the workshop. A certain *basisme* was developing.[24] This does not imply that the trade unions were absent from the whole process however. In her survey of strikes in 1968 Erbès-Seguin noted that only in a small minority of cases did employees strike independently of the trade unions. In the majority of cases strikes were called either by the employees and then backed by the trade unions or by the latter backed by the former.[25] It was not the case that the trade unions were absent from strike activity either in 1968 nor subsequently.

Did the events of May act as some form of watershed as to the type of demand leading to strike action? Was there a move from quantitative to qualitative demands - a distinction made particularly in 1968 between wages, hours and bonuses on the one hand and power within the workplace and a feeling of wellbeing on the other?[26] This is admittedly a distinction sometimes difficult to draw. Writing about strikes in 1970 and 1971, Clerc maintained that working conditions, in the widest sense of the term, would not only play a more important role in the origin of strikes but would be present at the level of industrial demands.[27] In his study Mallet claimed that May 68 had transformed the content of strike action. He noted that a number of strikes were called in 1969, CODER, Etablissements Quillery, Manufrance, Caterpillar, Peugeot-Sochaux,

---

[23] P. Dubois, 'La séquestration', *Sociologie du Travail* (October-December 1974), p. 410.

[24] J-D. Reynaud, *Les Syndicats en France* Vol I, (Paris: Seuil, 1975). p. 166.

[25] S. Erbès-Seguin, 'Militants et travailleurs: organisation des relations dans la grève' in P. Dubois et al., op. cit.

[26] J-D. Reynaud, *Les Syndicats en France*, op. cit., p. 154.

[27] J.M. Clerc, 'Les conflits sociaux en France en 1970 et 1971', *Droit Social* (January 1973), pp. 19-26.

which brought into question management's control over such areas as redundancies, qualifications, productivity, work regulation and time keeping. Wage claims as such did not often feature in the particular strikes that he had investigated.[28] More detailed studies do not support this view however. The Erbès-Seguin, Casassus and Kourchid survey demonstrated that wage increases both before and after 1968 accounted for the majority of reasons for going on strike - moreover this trend increased from 1966-7 to 1972.[29] Durand and Harff compared their results for 1971 with those of the 1964 Baumfeldner survey and noted that wages provided the major reason for going on strike. Their results disproved Clerc's thesis.[30] However there was a greater readiness to strike for across-the-board wage increases rather than percentage increases, thus eroding wage differentials within the firm.[31] Indeed Durand has described this type of wage demand as the interface between qualitative and quantitative demands.

This relative increase in the significance of strike activity may have been even greater had it not been for the relative flexibility demonstrated by the government and the *patronat*. As Durand has stated: 'le réveil ouvrier de Mai 68 n'a pas cessé, dix-huit mois plus tard, de hanter le pouvoir politique et d'ébranler partis politiques et organisations syndicales. Les revendications nouvelles, la cogestion, la démocratie sont largement "récupérées" par le pouvoir politique dans le slogan de la participation.'[32]

COLLECTIVE BARGAINING

Participation may take a number of different forms and various governments have indeed flirted with certain of them. Some months before the events of May the government had already introduced a law on profit sharing. In 1970 the government introduced a law

[28] S. Mallet, 'L'aprés-mai 1968: grèves pour le contrôle ouvrier', *Sociologie du Travail* (July-September 1970), pp. 309-327.

[29] S. Erbès-Seguin, C. Casassus and O. Kourchid, op. cit., p. 189.

[30] M. Durand M and Y. Harff, 'Panorama statistique des grèves', op. cit., pp. 365-369.

[31] S. Erbès-Seguin, C. Casassus and O. Kourchid, op. cit., p. 189.

[32] C. Durand, 'Ouvriers et techniciens en mai 1968', op. cit., p. 10.

enabling Renault employees to acquire shares in their company and in 1973 employees in nationalised banks and insurance companies were given the same opportunity. This provision was also extended to private companies.[33] There was also a half-hearted attempt to introduce some form of 'industrial democracy' with the Sudreau Report.[34] However the government and the employers put most of their energy at that time into the institutionalisation of industrial conflict through collective bargaining. As has already been seen, bargaining agreements were made with great alacrity in most industrial sectors just after the *de facto* breakdown of the negotiations in the rue de Grenelle.

From 1968 onwards there was an increase in the number of agreements signed and a generally higher number of collective bargaining agreements signed per year in the 1970s than in the 1960s.[35] Of course these figures give no information about the quality of the agreement reached and neither do they explain the extent to which collective bargaining had become custom and practice. This increase in consultation and negotiation can be explained in part at least by the change in attitude of the government and by the CNPF subsequent to the events of May. Indeed Jacques Moreau, one of the leaders of the CFDT, claimed that before the events of May neither the employers nor the government were prepared to negotiate.[36] After the presidential elections in 1969 Chaban-Delmas was appointed Prime Minister and in a speech to the National Assembly in September 1969 provided a blueprint for a new society in which collective bargaining would play a significant role. Moreover as he explained in his memoirs the development of collective bargaining was encouraged by the creation of plant level unions and by the events of May: 'la politique contractuelle que je développai fut largement facilitée par la reconnaissance de la section syndicale d'entreprise qu'avaient amorcée les accords de Grenelle; aussi par le jaillissement de mai 1968, qui avait dénoué quelques bâillons...'[37]

---

[33] J-D. Reynaud, *Les Syndicats en France*, op. cit., p. 252.

[34] For resumé and critique see R. Mouriaux, 'Antagonismes sociaux et réforme de l'entreprise', *Etudes* (April 1975), 483-496.

[35] C. Jezequel, 'Aperçus statistiques sur la vie conventionnelle en France', *Droit Social* (June 1981), p. 462.

[36] *Projet* (November 1970), 1042.

[37] J. Chaban-Delmas, *L'Ardeur* (Paris: Stock, 1975), p. 349.

Indeed Chaban-Delmas was particularly responsible for encouraging collective bargaining in the public sector and for replacing the much maligned 'Toutée procedure' for deciding wage levels with the self-styled *contrats de progrès*. The first agreement was signed in the civil service in October 1969 and this was followed two months later by an agreement in the electrical and gas industries (EGF). Afterwards there were agreements on the railways (SNCF), the mines (Charbonnages de France), the Paris metro (RATP) and Renault and also in the nuclear power industry (Commissariat à l'Energie Atomique), Air France, the radio and television broadcasting company (ORTF), the Mines de Potasse d'Alsace and the Aéroport de Paris.

In his book on industrial relations in the public sector *Mort de l'Etat-Patron*, Dubois identified three specific government objectives *vis-à-vis* the new form of public sector bargaining; firstly, to reduce wage increases in the public sector; secondly, to tie wage increases to the commercial success of the industry or company concerned; and thirdly, to introduce 'paix sociale' and 'concertation', a reduction in strike activity and consultation.[38] Indeed Chaban-Delmas proclaimed triumphantly, and also erroneously, at the time of the signing of the first agreement: 'aujourd'hui s'est produite une révolution, et cela sans que le sang coule, sans qu'une ville ou une civilisation soit cassée...Pendant deux ans ou plus exactement pendant vingt et un mois, vous pouvez considérer qu'il n'y aura plus de grèves.'[39] He explained that collective bargaining had become the normal means for fixing wages in the public sector. Indeed so great was his commitment to public sector bargaining as a result of the May events that he, and certain subsequent governments, were prepared to continue to support it even though it did not fulfil some of the original objectives. It did not produce multi-year agreements. It did not succeed in incorporating no-strike clauses into most agreements. It did not produce many agreements which actually linked the increase in wages to the performance of the particular industry or to France's GNP. It did not halt the increases in wages, since as Lebon has shown, by 1971 all the major agreements had a

---

[38] P. Dubois, *Mort de l'Etat-Patron* (Paris: Editions Ouvrières, 1974), Ch. 2.
[39] *Le Monde*, 12 December.1969.

price-indexing safeguard clause.[40] The 1971 agreement in the EGF for example stipulated that real wages were to increase by 2.5 per cent. As a result of the additional agreement signed in 1972 real wages were to increase by at least 2-2.5 per cent. In 1973 they were to increase by 5 per cent. It was not until the introduction of the Barre plan that these safeguard clauses were abandoned.

Jobert has identified three particular stages of public sector bargaining, *une phase de lancement* (October 1969-December 1970), *une phase de consolidation* (1971) and finally, borrowing an expression of Jacques Delors, *une phase mutilée* (from 1972 onwards).[41] Public sector bargaining started briskly but gradually lost most of its momentum as it became clearer that its objectives were not being attained and as other economic and political factors crowded into the sphere of French industrial relations.

This insistence on wage bargaining in the public sector was designed to act as an example to the private sector. Sellier and Silvestre claimed that increasingly since 1958 and above all since 1968 the state has put pressure on the CNPF to bargain with unions at the national level on particular subjects.[42] This was no doubt made more possible by the attitude of the *patronat* itself, which was collectively less interested in revenge in 1968 than it had been in 1936, at the time of the strike wave accompanying the Popular Front government. According to Weber, employers were experiencing a crisis of conscience and a desire to ensure that the events of May did not happen again.[43] This new approach was personified above all by François Ceyrac. Although he did not become the president of the CNPF until 1972, he had already been appointed head of the CNPF's *commission sociale* in December 1967, with the reputation of being a convinced supporter of collective bargaining. The events of May provided him with the opportunity of pressing ahead with the

---

[40] A. Lebon, 'Les principaux accords salariaux signés en 1970 et 1971 dans les secteurs public et nationalisé', *Droit Social* (July-August 1971), 441-449.

[41] A. Jobert, 'Vers un nouveau style de relations professionnelles?' *Droit Social* (September-October 1974), p. 400.

[42] F. Sellier and J-J. Silvestre, 'Union policies in the economic crisis in France', in R. Edwards et al (eds), *Unions in Crisis and Beyond* (Dover, Mass.; Auburn House, 1986), p. 173.

[43] H. Weber, *Le Parti des Patrons*, op. cit., p. 170.

negotiation of collective bargaining agreements. After the negotiations in the rue de Grenelle he threw himself into national inter-professional bargaining.[44] An agreement was signed in February 1969 by the CNPF and the trade union confederations on job security. The following year in April an agreement was signed on the subject of *mensualisation*, the introduction of salaried status to all employees. Moller reinforced the argument put forward by Sellier and Silvestre explaining that it was essentially as a result of government pressure that *mensualisation* came to figure in the first rank of recent social achievements.[45] In July 1970 there was an agreement on maternity benefits and another on vocational training; and in March 1972 there was an agreement signed relating to early retirement. These agreements on job security and vocational training were in fact direct consequences of the *constat de Grenelle*.

The CNPF represented the employers but did not have the ability to dictate to the individual employers. Even in 1969 after the change in the statutes of the CNPF which strengthened the position of its leadership there was never any real suggestion that the CNPF made social policy on behalf of the other employers; however it did set the tone.[46] It set the tone and in the case of the agreement on *mensualisation*, the national inter-professional agreement was complemented by the signing of 18 other industrial agreements.[47]

The government of Chaban-Delmas also introduced legislation in July 1971 with the aim of improving collective bargaining procedures in the private sector. The law passed unanimously in the National Assembly had three major objectives: 'organiser la négociation collective au niveau de l'entreprise et de l'interprofession... élargir le champ couvert par les conventions collectives; intensifier et approfondir la vie contractuelle.'[48] The figures advanced by Jezequel did in fact show an increase in the number of extensions to bargaining agreements from 1971

---

[44] Ibid ., pp. 181-2.

[45] L-A. Moller, 'La mensualisation: bilan des accords professionnels signés à la fin de 1970', *Droit Social* (March 1971), 165-187.

[46] J-D. Reynaud, S. Dassa, J. Dassa and P. Maclouf. 'Les événements de mai et juin 1968 et le système français de relations professionnelles (II)', *Sociologie du Travail* (April-June 1971) p. 196.

[47] L-A. Moller, op. cit., pp. 173-4.

[48] Notes du Ministère du Travail, de l'Emploi et de la Population. 22/1971.

onwards.[49] However this does not mean that collective bargaining as such has become established practice. According to Lyon-Caen writing some years later: '...Même si les conventions et les accords sont quantitativement nombreux, la négociation n'est qu'un faux-semblant. Des propositions sont faites par le patronat; on y souscrit ou on n'y souscrit pas. Est-ce négocier?'[50] This opinion would become increasingly valid as the seventies progressed and other factors impinged on collective bargaining in France. The memory of the events of May faded and the perceived need to draw the trade unions into the process of collective bargaining was felt less keenly.

CONCLUSION

In spite of the fact that 1968 saw the largest strike wave in modern French history, the impact of the events of May on French industrial relations was nevertheless relatively modest. In the wake of the *constats de Grenelle* French employees obtained certain significant short-term quantitative benefits, particularly in terms of wages and hours, and more significantly in the medium term for industrial relations in France, trade unions were able to reinforce their presence in the workplace. However there was no suggestion that the basic power relationship within the workplace should be transformed.

In the subsequent period the direct consequences of the events of May were less obvious. Industrial conflict, when measured in terms of the number of strikes and the number of strike participants, did indeed increase considerably after 1968, but then strike activity had in fact been on the increase since 1967. However in spite of numerous claims to the contrary, there were only marginal changes to the overall pattern of strike activity. Collective bargaining in the public and private sectors was to experience a brief period of expansion, particularly as a result of the example set by the Chaban-Delmas government. Although there was an increase in the number of agreements signed, there was no evidence to suggest that collective bargaining was becoming an established practice.

---

[49] C. Jezequel, 'Aperçus statistiques sur la vie conventionnelle en France', op. cit., p. 463.
[50] G. Lyon-Caen, 'Critique de la négociation collective', *Après-demain* (February 1980) pp. 7-9.

Reynaud, Dassa, Dassa and Maclouf have noted that:

> ...d'un premier bilan des négociations et des accords intervenus dans les douze ou quinze mois qui ont suivi mai 1968, il faut bien tirer une constation paradoxale: alors que chacun à l'envi a insisté sur les caractères nouveaux et originaux des grèves et revendications, les problémes traités à la suite de ce mouvement montrent une continuité à peu près parfaite avec la période antérieure.[51]

However it was the readiness to tackle these problems at this particular time which characterised the impact of the events of May. The intensification of strike activity led to a modification in general terms in the *rapport de force* between employees and the trade unions on the one hand and employers and the government on the other. The latter responded initially by attempting to draw the trade unions into some form of collective bargaining in the public and private sectors.

---

[51] J-D. Reynaud, S. Dassa, J. Dassa and P. Maclouf, 'Les évènements de mai et juin 1968 et le système français de relations professionnelles (I)', op. cit., p. 76.

8. TRADE UNION STRATEGIES AFTER MAY 1968

RENÉ MOURIAUX

The social movement of May-June 1968 was a shock to the trade union system in France but did not alter its internal balance significantly. After a pause, unity of action between the CGT and CFDT was resumed and would continue until the break-up of the union of the political left. The presence of the teachers' union FEN at the Grenelle negotiations, far from being anomalous, would turn out to be a portent of things to come and we may say that this is the moment when the FEN emerged as a significant actor on the national stage. The economic crisis which set in from 1974 gradually dictated its terms, and the May page only began to be turned late in 1977 or early in 1978.

THE CGT-CFDT AXIS

The CGT-CFDT agreement of 10 January 1966 was vital in mobilising the membership prior to the general strike. The aims it set out can be found, subject to corrections and qualifications, in the text of the Grenelle agreements.[1] But understanding between the two unions which was already shaky by the end of 1967 could not withstand the whirlwind of the 'events'. The CGT would never

---

[1] M. Bellas, 'Ambigüités des négotiations de Grenelle', *Projet*, 27 (July-August 1968), 809-813.

accept that Daniel Cohn-Bendit represented anything and sought to set up an agreement between the FGDS and the PCF, backed up by a union front. The CFDT plumped for the opposite choice. The joint reminder of the line agreed on 10 January 1966, which was issued on 22 May gave way to divergence which was clear at Grenelle and Charléty. From then on the two organisations were divided by sharp differences and it would take two years for them to return to the road to united action.

The phases of unity of action after 68

The aftermath of May saw no change in the climate which had set in during the 'events'. Unity of action was resumed in September 1970 and would go through four phases before petering out after September 1977.

After the general strike each union was taken up with making its own internal evaluation of the consequences of the strike and with implementing the gains of Grenelle. It looked as if there might be a change of alliances. The national confederal committee of the CGT-FO on 19-20 October 1968 came out in favour of resuming talks with the CFDT.[2] Georges Séguy referred to the virtues of the inter-union agreement of 10 January 1966 three days before its anniversary. The CGT administrative committee called on the same day for a national day of action which would later be set for 12 February 1969. The CFDT's reply was that the CGT move was political, unilateral and publicity-seeking; understanding between unions presupposed independence from political parties. The CFDT therefore began talks with FO which it saw on 3 and 18 February 1969 and later on 18 June 1970. 'Some convergence of views' was noted, especially on short-term matters and in view of the Tilsitt meeting of 6 March. But this was not enough to overcome persistent disagreement. FO absolutely ruled out any co-operation with the CGT, while Eugene Descamps' union wanted to involve the latter in a joint campaign for certain demands.

The *rapprochement* between the CFDT and FO came to nothing, and the CFDT and CGT continued to disagree. The two were certainly able to call for a 'no' vote in the referendum of 27 April

---

[2] E. Descamps, *Militer* (Paris: Fayard,1971), pp. 103-5 and 242-3.

1969, but disagreed as to what advice to give supporters for the second ballot of the presidential election on 15 June. Séguy's union urged abstention, whereas Descamps' came out in favour of Alain Poher. They also had differing approaches to the incomes policy which Jacques Delors, social affairs adviser to Chaban-Delmas and a CFDT member, was urging upon the public sector. The CFDT signed the wages agreement of 10 December 1969 with the state electricity company EDF while the CGT fought it.

The CFDT's 35th Congress of 6-10 May 1970 showed how much headway various left-wing elements had made within that union. The union proclaimed its official attachment to socialism, albeit to what it called *autogestionnaire* (self-managing) socialism. The report of the union president André Jeanson, *Perspectives et stratégies*,[3] which was adopted by a vote of 64.5 per cent, saw three planks in the construction of socialism: social ownership, workers' self-management (*autogestion*) and planning. Descamps' report lamented the obstacles to unity of action with the CGT,[4] and the motion on action recommended 'constant efforts to bring the strength of the unions together on as broad a basis as possible.'[5]

The CGT which had at its 37th Congress in 1969 called for the formation of a united union front and written to all the other unions on 26 February 1970 with its suggestions for creating one, pointed out the progress made by the CFDT's 35th Congress. The first meeting between the two took place on 4 June 1970 and an agreement was signed on 15 September.[6]

'Representatives of the CFDT and CGT met on 15 September to continue the debate which they began in June on essential demands and on the means recommended by the two unions to bring these demands to fruition.
Both unions have already pointed out separately to the government and the employers what the most urgent needs of working people are, particularly as regards an increase in

---

[3] A. Jeanson, 'Perspectives et stratégie', *Syndicalisme*, 1279a special number, (February 1970).
[4] *Syndicalisme*, 1291, 14 May 1970
[5] Ibid.
[6] Joint CFDT-CGT Communiqué in *L'Humanité* 16 September 1970.

purchasing power and better living conditions inside and outside the workplace.

Accordingly negotiations must be carried on at every level - individual firms, whole branches of industry and nationally - and in close co-ordination.

The two unions intend to specify appropriate means of action in support of each of their joint demands.

To this end they are ready to single out and campaign together for the following targets, which are among the most pressing issues facing working people:

1. the defence, guarantee and increase of purchasing power; the evening-out of disparities

2. a minimum guaranteed wage of 800 francs per month, with the aim of reaching a minimum remuneration of 1000 francs per month for both notionally agreed and take-home pay

3. the speedier and more widespread reduction of working hours; earlier retirement ages

4. the upgrading of pensions and benefits with the aim of reaching a minimum of 800 francs per month

5. the defence and extension of union freedom, particularly the one paid hour of information time per month

6. a democratic reform of the tax system

These aims will be achieved only through action by individual branches and trade federations as well as at departmental and national levels. Some of them call particularly for national initiatives, if union branches and their workers are to be brought into action.

The delegations have therefore decided to meet again soon after reporting back to the bodies to which they are responsible.'

Clearly there had been no complete reconciliation between the CGT and CFDT. It showed the limits of the policies applied by Jacques Chaban-Delmas, whose 'new society' appealed neither to conservatives nor to all the moderates. It was but a pale reflection of the movement of 68, and while the employers were committed to a strategy of pay rounds they were not ready to pay the price it would take to break up the union front as it was slowly being put back together.[7]

The first phase in the new understanding between the CGT and the CFDT stretches from September 1970 to June 1972. It included argument over doctrine, the organising of joint campaigns and some public controversy. By relaunching unity of action the CFDT was expressing its hope that the different parts of the union movement would exchange their views about socialism and how to bring it about. The CGT went along with this and on 31 March 1971 published its *Thèmes de réflexion sur les perspectives du socialisme pour la France et le rôle des syndicats.*[8] Georges Séguy's union favoured the setting up of a government that would express the interests of the working class and nationalise the major means of production, economic planning and democratic management of the economy. On 30 October 1971 came the CFDT's contribution which carried on from Jeanson's report by stressing alienation and domination as a counterweight to the CGT's economic reductionism.[9] These doctrinal arguments between the two unions shed light on their differences, bringing them into the open and giving them form; but they did not create these differences, nor indeed did they reduce them.

Parallel to this ideological debate rather than in conjunction with it, joint action was undertaken. The agreement of 15 September 1970 had set out general guidelines, and other meetings gave it precise form. Descamps' replacement by Edmond Maire on 1 September 1971 made no difference. The new General Secretary of the CFDT declared that unity of action was 'irreversible', 'in that it is a tried

---

[7] The renewal of the employers' organisation CNPF, which had been given a boost by the May 1968 crisis, was symbolised by the election of François Ceyrac to the head of its governing council in December 1972.

[8] The text is reprinted in H. Krasucki, *Syndicats et socialisme* (Paris: Editions Sociales, 1972), pp. 103-23.

[9] See E. Maire, *Pour un Socialisme démocratique*, contribution de la *CFDT* (Paris: Epi,1971), pp. 31-78.

and trusted weapon which we are determined to use whenever joint union action seems feasible and likely to bring results.'[10]

Three national campaigns were launched, on the lowering of retiring age, labour legislation and immigrants. Disagreement about methods of action surfaced, with the CGT favouring national days of action, whilst the CFDT preferred a more decentralised formula, spread out over a longer period of time. The disagreement between the two unions intensified in November 1971 with the civil service pay deal,[11] protests against unfair taxation on 17 February 1972 and especially the death of a young Maoist activist, René-Pierre Overney at Boulogne-Billancourt on 26 February.

The signing of a joint programme of government led to a new phase in union relations. At the meeting of 23 August 1972, the CGT said to the CFDT: 'we can't say that we will carry on united action with you as if the joint programme didn't exist.'[12] George Séguy spelled out his union's thinking at the public meeting in the Mutualité hall in Paris on 7 September. Support for the joint programme was a mark of specific class loyalty. But the CFDT national executive still had reservations which outweighed the approval it had given the joint PS-PCF document on 15 September 1972. It saw a risk of centralising statism and production for its own sake. It would not take part in the support committees for the joint programme. Moreover the CFDT came out in favour of strikes by the number of hours: a total stoppage time in hours would be agreed for a fixed period and then workers would be left free to carry out this instruction in the way that best suited them. Georges Séguy accused the CFDT of putting more obstacles in the way of unity, of preferring to get closer to leftists than to reach an understanding with the mainstream left and of being completely unrealistic with its notions of 'flexistrikes'.[13]

Perhaps as a result of the sacking of Jacques Chaban-Delmas and the 'shift to the right' of Georges Pompidou's presidency, the two unions did confirm their unity agreement despite their differences on 28 September 1972. They agreed in the words of one participant 'to

---

[10] *Syndicalisme* 2 September 1971.

[11] It gave rise to conflict even within the CFDT.

[12] Quoted in *CFDT aujourd'hui* 17 (January-February 1976), p. 81.

[13] Declaration by Georges Séguy in *Le Monde* 28 September 1972.

keep the torch alight.'[14] The general elections of March 1973 tended to strengthen relations between the unions. The CFDT's 36th Congress (30 May - 3 June 1973) saw some sharp attacks on the PCF, but what struck the CGT was the fact that the CFDT kept its distance from minority group actions and that its line on differentials was totally unrealistic.[15]

Tension grew again at the grass roots, when there were local conflicts like the Lip dispute. But the two unions were drawn closer by the adoption of a joint set of demands on social security on 11 July.[16] On 10 October 1973 the CGT published a document entitled *La Gestion démocratique des entreprises dans la démocratie économique et politique*. In this text Séguy's union attempted to refute the contrast postulated by the CFDT between a centralising tradition of socialism and a self-managing one.[17] But Maire's organisation strove to maintain the difference by developing its strategy of 'the union of popular forces'.[18] It did not invite the CGT to its symposium on autogestion held on 16 February 1974: 'If we're not careful, *autogestion* will be too popular for its own good and end up meaning all things to all men.'[19] Further friction was evident in the disputes at the Rateau and Saviem works and in banking, as the CGT secretary André Berteloot pointed out.[20] Albert Detraz, a CFDT leader, had an optimistic interpretation of these clashes between the unions:

'You have to feel things as well as understand them. The CFDT is better at feeling, and the CGT seems to understand better. We haven't yet got a blend between the two...We're stuck with

---

[14] *Le Monde* 30 September 1972.

[15] This view was shared by *Le Monde* for instance , which concluded its series of articles on the 36th Congress with a significant by-line: 'Autogestion seems to have come of age within the CFDT' (5 June 1973). Note also the subtitle, 'un réformisme révolutionnaire'.

[16] *L'Humanité* 24 July 1973.

[17] This theme was particularly developed in an interview given by Edmond Maire to *Le Nouvel Observateur* (9 June 1973).

[18] A document on this theme was adopted by the national council on 24-6 January, 1974.

[19] *Le Monde* 17-18 February 1974.

[20] *L'Humanité* 15 March 1974.

unity of action despite the conflict, because no-one wants to break up the class-front...The CGT has no business giving us lessons, because above the CFDT there's the union movement and above that there's the working class.'[21]

Georges Pompidou's death led to an early presidential election which pushed the disagreements into the background. The forward march of the left on 19 May 1974, which was undeniable albeit insufficient, unleashed a new political process. François Mitterrand pushed for the *Assises du socialisme* meetings which the CFDT at first supported strongly.[22] At this moment the understanding between the CGT and the CFDT was at its peak. On 26 June 1974 the two unions issued a joint declaration on aims and methods of action; this is the widest-ranging and most profound document that the two organisations ever put together.[23]

This high point of inter-union understanding was put under stress by the changing balance of strength between the PCF and the PS and by the differing analyses of the economic crisis made by the CGT and CFDT. Jacques Moreau's report to the national council of the CFDT (24-28 October 1974) stressed the reasons for Valéry Giscard d'Estaing's success and implied that the crisis would last for some time yet.

1975 and the first part of 1976 saw a third phase in the unions' relationship. The CFDT accused the CGT of preferring to act on its own. The CGT replied that it kept its promises but that the stage had not yet been reached 'where we can have everything in common and only act together.'[24] This view was confirmed by its 39th Congress of 22-26 June 1975, where it was justified by reference to frequent clashes at grass-roots level.

The two organisations reacted differently early in December 1975 when Jacques Chirac cracked down on anti-militarist campaigning. CFDT premises were searched and some activists arrested. Edmond

---

[21] *Le Monde* 28 March 1974.

[22] M. Kesselman and G. Groux (eds), *1968-1982: le Mouvement ouvrier français, crise économique et changement politique* (Paris: Editions Ouvrières, 1984), pp. 97-8.

[23] *L'Humanité* 27 June 1974. See also CFDT, *Textes de base 1* (Paris: CFDT, 1974), pp. 123-4.

[24] Georges Séguy interview with *L'Humanité* 18 February 1975.

Maire called for unflinching solidarity, whereas Georges Séguy demanded that irresponsible actions be condemned before he would join in a joint protest.

The tenth anniversary of the 1966 agreements passed unspectacularly; the affair of the soldiers' committees had left its mark. Moreover the CFDT was pondering its failures of the previous year in disputes at Renault, Usinor and the Post Office. At a meeting of 5 April 1975 the CFDT suggested bringing the FEN into the united union front. The CFDT's 37th Congress (25-9 May 1976) saw vigorous attacks on the CGT, and what were referred to as 'cuckoos in the nest'; unity of action was described as 'the central means for the CFDT to carry out its policy of class and mass struggle.[25]

Jacques Chirac's replacement as prime minister by Raymond Barre ushered in the last phase of unity of action, which was directed against the austerity plans. The days of action of 7 October 1976, 24 May 1977 and 1 December 1977 were the high points of a period which effectively came to an end in September 1977 with the failure to update the joint programme of government. Unity of action between the unions would be broken off formally in June 1980 ; but as Hervé Hamon and Patrick Rotman write, it was implied within the policy of *recentrage*.[26] The Moreau report which paved the way for abandoning the understanding with the CGT was put together in autumn 1977 and an advance version circulated in December.

Unity of action: what was at stake

Between 1968 and 1978 the relationship between the CGT and CFDT was very much an up-and-down one. But the life of the unions revolved around it. The debate to which it gave rise and the struggles it helped stimulate were the tangible expression of a dynamic process which by its very contradictions continued the movement of 1968. Three major issues were at stake in this inter-union relationship.

---

[25] CFDT, *Textes de base 2*, (Paris: CFDT,1977), p. 54.
[26] H. Hamon and P. Rotman, *La deuxième Gauche* (Paris: Ramsay, 1982), p. 332. Two events would provide the catalyst for the break-up : the march on Paris of 23 March 1979 and the invasion of Afghanistan.

The CGT and CFDT clashed over demands relating to wages, taxation, the nuclear industry and women's matters. Between 1968 and 1978 they did scale down their differences over trade-union law,[27] immigration problems,[28] social security[29] and conditions at work.[30]

The biggest and longest-lasting controversy concerned differentials. In September 1970 the CFDT ran a special number of *Syndicalisme* entitled 'Challenging differentials'. The national council of October 1970 developed the union's ideas further. Daily action could not be separated from the vision of self-managing socialism towards which they were working; but equally, tomorrow's revolution was no excuse for neglecting today's reforms.

Henri Krasucki was critical of the CFDT's idealism : 'Nobody can dream up demands - they're something working people feel as a need.' Edmond Maire thought there was more to it than that: there was always a choice to be made, but if it wasn't made with full awareness then it would be sidetracked.[31] The agreement of 1 December 1970 envisaged 'sorting out job gradings by fixing single salary scales for each category of workers within any industry'. The section on wages ended with a vague formula: 'solutions will be found in each branch of industry and each firm according to the real problems which exist and which vary from one place to another.'[32] René Bonéty explained that 'if some points in the text might not seem clear then this is because there is indeed considerable ambiguity. It can only be cleared up by carrying on with in-depth discussions.'[33] In firms, CFDT branches frequently asked for flat-

---

[27] The CFDT's legal experts, unlike those of the CGT, pushed for the introduction of penal sanctions into labour law. They also obtained a system of proportional representation for elections to arbitration tribunals (*conseils des prud'hommes*). See P. Cam, *Les Prud'hommes : juges ou arbitres?* (Paris: Presses de la FNSP, 1981).

[28] R. Mouriaux and C. Withold de Wenden, *Syndicalisme français et Islam* (Paris: AFSP-CERI,1982).

[29] N. Dada and R. Mouriaux, *Le Régime de la sécurité sociale en France et les syndicats de salariés* (Paris: AFERP- AFSP,1982).

[30] R. Mouriaux, 'Négociations sur les conditions de travail', *Etudes* (October 1973), 345-52.

[31] R. Mouriaux, *La CGT* (Paris: Seuil,1982), p. 128.

[32] *L'Humanité* 2 December 1970.

[33] M. Branciard, *La CFDT* (Paris: PUF, 1986), p. 68.

rate wage rises, unlike the CGT. In the shopping-list of demands for which it voted in June 1977, the CFDT national council stated its preference for a spread of differentials from one to six. At the same time the CGT brought out a special number of *Le Peuple*, 'Solutions et propositions', which went for a one to seven spread on differentials.[34]

Disagreements on taxation and nuclear energy were not so crucial as those on wages.[35] But women's matters would also serve to differentiate the two unions.

The CFDT accused the CGT of maintaining the gender division of labour by putting forward specifically female demands. It wanted immediate equality and was particularly hostile to any differential reducing of the retirement age. The difference between the two points of view was narrrowed and on 13 December 1974 Edmond Maire and Georges Séguy published an agreement on the demands of women workers. Apart from demands concerning the status of pregnant women and the problem of freely consented and conscious procreation, the rest of the package aimed at outlawing discrimination over wages, training, employment and living and working conditions. One demand was for 'a credit of two years per child to be taken into account in determining the age at which a woman can retire with full entitlement.'[36] The CGT continued to demand retirement at 55 for women, not least because it figured in the joint programme of the left.

The gap between the CGT's demands and the CFDT's suggestions grew slowly wider as the recession set in. The CGT organisation felt that the big depression called for drastic remedies and that this added new legitimacy to its basic demands. But the CFDT tended more to stress qualitative demands rather than quantitative, as shown in its 1976 booklet *La Crise* .

---

[34] CFDT, *Plate-forme de revendications et d'objectifs immédiats* (Paris: CFDT,1978). See also *Le Peuple* 15 June 1977.

[35] Public disagreement over taxation surfaced in September 1970 when the CGT and CFDT organised separate demonstrations against unfair taxation. The CFDT national bureau came out against the French nuclear energy programme in April 1975 whereas the CGT approved it for the most part.

[36] J. Laot, *Stratégie pour les femmes* (Paris: Stock, 1977), p. 242. The full text of the document of 19 December 1974 is reprinted in this book.

This difference in the demands that the CGT and CFDT were putting forward cannot be isolated from differences over methods of action. During the decade under consideration the CGT accused the CFDT of giving support to adventurist tactics and refusing to generalise action when necessary.

The CFDT returned the compliment by complaining that the CGT was putting the brakes on grass-roots struggles and trying to cobble together a front of people with any kind of grievance.[37] On 26 June 1974 the two unions adopted a document which reduced disagreement about ways of carrying out union activity. This document declared that the union branch was responsible for carrying out action, that the greatest number possible should be involved in deciding what demands to push for and what action to take in support thereof.[38]

Where unions are concerned a document can indicate a state of mind, but it does not alter people's way of doing things. Tactical disagreements between the CGT and CFDT carried on and on. In 1976 Maire's union analysed them clearly. An article in *CFDT Aujourd'hui*, which was edited at the time by Jacques Moreau and Pierre Rosanvallon, asked a number of quesions about the CGT's anti-leftist stance. The (anonymous) author felt that since the crisis of May 1968 the CGT had not been trying to put a brake on action so much as to bring it under its own control. After the break-up of the leftist movements in late 1972-early 1973 the CGT had changed its attitude so as not to encourage conservative behaviour among its membership.

The CFDT analysis of CGT behaviour seems quite relevant. Alongside this, it does seem correct to point out that the CFDT was wary of national days of action for two reasons: firstly because this tactic showed up the superior numbers of the CGT quite clearly, whereas within individual firms union strengths varied a great deal;

---

[37] For instance on 9 November 1973 the CFDT criticised an agreement it had signed with the CGT and the left-wing parties on the struggle against inflation because the farmers' union FNSEA was likely to be among the signatories.

[38] *L'Humanité* 27 June 1974.

and secondly because mobilising people for social ends ran directly into political campaigning.[39]

The third area of confrontation between the two unions was precisely this relationship between union action and the political sphere.

Ever since the Liberation the CFTC had accused the CGT of being subordinate to communism. The *Reconstruction* group within the CFTC was set up, as Paul Vignaux recalls in his book *De la CFTC à la CFDT: syndicalisme et socialisme*, to encourage the development of a class-based trade-unionism that would be really independent and strong enough to check any drift into Stalinism. The events of May-June 1968 showed the CFDT's continuing anxiety to avoid the 'slide from a union front into some kind of politico-union admixture.'[40] From 1968 to 1978 the CFDT never gave up the fight to stop the trade unions' action from being determined by communist strategy. This it did by putting forward other demands, other modes of action, a different system of alliances and objectives. It relied first on the far left, then at the 1974 *Assises* put its weight behind the building of a big socialist party. It put up a different analysis of socialism and was tireless in its criticism of the CGT's workerism, economic reductionism, obsession with politics and centralism.

Edmond Maire admitted in 1976 that 'one cannot deny how far the CFDT has moved, partly thanks to the CGT's influence' ; he also noted that the CGT had shifted in response to the actions as well as the ideas of the CFDT.[41] Likewise in 1980 Henri Krasucki felt that 'everyone has moved, but not in the same way.'[42] The break-up in 1978 put an end to this process of mutual enrichment.

UNION PLURALISM CONTINUES

Although unity of action between the CGT and CFDT was the major driving force in union affairs between 1968 and 1978, there were

---

[39] On this problem see R. Mouriaux, *Syndicalisme et politique* (Paris: Editions Ouvrières, 1985), pp. 138-50.

[40] P. Vignaux, *De la CFTC à la CFDT: syndicalisme et socialisme. 'Reconstruction', 1946-72* (Paris: Editions Ouvrières, 1980), p. 60.

[41] *CFDT Aujourd'hui* 17 (January-February 1976), 31.

[42] H. Krasucki, *Syndicats et unité* (Paris: Editions Sociales, 1980), p. 105.

other players in the game. There was still a trio of reformist unions with whom the FEN, whose power was growing, kept some links. But the independent unions never managed to grow beyond marginal status, even though the events of May-June 1968 had provoked some sharp reactions to the big unions.

The reformist three show their strength in the elections while the FEN's power grows

According to FO's own official declarations, its membership increased steadily from 1968 to 1978. Its score in elections to works committees (*comités d'entreprise*) rose slowly after a slight dip between 1968 and 1972. FO played a key rôle in the government's policy of public sector agreements, and Jean-Daniel Reynaud wrote that this policy of the union 'did not get its just deserts.'[43] Its image was rather woolly because of its heterogeneous character and its lack of punch. The CFDT won over some of the members of FO's Chemical Workers' Federation in 1972 and some of its postal workers in 1974 because of its greater willingness to put up a fight.

Although a quarter of the size of FO, the CFTC continued its slow build-up. In elections to works committees it scored between 2.1 and 3 per cent. This catholic union suffered from being in an extreme minority except for one or two sectors (mining, banking, private schools) or regions (Alsace, Lower Normandy).[44]

The CGC was the union hardest hit by the movement of May-June 1968. From 22 May there was a sit-in in its headquarters. This did not stop the union from enjoying increased support from managers keen to enjoy a peaceful social climate. However a controversy dating back to 1966, when an agreement was signed with EDF providing for a reduction of differentials, led to a split. In 1969 the *Union des cadres et techniciens* was set up. André Malterre's reply to this challenge was to modernise his union's rule book. Yvon Charpentié who took over from him in 1974 was unable to establish his authority and bring back internal harmony. In

---

[43] J.-D. Reynaud, *Les Syndicats en france* (Paris: Colin, 1975), Vol. I, p. 110.
[44] R. Mouriaux,' Le 39ᵉ Congrès de la CFTC', *Etudes* (January 1978), pp. 73-4.

October 1978 there was an open crisis which threatened the very existence of the union.[45] But none of this stopped the CGC's electorate from growing.

The FEN developed under the impulsion of James Marangé and then André Henry. It used public sector wage deals to secure a key position in that sector. Treating each situation on its merits, it would ally either with the CGT-CFDT axis or with FO. From 380,000 members in 1968 it grew to 550,000 in 1978. This growth was due to a widening of its area of unionisation and to an increase in its number of branches. The union also strengthened the network of mutual assurance companies and associations in its orbit. In 1972 it set up the CCOMCEN to rule over this 'empire'.

In 1976 the FEN proclaimed itself to be socialist and defined itself as an organisation for teaching, research and culture. It hoped to gain entry to the top committee for collective bargaining, but all it got was a letter from Jacques Chirac in August 1976 which 'confirmed the government's intention to consider the FEN as one of the most representative of the trade union organisations'. Under this head it received Ministry of Labour grants for the education of its members, like the five recognised unions.

The failure of the independent unions

The independent unions were hoping that the May upheavals would bring official recognition nearer. But Maurice Couve de Murville, Jacques Chaban-Delmas and Pierre Messmer were to disappoint them. As early as 1971 some CFT shopworkers' branches joined FO, and the CGSI merged with the CFTC in 1977.

But the CFT still carried on attacking the 'monopoly' enjoyed by the CGT, CFDT, FO, CFTC and CGC. An internal crisis in 1975 led to a split and the setting up of the UFT. In June 1977 a CGT activist was killed at Reims by a member of the CFT. To escape the opprobrium which descended on it, the organisation changed initials and became the CSL; but its future remained uncertain.

---

[45] G. Lavau, G. Grunberg and N. Mayer, *L'Univers politique des classes moyennes* (Paris: Presses de la FNSP, 1983), pp. 321-5.

CONCLUDING REMARKS

May-June 1968 did not turn the world of French trade unions upside down. Certainly new goals emerged, in the shape of working conditions and women's emancipation. Methods of action changed too. Work-ins became quite a normal means of applying pressure. Struggles were popularised in original ways, with products being sold not just to swell strike funds but also to show that the strikers were capable of running the firm.

The CGT and the PCF managed to get their 'frontist' strategy off the ground, although they had failed to do so in May 1968. They gave up on it at the end of 1977, as the PS surged ahead and disagreement remained widespread as to how to deal with the recession.

Unity of action between the CGT and CFDT barely survived the break-up of the union of the political left. Ten years after May 1968 a new era opened, dominated by the all- pervasive presence of the recession.

APPENDIX I. LIST OF THE MAIN NATIONALLY
APPLICABLE AGREEMENTS CONCLUDED BETWEEN THE
CNPF AND THE UNIONS, 1969-77.

10 February 1970: agreement setting up employment committees,
for individual trades and cross-industry, with equal representation for
employers and unions. It defined the rules of appeal to the works
committee before any mass dismissals for economic reasons and gave
employees guarantees, especially in the case of job changes and mass
redundancies on economic grounds. Signed by CFDT, CFTC, CGC,
CGT, FO.

20 April 1970: joint declaration inviting unions in all branches of
industry to begin negotiations on the monthly payment of wages.
Signed by CFDT, CFTC, CGC, CGT, FO.

22 April 1970: joint declaration on payment by the month.

22 June 1970: agreement on job security for sales representatives.

2 July 1970: draft agreement for raising the daily allowance
payable to women on maternity leave from 50 to 90 percent of pro
rata wage.

9 July 1970: agreement giving all employees the right to training
and improvement of skills. This agreement was broadened out on 30
April 1971 to include an additional section for executive grades and
also on 2 February 1973 to take account of the law of 16 July 1971.
Signed by CFDT, CFTC, CGT, FO.

30 April 1971: executive grade addition to above. Signed by
CFDT, CFTC, CGC, CGT, FO.

27 March 1972: agreement to provide a guaranteed income for
employees made redundant at 60. Until the age of 65 beneficiaries
were entitled to membership of a guaranteed income scheme and to a
special status, distinct from that of the unemployed (mainly by being
exempted from signing on).

16 March 1973: youngsters admitted to occupational pension schemes (supplement to the agreement of 8 December 1961); removal of the age clause.

19 March 1973: agreement on youngsters joining occupational pension schemes directly on starting work.

6 June 1973: agreement on extending compulsory payment of national insurance contribution (T1) to all executive grades.

25 June 1973: supplement to the agreement of 27 March 1972; the scheme was improved in five areas.

30 October 1973: extension of the agreement of 2 March 1972 to agricultural workers.

4 March 1974: improved conditions for payment of special unemployment benefits, especially for those over 50 (supplement to the agreement of 31 December 1958).

14 October 1974: agreement to set up a system of interim payments to workers dismissed for economic reasons.

21 October 1974: agreement on new guarantees in the case of mass redundancies. Signed by CFTC, CGC, FO.

25 February 1975: extension of the agreement of 14 October 1974 to workers finishing contracts in the construction industry. Signed by CGPME (small employers' federation), CFDT, CFTC, CGC, CGT, FO.

17 March 1975: agreement on working conditions. Signed by CFTC, CGC, FO.

8 April 1975: agreement on short-time working. Signed by FO.

23 June 1975: agreement on short-time working with all the unions.

3 October 1975: national cross-industry agreement on sales representatives. 3 February 1976: addendum to the national cross-industry agreement of 21 February 1968 on compensation for short-time working.

9 July 1976: agreement on vocational training.

14 September 1976: addendum to the cross-industry agreement of 21 February 1968 on compensation for short-time working.

25 February 1977: agreement on compensation for short-time working (modifies above agreement).

16 May 1977: agreement between CGT, CFDT, FO and CFTC and CNPF in favour of agricultural workers.

25 May 1977: addendum to the addendum of 25 February 1975 dealing with the rules of the national special allowance scheme for the unemployed in industry and commerce.

13 June 1977: national cross-industry agreement filling out and modifying the appendix to the agreement of 31 December 1958 (guarantee of income for those made redundant at 60).

10 December 1977: national cross-industry agreement on payment by the month.

12 December 1977: addendum modifying Appendix I of the national agreement of 25 February 1977 on compensation for short-time working.

APPENDIX II. MAIN MEETINGS BETWEEN CGT AND CFDT, 1970-77.

15 September 1970: joint statement. Seven demands put forward.

1 December 1970: joint statement. Three inter-union campaigns on pensions, trade union law and immigrants.

25 August 1971: joint statement.

6 September 1971: joint statement.

14 March 1972: failure to agree on response to police repression.

11 June 1972: joint appeal for the day of action on 23 June.

28 September 1972: joint statement. Eight demands put forward.

4 April 1973: joint declaration. Five campaigns (the three existing ones, plus the minimum wage and family allowances).

26 April 1973: joint statement. Appeal for action.

14 June 1973: joint declaration after Pierre Messmer's refusal of talks.

5 July 1973: joint press conference on current industrial disputes.

11 July 1973: joint platform on social security.

5 February 1974: launch of national campaign for union freedom.

23 February 1974: joint statement. Action on wages and jobs.

6 May 1974: joint appeal for victory for François Mitterrand.

26 June 1974: joint declaration on the aims and conduct of industrial disputes.

28 August 1974: joint statement on development of united union action.

7 October 1974: declaration on action campaign.

29 November 1974: joint declaration on jobs.

19 December 1974: joint platform on workers' special demands.

4 March 1975: joint protest at the prime minister's attacks on industrial action at the Renault works.

9 April 1975: joint statement on differing forms of action.

28 May 1975: joint declaration on industrial action.

10 June 1975: joint appeal for defence of union freedoms.

28 August 1975: joint appeal for action.

13 September 1975: joint appeal for stoppages on 23 September.

18 November 1975: joint appeal for the day of action on 2 December.

3 December 1975: joint appeal for a demonstration during the parliamentary debate on working hours and retirement.

6 April 1976: joint declaration on action in pursuit of claims.

15 April 1976: joint declaration for Labour Day (1 May).

20 April 1976: joint declaration for 6 and 13 May.

21 March 1977: joint declaration on minimum wage.

7 April 1977: joint declaration on the action to be taken on 21 April in support of the social security system.

21 April 1977: joint declaration on action to be taken on 28 April.

26 September 1977: exchange of views on the consequences of the break-up of the Union of the Left.

APPENDIX III. NATIONAL DAYS OF ACTION, 1969-78.

The unions in brackets are those which supported action on the day
in question.

12 February 1969 (CGT); 11 March 1969 (CGT, CFDT, FO, FEN);
27 April 1970 (CGT); 27 May 1971 (CGT, CFDT); 1 December
1971 (CGT, CFDT); 7 June 1972 (CGT); 23 June 1972 (CGT,
CFDT); 6 December 1973 (CGT, CFDT, FEN); 19 November 1974
(CGT, CFDT); 2 December 1975 (CGT, CFDT); 13 May 1976
(CGT, CFDT); 7 October 1976 (CGT, CFDT, FEN, FO, CGC); 24
May 1977 (CGT, CFDT, FEN, FO, CFTC, CGC); 1 December 1977
(CGT, CFDT, FEN).

9. THE TRADE UNIONS AND WOMEN WORKERS AFTER 1968

MARGARET GIBBON

In this chapter I will examine some of the most salient developments in the social consciousness of working-class Frenchwomen since May 1968. I will relate these developments to what I shall term the 'culture' of May 68 and shall go on to discuss the responses of the CGT and CFDT trade-union confederations to some of the challenges brought to them by their women members.

The culture of May 68 may be understood primarily in terms of a challenge to unicity and a concomitant awareness of and promotion of diversity. This unicity is found not only in the State and its primary institutions but also in the mainstream counter-institutions such as the PCF and the trade-union movement. With regard to this labour movement, this charge applies most clearly to the CGT. Nevertheless, it may also be levelled at the provincial CFDT, if not at its Parisian leadership. Within these left and labour formations, unicity assumes the form of a stylised rhetoric which describes the fortunes of a unitary working class whose social being determines the quality of its social consciousness and equips it, pre-eminently, to effect the historical project of human liberation.

1968 was a period of immense and wide-ranging challenge to the trade-union movement: to its economism, its vision, its cultural model and to its organisation and structure. In the years immediately following 1968, there was clearly a significant reversal in the motives underlying or precipitating industrial action by manual workers.[1] During the 1950s and 1960s strikes were usually called to support pay-claims for the trade unions ' core membership: white, male, skilled workers - *ouvriers professionnels*. These quantitative demands began to give way after 1968 to the more qualitative demands of the ever-increasing semi-skilled contingent of the French working class, the *ouvriers specialisés* and *ouvrières spécialisées*. Their demands were, however, often considered too specific to be fought for by the movement as a whole, as in the case for the abolition of payment-by-results, or else were converted, inappropriately, into pay-claims by the trade unions.

Concurrent with this development, a glaring chink appeared in the formerly sacrosanct unity of the French working class. Women workers, immigrants, young workers and ethnic minorities such as Bretons, who were made aware of their distinctiveness by the strikes in which they engaged, began to aspire to more than the nominal equality which underpinned their mythic unity. They began to seek greater autonomy in defining their own problems - which more often than not spilled over into non-workplace domains - thereby maintaining and promoting the more libertarian spirit of 1968 and seriously challenging the representativeness of the established trade unions. They did this by claiming to be specific groups with specific needs and, more pertinently, by proclaiming their desire for autonomous structures within the unions to promote their own interests, feeling themselves to be unrepresented or misrepresented by others. The emergence, then, of the theme of specificity is one clear aspect, at grass-roots level, of what I have called the culture of May 68. It is paralleled, in the intellectual stratum of French society, by the rise to celebrity of such writers as Derrida, Foucault, Lacan and Kristeva whose critiques resonate strongly with the ethos of this period.

In order to study women's social consciousness and their relationship to trade-unionism in France, it is useful to reflect upon Marx's idea that social consciousness is determined by social being. It is also instructive to reflect upon the way the critical promise of this idea is put to use by contemporary discourses of the left. I will focus here on the conditions of women's social being and the

---

[1] D. Auffray, T. Baudouin and M. Collin, *Le Travail, et après* (Paris: Jean-Pierre Delarge/LSC, 1978), *passim*.

determining influences these conditions may be found to exert over women's social consciousness.

Women's social being is clearly rooted both in the world of paid employment and in the home and associated community. As Gardiner[2] points out: 'The domestic labouring role overlaps for the majority of women for considerable periods of their lives with other class positions and is crucial in affecting questions of consciousness and organisation.'

Yet social being has been defined by sociologists and political theorists in such a way as to restrict its application to the sphere of social production. Pierre Rolle,[3] for example, writes:

Les opérations sociales auxquelles nous prenons part plus ou moins consciemment, comme l'ensemble des rapports qui nous lient et nous opposent les uns aux autres, se créent et s'éprouvent d'abord dans la production... Le mode de participation des individus au système économique les types particuliers de travail, d'éducation, d'échange qui y règnent, non seulement leur procure quelques-unes de leurs expériences les plus fondamentales, mais encore leur impose en grande partie la structure même de leur individualité.

Studies relating to the social or class-consciousness of male industrial workers have been carried out with an underlying assumption that workplace relations are the primary determinants of social consciousness. Experiences outside paid work are ignored or considered irrelevant to them. Moreover, the family is perceived as a solidary unit, as private, pre-social or natural. In other words, the home and the shop-floor are discrete spheres of being and, for men, life at home, family roles and gender divisions are not considered to have any determining influence over their social or class-consciousness. Men's industrial experience is not recognised as specific to them but is granted the status of a norm by which women's experience is measured as deviant or particularised.

[2] J. Gardiner, 'Political Economy of Domestic Labour in Capitalist Society' in D. Barker and S. Allen (eds), *Dependence and Exploitation in Work and Marriage* (London: Longman, 1976), p.120.
[3] P. Rolle, *Introduction à la Sociologie du Travail* (Paris: Larousse, 1971), p. 275.

The class-consciousness of the male industrial worker has, in this way, been the yardstick by which the consciousness of women workers and of male workers' wives has been measured and, generally found wanting. Women workers are often considered by trade unions to be passive, docile workers, difficult to organise, reluctant to assume trade-union responsibility and profoundly apolitical. Rather than seeking to explain differences in politicisation by references to situational variables relating to the different working environments of the genders, many sociologists have invoked an inherently conservative female nature.[4] Similarly, trade unions have been happy to accept such reasoning, now roundly refuted,[5] rather than examining the trade-union movement itself to assess how far its own organisation and ethos militate against the more active involvement of women workers.

Women's involvement in trade unions is determined by factors extrinsic to their sex and intrinsic to the nature of their work experience and to the organisation, ideology and practice of the unions. If social consciousness - and membership of a trade union is often considered a necessary and sufficient indicator of it - is determined by social being, then it would seem important to recognise that the social being of men and women is radically different, even in the shared setting of the factory floor. The actual working conditions of men and women are remarkably dissimilar in industrial production[6] and an examination of the wider social context, particularly the domestic environment, unveils even greater differences in the social being of women and men. By taking account of these very different social conditions under which men and women live, it becomes clear that it is facile and inappropriate to judge their social consciousness by the same criteria.

Furthermore, evidence of women's social militancy often escapes unnoticed, or is even denied, because of a tendency to assume

---

[4] For example, F. Parkin, 'Working class Conservatives: A Theory of Political Deviance', *British Journal of Sociology*, vol. XVIII (1967), 278-90. He claims that 'women are less prone than men to the attraction of socialism'.

[5] J. Siltanen and M. Stanworth, *Women and the Public Sphere: a critique of sociology and politics* (London: Hutchinson, 1984).

[6] A. F. Molinie and S. Volkoff, 'Les Conditions de travail des ouvriers....et des ouvrières', *Economie et Statistiques*, 118 (Jan. 1980), 25-39.

similarity between the sexes. Kergoat[7] points out: 'La combativité ouvrière feminine existe ... si leur combativité passe souvent inaperçue, c'est parce qu'elle se manifeste sur d'autres terrains que ceux auquels tant les sociologues que les syndicalistes sont habitués à referer la revendication ouvrière, c'est à dire ceux des hommes.'

As I have suggested, militancy and class-consciousness are assessed by reference to levels of involvement in the labour movement. The 'life-world' of the shop floor is the sole or primary site of social being. Feminism has challenged the salience of the home/work divide and pointed out that the family and the community are equally important sites for the construction of classed, as well as gendered, individuals. There is clear evidence that women are actively involved in significant social struggles. The peace movement is one obvious example. Significantly though, many areas of women's activism - the consumers' rights movement, parent-teacher organisations, feminism itself - are more often than not viewed as non-political because of a limited definition of what constitutes political activity. Various theorists have argued that political science operates with a narrow and exclusive definition of politics which limits political activity to a set of roles which are in this society, and many others, stereotyped as male.[8]

The French trade unions, particularly the CGT, themselves accept the traditional definition of political and economic struggles, leaving politics to the politicians and maintaining their own hegemony in the workplace. 'Il existe... des domaines politiques et idéologiques où les syndicats, organisations de masse indépendantes, dont la vocation première est la défense des intérêts des travailleurs, sont tenus à une certaine réserve et par conséquent, il existe des domaines spécifiques des syndicats et des partis.'[9]

The trade unions then, up to 1968, deliberately and voluntarily limited their sphere of intervention to the workplace and to waged workers. After 1968, this economism was challenged in various ways and the unions were invited to play a far greater part in social

[7] D. Kergoat, *Les Ouvrières* (Paris: Le Sycomore, 1983), p. 133.
[8] S. Bourque and J. Grossholtz, 'Politics, an unnatural practice: political science looks at female participation', *Politics and Society*, vol. 4, no 2 (winter 1974), p. 225.
[9] CGT, *Vie Ouvrière*, 18 February 1976.

struggles beyond the workplace. The CFDT was far quicker in taking up this invitation.

During the 1970s, to give one example, conscripted soldiers on the one-year military service actively sought trade-union membership and support for what became a heterogeneous social movement which sheltered activists whose aspirations ranged from basic civil rights for conscripts to the overthrow of world imperialism and militarism. While the CGT quickly attempted to channel all these aspirations into well-tried, formulaic 'pay and conditions' demands and stressed the class difference between the conscripts and their officers, the CFDT response was less than monolithic. The lack of a clear policy on the issue led the usually innovative Parisian hierarchy to be overtaken on its left by several departmental offices, including that of Besançon, who were later severely reprimanded and censored for their support to local conscripts.

Feminism, obviously, was another major counter-hegemonic social movement to derive inspiration from this period, and from the beginning of the 1970s began to inspire women to bring their problems to their union leadership and also, in the light of considerable disenchantment, to organise separately as women within unions to promote awareness of their specific interests. It is a commonplace to hear that feminism is a petty-bourgeois phenomenon associated, in France, with the Parisian intelligentsia. The 1970s proved otherwise. Not only did employed women become more and more articulate and militant within their unions, but also housewives in the provinces attempted to become union members within the CFDT. Inevitably, they were turned down: the union was *une organisation de salariés* and housewives are not wage-earners.

The proliferation during the 1970s of various social movements pointed up the inadequacy of the classical left formations to express the range of aspirations and interests of their members. This was particularly true for women. Eventually, however, both trade-union confederations were led by feminists within their ranks to take principled decisions and to formulate policy on such questions as contraception, abortion, childcare and sexual harassment. Hitherto, such issues were beyond what the unions considered their legitimate realm of concern. The inclusion of such issues on trade union platforms signals, then, a significant change in the role trade unions are being called upon to play. More significantly, it marks a major success for feminism which argues that the trade unions and parties of the left have limited their chances of effecting radical social change by accepting capitalism's division of social being into two discrete spheres - the public sphere of politics and employment and the private sphere of domestic life, the family, procreation and sexuality. Although as feminists we may congratulate ourselves that the trade unions can mobilise thousands of workers to march for women's right to control their own fertility, it is far from clear whether the unions' motives in supporting women's reproductive rights are the same as those motivating women to formulate such demands. The fear of co-optation has, among French feminists, been justifiably rife.[10]

It is not clear either whether the connection has definitively been made between politics and so-called personal life, or whether the trade unions have glimpsed the magnitude of the role they are being called upon to play. In his book on the consumer movement, Michel Wieviorka[11] outlines the two possible forms trade unionism can take in contemporary French society. On the one hand, unions can play their traditional economistic role, in which case Wieviorka calls their action 'le niveau bas de l'intervention syndicale'; on the other hand, as was the case for the CFDT when it acted as umbrella for many anti-nuclear organisations, unions can play a more encompassing role.

Le niveau haut de l'intervention syndicale est celui par lequel le syndicat, de par son rôle unificateur et catalyseur, déclenche une action qui met en jeu, directement, les grandes orientations de la société. Il ne s'agit plus alors de peser sur les modalités du produit social, ou de contribuer à un assainissement de la production ou du commerce, mais de développer une action allant bien au-delà de revendications économiques et posant la

---

[10] S. de Beauvoir, 'Feminism - Alive, Well and in Constant Danger' in R. Morgan (ed.), *Sisterhood is Global* (Harmondsworth: Penguin, 1984), pp. 232-8.

[11] M. Wieviorka, *L'État, le patronat, les consommateurs* (Paris: PUF, 1977).

question de l'avenir de la société et de son futur modèle culturel.[12]

The subordination and oppression of women is clearly one of the 'grandes orientations de la société'. In order to fight against this oppression, one of the most pressing tasks involves the deconstruction of the divide between the public and the private spheres of social being: 'la contestation, par les femmes, de leur situation porte en bonne partie sur le décloisonnement, la réunification de différents aspects de la vie sociale, c'est à dire sur la négation ou la redéfinition des clivages travail/hors travail, public/privé.[13]

Feminists have pioneered reflection on this subject for fifteen years, and Marxists, perhaps for different reasons, have also attached importance to it. Michael Mann[14] rather generously claims that: 'Marxists are well aware that the segmentation of life in capitalist society constitutes an obstacle to the realisation of class-consciousness. For the latter to develop, the worker must make 'connections' between his work and his family life and between his industrial and political activity.'

In fact, it would appear that when workers have made connections between their domestic lives and their paid work, it has been the unions themselves which have acted as a brake upon consciousness by narrowly construing their role in economic terms and outlawing consideration of extra-economic issues. I would like to consider the subject of women's double-shift of paid and unpaid work in the light of this claim and to examine the positions and policies of the CGT and CFDT on this most specific of women's specificities.

The two unions differ quite substantially in their interpretations of the causes of women's social subordination and their differing analyses lead them to adopt different goals, strategies and tactics in dealing with it. Schematically, the CGT was unwilling, until around 1977, to consider anything other than the capitalist system itself as

---

[12] Ibid., pp. 253-4.

[13] M. Maruani, *Les Syndicats a l'épreuve du féminisme* (Paris: Editions Syros/CNRS, 1979), p. 28.

[14] M. Mann, 'Industrial Relations in Advanced Capitalism and the Explosion of Consciousness' in T. Clarke and L. Clements (eds), *Trade Unions Under Capitalism* (London: Fontana, 1977) pp. 294-5.

the cause of women's inferior status in society. The CFDT on the other hand, has, since the late 1960s, considered that the precise condition of women under capitalism is multi-faceted and that many of the root-causes of women's oppression and subordination pre-date capitalism and are not strictly economic in nature. The CFDT appears, therefore, to have adopted a more radical position than the CGT. Moreover, it has made major strides forward since its CFTC days (up until 1964) when it considered that: 'le rôle et la vocation des femmes était d'assumer les fonctions d'épouse et de mère et les taches ménagères.'[15]

Whereas for the CGT, up until 1977, the specific cause of women's subordination was their unfavourable economic situation which made them liable, like other 'formes dévalorisées du travail' to be 'sur-exploitées', for the CFDT a major facet of women's situation was what it called 'les rôles sociaux prédéterminés'. This term essentially covered gender socialisation and its main underpinnings such as the domestic division of labour. The CGT, meanwhile, considered such an issue was well beyond the sphere of intervention it had traditionally seen as appropriate to a trade union. Consequently, it referred to the CFDT position - 'l'égalitarisme intégral' - as utopian. Up until 1977, considered by many feminists within the CGT as a turning-point, the union was not convinced of the good sense, opportuneness or desirability of challenging gender roles in this way and, like Marx and Engels a century before, argued that women's liberation depended upon their entry into paid employment: 'en fait la participation accrue des femmes au travail salarié, la lutte contre les discriminations de tous ordres qui les frappent, sont beaucoup plus efficaces pour une meilleure conception de la vie du couple et le partage des responsabilités dans la famille qui de prôner l'égalitarisme intégral.'[16]

Ann Oakley has pointed out that this emphasis on paid employment as the panacea to women's oppression is a piece of confused thinking: 'if the liberation of women requires an assertion of the right to productive activity, then the liberation of men demands their re-involvement in the labour of producing families.

[15] J. Laot, cited in M. Maruani, op. cit., p. 35.
[16] CGT, *Les Femmes salariées* (Paris: Editions Sociales, 1973), p. 21.

Women's employment is a red-herring, half an equation, a piece of double-think; it is not a path to paradise.'[17]

It is also clear in the CGT extract above, that the union speaks of housework as if it were performed only by women outside paid employment when, in fact, it was of course *employed women* who first brought the subject of the unfair division of household tasks to the unions precisely because their participation in the labour force had not significantly altered their burden of responsibilities in the home.

The CFDT, on the other hand, recognised early on the political nature of the private sphere and the ideological dimension of the public/private division. For these reasons, it has adopted a wider societal role than the CGT and integrates private and public dimensions in its analysis of women's subordination:

> Pour mettre fin à la surexploitation des travailleuses et élaborer avec elles dans ce but des revendications efficaces, *notre pratique syndicale doit faire apparaître constamment le rapport entre cette situation dans l'entreprise et celle des femmes dans la société.* La libération des femmes conditionnant la réalisation de leur objectif, les organisations de la CFDT doivent donc prendre de plus en plus encompte la totalité de la condition des travailleuses, composante de la condition ouvrière.[18]

However, it should in fairness be noted that the positions and policies of the national CFDT do not always filter down intact to provincial departmental officials. I would like to quote briefly here from an interview I conducted in 1981 with a male CFDT leader in Finistère, in order to underline this point:

> M.G.: 'On dit que les femmes sont moins souvent syndiquées que les hommes. Y a-t-il, d'après vous, des raisons d'ordre matériel ou psychologique pour expliquer ce manque d'intérêt pour le fait syndical?'

---

[17] A. Oakley, *Subject Woman* (London: Fontana, 1981), p. 162.
[18] CFDT, *Rapport General au 36ᵉ Congrés* (Paris: CFDT, 1973); my emphasis.

CFDT official: 'Certains veulent mettre des problèmes où il n'y en a pas. Jeannette Laot, par exemple ... Bon, le fait est qu'elles ne se présentent pas, ici on a eu un mal fou pour trouver des femmes à se présenter.'

M.G.: 'Elles ont quand-même beaucoup d'autres responsa– bilités...'

CFDT official: 'Oui, il y a le partage des tâches. La CFDT ne s'occupe que des femmes qui travaillent (sic). Ça, c'est un problème de couple, ce n'est pas un probleme de société, ça - ce n'est pas un problème de la CFDT.'

Again we note that there seems to be, for mar_y male trade-unionists, a clash between the identities of worker and housewife, so that the fact that women employees accumulate both these functions appears to escape them. Nevertheless, at national level, the CFDT does attempt to fight against women's double shift and has linked this demand for a shorter working week to the ideal of more male involvement in unpaid domestic labour in its slogan: *les 35 heures pour le partage des tâches.*

Theoretically, the notion of specificity should serve to throw light upon women's double shift. In practice, however, I believe that the specificity theme has helped to maintain and consolidate the domestic division of labour rather than challenging it. For example, negotiating fleximtime and free Wednesdays for women with school-age children may well be appreciated by those mothers who effectively have to reconcile their two jobs. In the long term, such policies, if not extended to fathers, only serve to allow women to manage, at great cost to their health and well-being, a double shift of paid and unpaid work. The CGT commonly promotes such 'solutions', which are deplored by the CFDT, who consider that these solutions in fact fail to challenge the foundation of women's double burden. Sociologist Andrée Michel analyses the CGT's specificity themes, such as earlier retirement for women, from a similar perspective:

Il semble que la CGT n'ait pas su rompre avec l'idéologie traditionnelle qui consiste à abandonner aux femmes le monopole des taches domestiques et l'éducation des enfants. Par suite elle multiplie les demandes de mesures spécifiques qui ont pour but - directement ou indirectement - de maintenir les rôles traditionnels des sexes et d'enfermer la femme dans ses taches domestiques.[19]

Evelyne Le Garrec, a participant observer of the famous strike at Lip, is one of the most eloquent opponents of the CGT's specific measures for women. She sees them as: 'une manière détournée de partager les revendications en deux categories hiérarchisées.'[20]

She is particularly scathing on the subject of the CGT's policy for women's earlier retirement, which she links to the domestic division of labour: 'Contre cinq ans de travail en moins pour les femmes, les hommes achètent le droit de se décharger définitivement pendant toute leur vie des basses besognes sur les femmes.'[21]

I would like to conclude by reiterating and substantiating two of my previous points: that it is the impact of feminism which has brought about a marked politicisation of women workers since 1968; and that the French trade unions have been, in practice, inadequately receptive to women's demands for change in union roles, positions and organisation. I would like to quote a CGT shop steward from a large State tobacco factory in Finistére speaking on the subject of some women colleagues who raised the subject of domestic labour as a union issue.

CGT shop-steward: 'J'ai discuté avec certaines femmes qui se défendaient sur, enfin qui voulaient presque se syndiquer pour se défendre sur l'histoire du partage des tâches et qui, bon, j'ai jamais été d'accord avec ça quoi par exemple - et puis ils (*sic*) envoyaient dans leurs revendications des problèmes qui étaient intérieurs à leur couple dans le fond donc qui n'avaient rien à voir avec l'intérêt général.'

While the public/private divide may have some salience for men, women working a double shift who confront conflicting demands and expectations of them at home and at work effectively straddle

---

[19] A. Michel, *Travail Féminin: un point de vue* (Paris: Documentation Française, 1975), p. 120.
[20] E. Le Garrec, *Les Messagères* (Paris: Editions des Femmes, 1976), p. 161.
[21] Ibid., p. 161.

that divide. Those who make connections between their home and work lives are those whose social awareness is the most encompassing. However, such women are often accused of bringing division into the labour movement. It became apparent, after 1968 particularly, that the established trade unions do not adequately represent the motives and aspirations of their women members. Indeed, in the light of feminist disenchantment, it seems likely that this may well constitute one salient and potentially divisive dimension in critical diagnoses of the trade unions' current crisis of representativeness.

10. 'NOT LOOKING BACK AT 68': CONTEMPORARY FRENCH WOMEN FILM MAKERS

GINETTE VINCENDEAU

In August 1968, the editors of *Cahiers du cinéma* called for 'revolution in and through the cinema' - a feeling echoed by the radical film groups which emerged in the wake of the *événements*. Ambitious claims were made for changes in modes of production, distribution and exhibition of films in France and the structures of the French film industry (and particularly the CNC), for a radical shift in the status of film from commodity to political weapon as well as work of art, for a drastic re-thinking of the relationship between films and their 'alienated' spectators, for a challenge to individual authorship and a move to collective work, and for a new film language - in short, in the notorious words of Jean-Luc Godard, to 'make politically a political cinema'. Equally important, and of international resonance, were the profoundly new directions taken by the discourses about the cinema initiated in France around 1968. As Sylvia Harvey put it in her monograph *May 68 and Film Culture* (published in 1978), 'the landscape of film studies in Britain and in the United States has been transformed by post-68 developments in French film theory'.

Twenty (or so) years on, unsurprisingly, the French box-office is still dominated by American spectaculars, French comedies and the routine yearly Belmondo and Delon adventures. More disturbingly perhaps, the French film journals that were at the vanguard of ideologically aware criticism (*Cahiers du cinéma, Cinéthique*) have either disappeared or, like *Cahiers du cinéma*, have returned to a pre-1968 concentration on individual *auteurs*. Film theory, meanwhile, has become the almost exclusive province of the university and is largely dominated by formalist analyses which are often brilliant but lack any concern for ideological constructs such as class and gender, considered in France at best irrelevant and at worst simply out of date. For me, equally disturbing in this respect are developments in recent French *auteur* cinema, which, again often brilliantly, manifest three broad tendencies, all equally remote from the immediate political concerns of 1968: a re-exploration of familiar popular genres by established directors (Resnais, Pialat, Godard); a youth-market-orientated 'post-modernism' (Beneix, Besson, Carax); and a return to the romantic notion of the sufferings of angst-ridden (mostly male) individuals (Téchiné, Doillon, Zulawski, Assayas). The list of films that have won *Césars* (the French Oscars) in the last four years is representative of this general picture: Pialat's *A nos Amours*, Zidi's *Les Ripoux*, Serreau's *Trois Hommes et un couffin*, Cavalier's *Thérèse*. Perhaps 'turning their backs on 68' might have been a more appropriate title.

Whether this situation, contrasting sharply with the 1970s concern with 'contemporary issues' bespeaks a (right-wing) backlash, or whether things never really changed in French cinema at all is a question that probably cannot be answered at this stage. Rather than attempt a general overview of French films of the last 20 years I have chosen instead to concentrate on a specific sample - films made by women - for the following reasons:

1. Women's cinema as a category, in France as elsewhere, has existed only since, and to some extent, because of, May 1968.

2. Thus, as an ideologically overdetermined category, and an oppositional force (at least theoretically), women film makers - a category including, but not reduceable to, feminists - might be expected to show in a more illuminating way than the rest of cinematic production the repercussions of 1968. They might also be expected to be politically more radical than their male counterparts.

3. Concurrently, and somewhat paradoxically, women's cinema in

France (as elsewhere) tends to mirror, in genres and modes of production especially, that of men. It is thus quite a good gauge of what is going on in the rest of the industry.

The relationship between May 1968 and women's cinema in France is an ambiguous one. Just as women were largely absent from the decision-making and creative apparatus of French cinema before 1968 - and notably at the time of the New Wave - they were not exactly prominent during the *événementts* either behind the cameras or in front of them. Even in post-1968 Godard films, women do little more than prettily hand out little red books. Yet undoubtedly the post-1968 climate, together with international feminism, gave the needed impetus for the emergence of a specifically feminine and feminist cinema in France.

Women's cinema in France went through a militant leftist and feminist phase in the 1970s. The *Musidora* group was formed (named after a silent cinema actress who became a director), organised a festival in Paris in 1973 and published a book called *Parole, elles tournent*. Roughly at the same time, historians were rediscovering 'forgotten' women directors such as the pioneer Alice Guy. In 1978, the first regular French women's festival was set up in Sceaux - still going now and headed by the same team of two women, though in a different location (Créteil) and with very different aims and scope.[1] Films about 'women's issues' - what one (woman) critic facetiously called 'our mirror phase' - were, as in American and British cinema, part of that stage: films about women's work, abortion (*Histoires d'A*), motherhood, relationships between women of different generations, etc. Explicitly feminist feature films also reached regular cinema circuits - such as Coline Serreau's documentary *Mais qu'est-ce qu'elles veulent?* and her utopian fantasy *Pourquoi Pas!*, Varda's *L'une chante l'autre pas*, Yannick Bellon's *L'Amour violé*, etc. 'Strong' heroines also appeared in a few mainstream films made by men, usually played by Annie Girardot or Miou-Miou.

---

[1] G. Vincendeau, 'Women as *auteur-e-s*', *Screen* XXVII, 3 (May/June 1986) and 'Women's cinema, film theory, and feminism in France', *Screen*, XXXVIII (Autumn 1987).

The fact that this is now, barely 10 years later, seen as 'a phase' rather than as a base for future developments was neatly summed up by Chantal Akerman's public declaration at Créteil in April 1987 (at a women's film festival of which she was the star) that the notion of 'women's cinema', let alone feminist fiction, is out of date. This attitude of course belongs to the general retrenchment of feminism in France since the early 1980s - and the similar fate of a number of so-called *soixante-huitard* ideologies, as well as of psychoanalysis, as Catherine Clément reminds us in an article published in a recent issue of the *New Statesman*.[2] As Guy Hennebelle (editor of *CinemAction*, one of the few journals interested in political issues in the cinema) put it: 'Tout ce qui est féministe, tiers-mondiste, et 'iste' en general fait fuir.'[3] A good example, among others, of this phenomenon applied to women's film making is the trajectory of Danielle Dubroux, an ex-*Cahiers du cinéma* critic and co-author in 1976 of *L'Olivier* (a film about the Palestinian question), whose last feature is an 'erotic comedy' entitled *La petite Allumeuse*.

To understand why such a shift is taking place so quickly in the cinema, one also needs to look at the more specific context of French film culture. The crucial elements here are the continued focus in France on the *auteur* both as a practical strategy and as a critical category and the virtual absence of indigenous feminist film theory or theorising of gender and sexual difference in relation to the cinema. As I mentioned above, academic theory on the whole ignores the categories of class and gender. In *cinéphile* journals, the accent is still single-mindedly on the *auteur*, within a romantic tradition of humanist individualism which constitutes the bedrock of French critical approaches to film (and has done so since the 1920s) and which currently suppresses other considerations such as ideology. For example, the much admired (that is on this side of the Channel) work on ideology done by *Cahiers du cinéma* and others in the 1970s, has, in France, fallen into the same kind of critical disrepute, or indifference, as feminism. Reviews of contemporary films in French journals are in this respect indicative. An avoidance

---

[2] *New Statesman*, 13 September 1987.
[3] Letter to the author, August 1987.

of ideology in films is often commented on positively and by a
perverse logic, films that still show commitment to a particular
political or sociological position are either criticised (as old-
fashioned) or praised for the extent to which they *avoid* such
positions. For example, Issermann's first film, *Le Destin de Juliette*
(a film which recounts the slow and painful emancipation of a
woman whose life is ruined by an alcoholic father and husband, an
insane mother, a suicidal brother, and uncooperative social services),
has been praised by various French critics for its 'remoteness from
naturalism, feminism, miserabilism, sociological dryness,
melodrama, narrow psychology, stuffy intimacy.'[4] One wonders
what is left. A *Positif* review of Pomme Meffre's *Le Grain de sable*
(the story of a woman, played by Delphine Seyrig, who is driven to
suicide by unemployment) praises it 'above all for what it is not: a
film about unemployment or the female condition.'[5] I could go on.
In short, feminism, associated with the sociological, is scorned by
academic film theory for being non-theoretical, and by *cinéphile*
critics for distracting from the individual *auteur's* supposedly
detached personal expression
In the light of this critical context, the current position of French
women film makers could be described as falling between two
stools. On the one hand they lack a credible ideological framework
in terms of group allegiance, on the other they still hold only
marginal positions in the industry - even women with the career and
reputation of Agnès Varda or Marguerite Duras.

  This means that for most women work is restricted to low- and
medium- budget features, and it is logical that the defence of *auteur*
cinema should have become, as it were, their only political issue, the
point of resistance against economic strictures and industrial changes
represented by the three *bêtes noires* of French *auteur* cinema:
Hollywood, French super-productions (e.g. *Jean de Florette*), and the
ever-encroaching power of television. Given that the model for the
auteur is still the individual genius, or at least the artist driven by
'internal necessity' towards self-expression, this has had the

---

[4] *Positif*, 273 (November 1983).
[5] *Positif*, 274 (December 1983).

consequence of pushing French women directors into heightened
individualism and alignment with male 'colleagues'. The refrain from
French women directors is 'men have the same problems'. The
paralysing nature of this position is matched by a general reluctance
to discuss it. One lucid exception is Jeanne Labrune, who is worth
quoting here:

> Our history is different from that of German film makers who
> received help *as women*, and who structured themselves as
> such right from the start. Thus they have a collective identity
> which has allowed them to make claims for themselves as
> wonem film makers with a positive image, because they have
> fought collectively. The French inability to think collectively
> means that French women cannot experience their practice in
> any other way than as *auteurs*, thinking that they are doing very
> well out of this individualistic game, whereas very often they
> are at the same time being 'had', in terms of their contracts, of
> distribution, etc.[6]

The problem isolated by Labrune operates in all areas. For instance
the absence of a feminist distribution network precludes any positive
promotion of women's films as 'women's products', while
mainstream distributors handling women's films treat them as low-
priority commodities, even when they are made by Marguerite Duras
or Yannick Bellon.

The same paradox (refusing a collective identity but suffering the
drawbacks of an individualistic stance) is evident in the reaction to
press coverage. Though they are aware that they are being
discriminated against, most French women directors are reluctant,
and sometimes hostile, to ideological frameworks that might give
them support. For example Aline Issermann (the only French
director who bothered to come to a Franco-German debate at the
1987 Créteil festival, compared with an impressive German
presence) deplored the 'hysterical' response by male critics to her
second film *L'Amant magnifique*, but a few minutes later launched a

---

[6] Interview with Jeanne Labrune, by Joelle Youiton, Paris, April, 1987.

virulent attack on film theory and criticism, feminist or otherwise.

'I want to explore all the possibilities of my aesthetic project.' Jeanne Labrune's professed aim could serve as a motto for French women directors in the 1980s, in contrast to the ideological objectives of the 1970s. That women's cinema cannot be equated with feminist cinema is now a commonplace, but it is perhaps in France that this is most obvious. Clearly it is no coincidence that it is there that women have achieved the highest degree of integration into mainstream cinema (pathetically small though it is).

Most recent productions by French women (with the notable exception of Duras) - films such as *La Triche, Coup de Foudre, Rouge Baiser, Le Destin de Juliette, Trois Hommes et un couffin, Le Jupon rouge, Vertiges, Sans Toit ni loi* - are variations on medium-budget art cinema. They have the usual production values for the genre: tasteful photography, decors and music, stars, mostly French (Isabelle Huppert, Miou-Miou, Lambert Wilson, Alida Valli, Marie-Christine Barrault, Sandrine Bonnaire) and, in the case of *Coup de Foudre* and *Rouge Baiser*, both set in the 1950s, careful recreation of the period. Formally, most women's films fit into the tradition of French *auteur* cinema: a classic realist narrative cinema, little inclined to explore the fantastic or the grotesque. It tends to be an 'intimate' cinema which focuses on psychological motivation and behaviour rather than the historical, social, and political referent. Varda's *Sans toit ni loi*, for instance, despite its precisely observed milieu, is less a sociological statement on post-1968 France than an exploration of an individual's journey and the mythical resonances of that theme. Geneviève Lefebvre, director of *Le Jupon rouge*, the story of close relationships between three women, recently declared that the (scanty) historical background to her three characters, one of whom has spent time in a concentration camp, was there just 'to locate the characters in terms of their jobs. I would have loved to make an allegorical film without any reference to the social, but that's difficult. I will try to do it in my second film.'[7]

Lefebvre's aspiration is completely consistent with the critical

---

[7] Interview with Geneviève Lefebvre by Ginette Vincendeau, Créteil festival, April 1987.

climate mentioned earlier and charts a similar trajectory to that of other women who have completed more than one film. It is the case, for instance, with Issermann, whose second feature, *L'Amant magnifique*, focuses on sexual passion, and for Juliet Berto (whose first film *Neige* portrays immigrants and drug dealers in Barbès). Even allowing for the fact that drug-peddling is a generically overdetermined area, both in the gangster thriller and in French narratives of the 'lower depths', it is significant that Berto's subsequent two features, and in particular the latest, *Havre*, have departed from any precisely coded milieu, to arrive at a rather obscure allegorical 'post-modern' puzzle.

The insistence on the personal is another clue to understanding why in French women's cinema there has not been the intense engagement with their country's history (of any period) such as is found in German or Latin American films by women. There are, of course a few exceptions such as Vera Belmont's *Rouge Baiser*. This semi-autobiographical film recreates the communist milieu of the early 1950s, but uses the period more as a background to the young heroine's personal development than as its subject; it also feeds off the 1950s nostalgia of St Germain des Prés nightclubs, jazz, etc. It is however one of the rare occurrences in French cinema of a fiction film explictly dealing with Left ideology, and even rarer, with a woman at its centre. It remains to be seen whether Belmont and Charlotte Silvera (the director of *Louise l'insoumise*) will follow the Issermann/Berto route or will continue their investigation of the interaction between personal story and history. It is worth noting here that one film by a woman which dealt directly with May 1968, Diane Kurys' *Cocktail Molotov*, was her only box-office failure to date. Interestingly, when socio-economic realities are evoked, they tend to include immigrants. This is the case in *Rouge Baiser* (Eastern European Jews) and in Silvera's autobiographical *Louise l'insoumise*, which studies the North African Jewish milieu in a Parisian suburb in the early 1960s. It is also the case in Euzhan Palcy's *Rue Cases-Nègres*, which looks at the French colonial past of the 1930s. Otherwise, an interest in the social would seem to be confined to a few documentary features such as Nicole Le Garrec's *Plogoff* (the resistance of a village against a nuclear power station) or Marie-Claude Treilhou's *Il était une fois la télé* (the impact of the media on a small community) though again Treilhou was praised for not making a 'sociological statement'.

The accent on the centrality of the *auteur* and of personal aesthetic choice, as expressed by Jeanne Labrune earlier, retains its stranglehold on French cinema partly because it comes from a long established tradition of links between film makers, artists and intellectuals - going as far back as the 1920s. This tradition values originality above all and thus runs contrary to the collective impetus of much feminist work.

Auteur cinema, however, has served as a model (even a myth, with recurrent fantasies of being 'threatened') and a support system to directors, particularly those beginning their careers, and hence women directors; the financial aids channelled through the *avance sur recettes*, for instance, have been particularly beneficial to women and help to understand their relatively high numbers in France. It has also served as a 'cultural support' to avant-garde film makers like Duras.

The recourse by French women film makers to *auteur* cinema is, on the other hand, open to two charges which have particular relevance to women directors and the notion of a women's cinema as potentially politically progressive:

One is the accusation of excessive aestheticism and élitism - certainly a justifiable criticism of films such as Christine Laurent's *Vertiges*, or Jeanne Labrune's *La Digue* and *La Part de l'autre* as well as Berto's work.The other is that the encouragement to make films relatively free from box-office constraints, with financial help such as the *avance sur recettes*, contains its own weakness in removing the need to conceptualise a specific audience, something which has been of enormous importance to women's cinema in Britain and Germany. Hence French directors' impatient or frankly bored attitude when asked to discuss their films with the Créteil audience, an activity which Chantal Akerman brutally and revealingly described as 'after-sales service'. However, another term in the equation is fast altering the rules of the game - television. Though scorned by most of the French film establishment (and by Créteil), television has become one of the forces of French cinema and of course co-finances practically all *auteur* cinema. Though many of their films are shown by the French TV channels, women still have to engage with the medium other than just as a source of funds: for example as a means of reaching a different audience than that of the *art et essai* circuit. This might be a way to heed the 1968 calls for creating different rapport between producers and consumers of films.

Some French women are attempting to break out of the traditional *auteur* cinema mould by joining the mainstream industry. One way of doing this is by international coproductions; *Un Homme amoureux*, Diane Kurys' last film was shot at Cinecittà with an international cast. Similarly, Nathalie Delon's *Sweet Lies* was partly shot in Hollywood with a Franco-American cast. Another is by comedies produced in France. The success of Coline Serreau is well-known, though *Trois Hommes et un couffin* did not really succeed outside France (old-fashioned French comedy does not travel well); its American remake, however, is apparently now doing very good business in the United States.

Such attempts are interesting in so far as they have the potential to inject a 'liberal feminist' ideology into popular cinema. However, the danger in including elements of feminism in popular films is that they become so easily debased. This is visible in, for instance, Camille de Casabianca's *Pékin-Central* and Annick Lanoé's *Les Nanas*. Casabianca's film is an amusing if slender comedy of manners which aims some well-deserved digs at French machismo, but Lanoé's film does little more than turn 'liberated' women into the worn-out clichés of trendy women's magazines.

In this period of transition some younger women directors are attempting to steer a course between New-Wave-style *auteur* cinema and popular box-office genres, by appealing to a knowing, trendy, and most importantly, young audience; this is what a *Cahiers du cinéma* critic calls the 'Forum des Halles' genre. Films such as those directed by Beneix, Besson, and Carax blatantly cater for such a clientele. The way French women directors have followed the trend is by taking on soft-core eroticism and androgyny, neatly combining 'post-feminist' attitudes to gender with a certain sexual explictness. In this category fall films such as Virginie Thévenet's *La Nuit porte jarretelles*, and *Jeux d'artifice*, Caroline Roboh's *Clémentine Tango*, Arielle Dombasle's *La Novice*, Dominique Crèvecoeur's *Contes Clandestins*, Claire Devers's *Noir et Blanc*. *La Nuit porte jarretelles* and *Clémentine Tango* have both achieved cult status (the latter on the festival circuit). *Clémentine Tango* (in fact a student film) is a collage of cabaret acts by various transvestite artists, including a couple highly ambiguous in sexual terms. Some of the acts are wonderful, and the *roman-photo* manner of the film is hilarious. *Noir et blanc*, very expertly directed by Claire Devers, is a far-reaching and grim exploration of a sado-masochistic relationship between a black and a white man. Ultimately though, despite the insistence on gender bending, the play on sexual ambiguity remains just that. The exploration of sexuality in these films is less than subversive and could justify the accusation that taking on explicit eroticism is another way for women directors of getting male recognition.

What is significant, but accords with the current cultural *laissez-faire* about gender representation in France as well as the individualistic stance, is that French women's films are overwhelmingly white, middle-class and heterosexual. This brings me back to how difficult it is for French women directors to find a credible position from which to explore problems of gender and class without being accused of producing old-fashioned sociological statements. Between a rearguard battle to uphold conventional *auteur* cinema on the one hand, and the post-modern, fashionable avoidance of clear ideological and gender positions on the other, women directors in France have short-circuited the possibilities of both organised struggle and of a politics of representation.

11. THE REPRESENTATION OF VIETNAM IN FRENCH FILMS BEFORE AND AFTER 1968

CELIA BRITTON

The American war in Vietnam is often cited as one of the main politicising factors of the student left in Western Europe in the mid to late sixties. In France, for instance, the arrest of members of the National Vietnam Committee at Nanterre in March 1968 was one of the events which sparked off much larger-scale action. But, while Vietnam is closely linked with the events of 68 on the level of political consciousness, the actual situation of the Vietnamese was of course entirely different from that of the intellectual French left; and the juxtaposition of these two facts raises some interesting questions about the representation of Vietnam in French cinema. What is at issue is not a simple relation of cause and effect; it is not a question of the 'impact' of the events of May on perceptions of Vietnam, or *vice versa*, but rather of seeing how the relations between them are defined, implicitly or explicitly, by the films in question - how these go about articulating the Vietnamese situation *from within* France in the sixties.

The films that I shall be discussing are the following: *Loin du Vietnam*, produced by the collective SLON (Société pour le Lancement des Œuvres Nouvelles) which was formed for the occasion by Chris Marker, directed by Alain Resnais, Joris Ivens, Claude Lelouch, William Klein, Jean-Luc Godard and Agnès Varda, and edited by Marker; *Le Dix-septième parallèle*, by Joris Ivens and Marceline Loridan; *La Chinoise*, by Godard; *Vivre pour vivre*, by

163

Lelouch - all of which were released in 1967; *Le Peuple et ses fusils*, by Ivens and Loridan (1969) and finally Godard and Jean-Pierre Gorin's *Letter to Jane* (1972).

They include both fiction films and documentaries. This mixture of genres might appear to rule out any very rigorous comparisons, but in fact the main filmic issues raised are on a sufficiently general level to be able to accommodate the differences. The theoretical parameters that will be involved are, firstly, the question of whether or not cinematic representation can be realistic or truthful - i.e. of its adequacy to its (real or fictional) object; and, secondly, the related but slightly more specific question of audience identification, in other words, the extent to which spectators feel personally involved with what they are shown - covering a range of responses, from simple recognition and understanding of the situation to a more emotional identifying with the people shown on screen. The ideological significance of identification, whether in film or in fiction or drama, has been extensively debated. Figures as influential (and as disparate) as Eisenstein and Brecht consider it to be entirely negative because it produces a passive, self-indulgent spectator who remains immersed in his own emotional reactions, and is 'fascinated' rather than either analytical or mobilised. As against this, however, another more liberal left-wing aesthetic sees identification as politically effective in creating militancy through compassion, shared indignation, and so on. What I hope to show in this chapter is that the ways in which these general issues of film theory manifest themselves in the particular object of representation constituted by the Vietnam war are partly determined by the political situation.

France's attitude to the American intervention in Vietnam was different from that of other West European countries, because of the French colonial war in Indo-China ten years earlier. Not only could the French, in having let the Japanese take over the colony in 1940, consider themselves to some extent responsible for the initial American presence there, but their defeat at the hands of Ho Chi Minh at Dien Bien Phu in 1954 remained a humiliating memory. Civilian French public opinion had never really mobilised against the Indo-Chinese war, but from the beginning of the sixties a series of events led to a greater consciousness in France of the political significance of the Third World. The first of these was France's next colonial conflict, in Algeria, which did have a radicalising effect on the population - particularly the intelligentsia, through the involvement of leading intellectuals such as Sartre. Another important factor was the Cuban revolution in 1959: for instance, three of the directors who would later be involved in *Loin du Vietnam* went to Cuba and made documentaries there: Marker and Ivens in 1961 (Ivens also went back the following year and taught in the Cuban film institute), and Varda in 1963. Finally, the Cultural Revolution in China resulted in the formation of Maoist student groups all over Western Europe. In this context it is not surprising that the American intervention in Vietnam quickly became a focus for political opposition throughout the West - despite the fact that Ho Chi Minh was first and foremost a nationalist leader (lacking the internationalist outlook of, for instance, Castro).

But for the left of the sixties in France, specifically, there are good reasons as to why Vietnam might be a more problematic issue than it was for the equivalent groups in Britain or, indeed, America. In the first place, de Gaulle, unlike Wilson, had vigorously condemned the American presence in Vietnam, and this meant that support for the Vietcong could not be equated with opposition to the French government; there was, so to speak, no very accessible target for demonstrations or other forms of protest. More importantly, perhaps, opposition to the Soviet Union was a more central and prominent issue for the French *gauchistes* than it was for either the British or the American left; and the North Vietnamese were supported by the Soviet Union, who supplied them with most of their arms. Conversely, Ho Chi Minh's relations with China quickly deteriorated once the Cultural Revolution started in August 1966, both because the Vietnamese were strongly opposed to it on ideological grounds, and also for practical reasons, because the general disruption in China meant that a lot of the goods it was supplying to Vietnam failed to reach them; it was therefore, at least in principle, difficult for French Maoists to support the North Vietnamese unreservedly. As for the French Trotskyists, their expressions of solidarity with Ho Chi Minh may have been inhibited by the fact that there was good reason to suppose he had been responsible in some way for the murder of all the leading Trotskyists in Vietnam in 1945 - although this was not very widely known.

It is perhaps for the above reasons, then, that there was on the French left a discernible undercurrent of uneasiness about what would be the most intellectually honest and politically effective position to adopt in relation to Vietnam. On the one hand, the idea that all revolutionaries were involved in the 'same' struggle was an influential one at the time; it derives loosely from the Maoist position, in so far as this represents a move away from the traditional PCF exclusive stress on the industrial proletariat: hence its popularity, since it served to legitimise students as agents of revolution as well as providing an ideological matrix for interpreting struggles in the Third World. From this perspective, French workers and students on the one hand and the Vietcong and North Vietnamese on the other were fighting the same enemy, namely imperialist capitalism. On the other hand is the perception that things are perhaps not so simple, and hence a resistance to any automatic or facile assumption of unity, or any attempt to annex as it were the Vietnamese communists for the purposes of the French left, both students and workers.

This sense of the complexity of the political issues shows up, in cinematic terms, in a sense of the problems of representational documentary 'objectivity' - an awareness that there is no automatically given point of view from which to represent the situation. It also affects the question of identification which, in addition to its aesthetic and psychological dimensions, in this context acquires a new political one: that is, the possibility and desirability of French students and workers identifying with the Vietnamese on screen becomes enmeshed with the question of the interconnectedness or otherwise of their respective political struggles.[1] Thus the political factors involved mean that the Vietnam

---

[1] At the same time the 'cinétracts' of 68 were creating a new and far more real form of identification as those involved saw, and made, films that were quite literally about themselves. This was very positive in that it inaugurated a new relationship between filmmaker and the people filmed. Equally, however, the more theoretically orientated proponents of

war poses the general theoretical questions of truth and identification in a particularly acute form, and therefore proves to be a peculiarly revealing object of representation.

The first film on Vietnam by major French directors was *Loin du Vietnam*; and the concept of the 'same struggle', of revolutionary unity, is a dominant emphasis in it. It appears right at the beginning as the pre-credit sequence cuts from a shot of Vietcong guerrillas to a matched shot of Castro and a group of Cubans - both walking from right to left against an identical background of yellow maize - while the commentary says: 'A great number of the smaller nations have understood that they stand or fall with Vietnam...' Most reviewers also chose to emphasise this aspect; *Positif*, for instance, wrote: 'sa force est de s'élargir progressivement, de donner au Vietnam sa dimension mondiale, d'en faire le reflet de notre monde.'[2]

Equally, the film was premiered in Besançon, because the same team had just made another film there on a strike at the Rhodiacéta factory (clips of which are included in *Loin du Vietnam*) - thus inserting it immediately into the context of industrial militancy in France. The screening was introduced by one of the striking workers, who, again, stressed the need to build a sense of unity between different sectors of the revolutionary struggle: 'Et si ce film nous est offert en hommage à la grève "Rhodia"... nous y voyons un encouragement à poursuivre notre lutte et la nécessité de nous unir de plus en plus.'[3] And in the discussion that followed the screening, Resnais summed it up in similar terms: 'le film tend justement à

'materialist cinema' (such as *Cinéthique*, in particular) thought that it could induce a dangerous kind of narcissistic euphoria. Paul Séban, who made *La CGT en mai '68*, mentions both positive and negative aspects of the phenomenon: 'The workers' reaction was: "It's our strike, we can see ourselves." There's a deep identification. For my part, I find that important. But this identification rules out analysis, it's dangerous' (interview in *Cinéthique* 5, 1969, quoted in English by Sylvia Harvey, *May '68 and Film Culture*, London: BFI publications,1978), p.143.

[2] *Positif* 89 (November 1967), 11-13.

[3] This speech and the ensuing discussion are reproduced in *Cinéma 68*, no. 122, 37-55.

montrer les relations entre le Vietnam et un mouvement mondial
révolutionnaire...'

It is noticeable, however, that this very confident definition is
immediately qualified in a way that seems to reflect a countervailing
anxiety about the validity of these connections. Resnais continues:
'seulement il le fait, évidemment, avec, parfois... gaucherie, naïveté,
précaution, il pose plutôt les questions qu'il ne cherche à y répondre'
- expressing a rather different position: a recognition of the difficulty
that Western audiences have in understanding the Vietcong, a
recognition of their difference, and our cultural alienation from
them. The promotion of revolutionary unity, in other words, needs to
be carefully distinguished from the assumption that the Vietnamese
share our view of the world - an assumption which is, after all, *also* a
recognisable element of imperialist ideology. Solidarity is not a
question of reducing everything to the 'same' situation, of
assimilating Vietnam to France.

Within the film itself, Godard's commentary in his section of it
manifests precisely this same ambiguity. On the one hand it too
foregrounds the dimension of international equivalence: 'Che
Guevara dit:"Créons deux ou trois autres Vietnam"'; but it also
points to the 'coupures' between French intellectuals, workers and
the Vietcong: 'le public ouvrier ne va pas voir mes films et entre moi
et lui disons il y a la même coupure qu'entre moi et le Vietnam ou
bien lui et le Vietnam'.

The film as a whole, in its central aim of building solidarity with
Vietnam, is thus marked by the tension between these two political
perceptions: the Vietnamese both are, and are not, fighting the same
fight as us. And this tension shows in the construction and style of
film as well as the statements made in it. Thus on the one hand, there
is a concern to present the audience with an immediately intelligible
situation; the first sequence, for instance, although it alternates
dramatically between North and South, Vietnamese and Americans,
at the same time constructs a very coherent and explanatory
narrative: shots of the American bombers being loaded, followed by
close-ups of fragmentation bombs recovered from the North
Vietnamese countryside, then the departure of the bombers from the
South, then women making bomb shelters in Hanoi, and finally an

actual air-raid on Hanoi - so that the audience never feels confused or at a loss. Also, the film builds a sense of interconnectedness on the basis of purely visual links: as well as the pre-credits sequence mentioned above, the later episode based on the wife of Norman Morrison (the Quaker who burned himself to death on the steps of the Pentagon as a protest against the napalm bombing) cuts repeatedly between her and a Vietnamese woman living in Paris, and both women are shown with their children, eating a meal and then playing in their respective gardens. A sense of emotional identification is also encouraged, some of the time, by the use of camera angles, the commentary, and so on. This is especially evident in the footage shot by Ivens; in the sequence of the women making the bomb shelters, for instance, we are given a series of low-angled close-ups of their faces as they look down at their hands working, alternating with reverse shots of what they're looking at - that is we look *with* them at parts of their bodies; then the camera focuses on one (particularly pretty) woman's face as we hear *with her* the air-raid siren, and share her reaction as she looks up in alarm; meanwhile the commentary reinforces the identification by reading an extract from a letter to Marker from Ivens saying: 'Just by being with the Vietnamese, one becomes calm *like them*' [my italics].

As against this, however, many other features of the shooting and editing work in the opposite direction, in a way that resists smooth or quick interpretation - there is evidence of a conscious refusal to make the film easy to watch. The basic fact that the various directors have in any case very different styles of camera-work is accentuated by an editing style based on contrast: one is reminded throughout of Eisenstein's conception of montage as a 'collision of opposites'. Thus, returning again to the pre-credits sequence, Lelouch's shots of American bombers require a very mobile camera, alternating between dramatic low and high angles, with the dominant steely blue-grey of the military hardware echoed in the dark cloudy sky - then the film cuts to Ivens' footage of the camouflaged guerrillas against a yellow-brown background, shot in a single take with a fixed camera. As well as several directors, the film also employs a considerable diversity of genres - Resnais's fictional episode, interviews, newsreel footage, animation, titles, stills, radio news bulletins, letters from Ivens and Michèle Ray (a news photographer who was held captive by Vietcong guerrillas for three weeks) - and this heterogeneity itself makes for a very jerky presentation. Thirdly, the audience is also at various points faced with a simple visual difficulty in reading the image: the film camera amplifies the distortions in the pictures of a badly adjusted TV set, showing a speech by General Westmoreland; and the fact that Ray's camera broke down halfway through her assignment is exploited by incorporating the resulting fragmented, half-obliterated images into the film as a strikingly effective expression of the dislocation and chaos of the war situation.

Finally, the film contains one particular visual theme that seems to sum up the ambiguity which I have been discussing - namely that of the invisibility of Vietnamese, whom we first see as camouflaged guerrillas, and later as civilians in Hanoi hiding underground in air-raid shelters. This is further accentuated by the contrasting high-profile visibility of the Americans, whose huge machines in the sky seem to be offering us a vision of warfare as spectacle, as against the necessarily and essentially invisible nature of guerrilla warfare. (A later episode shows a play in a North Vietnamese village in which the actors caricature Johnson and his advisors - once again, from a different point of view, presenting the Americans as spectacle.) I think the invisibility of the Vietnamese is ambiguous because on the one hand we could interpret it as a metaphor for the difficulty we have in 'seeing', that is understanding and identifying with, them (an idea which is developed further in Resnais's contribution to the film, in which a (fictional) anguished liberal intellectual points to the illusory 'visibility' of Vietnam via TV: 'c'est la première guerre que tout le monde peut voir' - but what we see is facile, misleading and finally meaningless). On the other hand, however, the fact that the film *does* enable us to see them means that, when we do, we are so to speak given a privileged revelation; the feeling is one of being let in on a secret, and it produces a perhaps illusory feeling of shared intimacy and complicity. It is in this sense that the visual *seme* of the 'invisible Vietnamese' seems to me to contribute to the more general ambivalence discernible in the film.

Three of the directors involved in *Loin du Vietnam* also released films of their own in the same year, all involving reference to Vietnam - Lelouch's *Vivre pour vivre*, Ivens' *Le Dix-septième parallèle*, and Godard's *La Chinoise* [4] - and they exemplify three totally different approaches to the representation of Vietnam. Lelouch's is a feature film starring Yves Montand as a TV reporter who has affairs while on location abroad, and Annie Girardot as his long-suffering wife back home, and it includes an episode in which Montand, assigned to Saigon, is captured by the Vietcong. It was in fact while on location in South Vietnam that Lelouch also shot the sequences of the American air-force that figure in *Loin du Vietnam*. But *Vivre pour vivre* is essentially a romance which simply exploits the topicality of Vietnam to bolster up its plot with a little spurious political commitment; and as such it received uniformly negative reviews. Tom Milne in *The Observer* (7 April 1968) for instance wrote: '...what makes the whole thing so peculiarly repulsive... is Lelouch's gross pretension... The effect is as though a particularly crass TV commercial had decided to use that newsreel of a Vietcong prisoner being summarily shot through the head to advertise the exorcising power of a new underarm deodorant.'

The other two are both far more serious in their treatment of Vietnam, but they adopt diametrically opposed positions on the status of representation, that is, on the relationship between images and truth. Ivens' film is a documentary, shot in very difficult conditions in the village of Vinh Linh just north of the border between North and South Vietnam (i.e., the seventeenth parallel). He worked with Vietnamese cameramen and spent two months in the village getting to know the people and sharing their daily life under the American bombers.

For him, it is this experience that guarantees the truth of his representation; while he does not claim to be impartial, and is openly committed to the cause of the North Vietnamese, he does claim to have constructed his film in such a way as to reveal and analyse the

---

[4] In fact Godard released no fewer than four feature films in 1967 - *Made in U.S.A, Deux ou trois choses que je sais d'elle*, and *Weekend* as well as *La Chinoise*.

underlying reality of the situation. Thus the aim is to explain and to
move/mobilise the audience at the same time - as he says elsewhere:
'we are learning to conceive documentary film as an *emotional*
presentation of *facts*' [my italics].[5] In line with this stance, therefore,
Le Dix-septième parallèle is above all a methodical investigation of
all the different aspects of the village's life: it shows us men and
women, old people and children, working in the fields, fighting the
enemy, digging shelters, the underground printing press and
hospital, etc. Everything is carefully made intelligible to the
audience, either by being explained directly to camera (for example,
the operation of the printing press is explained to us by the man
working it), or by means of the commentary, or through various
other devices, such as showing a teacher addressing his class, or a
journalist from Hanoi interviewing one of the women on the party
committee. In all of these cases, the sound-track is responsible for
providing the relevant information. It is equally important in
assuring the more 'emotional' level of the film's effectiveness:
although the commentary is in French, it is spoken by a Vietnamese
woman (the camera team's doctor and translator) with a strong
accent, thereby declaring itself to be part of the represented situation,
rather than an impartial point of view imposed from the outside - she
says 'nous' rather than 'ils' - and thereby also fudging the issue as far
as 'objectivity' is concerned, since her vehement expressions of
hatred for the Americans are as it were co-opted by the *film's* point
of view while retaining the alibi of being the sentiments of the North
Vietnamese. In addition to this Ivens in this film is, thanks to the
participation of Marceline Loridan, using direct sound for first time,
which enables him to include a lot of dialogue between the villagers
in Vietnamese (with subtitles) - and this, together with the prominent
use throughout the film of close-ups of faces looking sad, angry,
resolute, etc., is an important factor in achieving a feeling of
authentic contact with the people shown on screen. Ivens, in other

---

[5] In an article called 'Collaboration in Documentary', reprinted in Rosalind
Delmar's *Joris Ivens: 50 years of film-making*, (London: BFI publications,
1979), pp. 104-5.

words, relies also on an intuitive level of understanding and empathy in the audience.

On a purely visual level, the double effect of intelligibility and identification is acheived with equal economy of means, largely through the editing techniques. The sequence showing a bombing raid, near the end of the film, is put together in such a way as to give an effect of simultaneity - showing different things happening at the same time: capturing an American pilot and putting out fires and carrying the wounded to hospital - without sacrificing the overall coherence of the representation. At the same time our sympathy is engaged by, for instance, having a shot of the villagers shouting and shaking their fists at the pilot immediately preceded by one showing a row of children's corpses laid out on the ground, and followed by a very sudden cut, matched on two images of a woman holding a crying baby and heightened by a sudden silence on the sound-track, to a scene of a child's burial - both cuts thus serving to justify the Vietnamese hatred of the Americans. The commentary is silent for most of this sequence, and on the single occasion that it does intervene it is not to provide information but just as a very forceful expression of the people's feelings: 'les Américains bombardent, brûlent, pillent, tuent, mais chaque jour notre peuple s'enflamme davantage de colère et de haine'.

The film's emotional impact also derives from an at times very dramatic visual style - the sequences in the underground shelters especially make full use of the potential of darkness, lamplight, and the strong vertical framing of the tunnels. The scene of the cadre's weekly meeting is a good example of how this can be combined with the informational function - and also of the point I made earlier about the 'hidden' nature of the Vietnamese producing a kind of visual complicity: with the cramped confines of the shelter removing any possibility of distance and perspective, and the faces of the men only intermittently visible in the darkness, the camera's presence produces a strong feeling that we are being initiated into a clandestine society: a feeling reinforced by the cautious pace of the editing as it constructs a gentle rhythm of alternating close-ups of hands and faces. Occasionally the film's emotional aspect becomes a little contrived: for instance when we hear children's laughter together with the sound of the bombers, initially without seeing the children, so that the poignant juxtaposition of sounds is given greater prominence - and then the camera tracks across to a group of very appealing little boys playing cards outside a shelter. But the film as a whole undeniably stands as a powerful and convincing tribute to the North Vietnamese and the justice of their cause.

Ivens' view is that the truthfulness of a documentary is ultimately determined by the personality of the film maker. He says: 'the success of his film depends both on the confidence the masses have in his personality, and, born from this confidence, on an individual human personality which chooses only the one side of reality that seems important and leaves all else aside. In other kinds of film there can be no such real and important criterion by which to evaluate the personality of the film maker.'[6] In other words, telling the truth is purely a problem of individual integrity - 'in documentaries, in the same way as in fiction films, you can lie or you can tell the truth. It's up to you.'[7] It has nothing to do with the status of the medium or the ideological context in which it functions. That is, it is not a theoretical problem.

Whereas for Godard, it is precisely that. And he adopts two very different approaches to it in *Loin du Vietnam* and *La Chinoise*. This is to some extent inevitable, since the latter is a fiction film, but his treatment exaggerates the difference already inherent in the two genres; it is principally a question of the presence or absence of an overtly stated point of view.

One section of *Loin du Vietnam* consists of a monologue by him, as he is shown operating a camera, interspersed with a fast-moving and rather complicated montage of shots taken from a variety of sources: newsreel footage, Marker's film of the Rhodiacéta strike, *La Chinoise* itself, and so on. The emphasis throughout is Godard's personal response to the invitation he received to participate in the film, but, through the doubts he formulates, voice and images work together to interrogate the whole process of film-making as a

---

[6] 'Some reflections on avant-garde documentaries', reprinted in Delmar op.cit., pp. 98-9.

[7] Quoted in Delmar op.cit., p. 121.

contribution to political struggle. He says, for instance, that all his ideas about what he could show on screen are undermined by his lack of direct involvement in the Vietnamese situation:

> ...le fait que Hanoï ait refusé que j'aille chez eux - et je trouve qu'ils avaient raison parce que j'aurais pu faire des choses qui leur faisaient plus de mal que de bien - fait que toutes ces idées, c'est des idées faussement généreuses... ça me paraît difficile de... parler des bombes alors qu'on ne les reçoit pas sur la tête... On a beau dire que notre cœur saigne... mais ce sang n'a aucun rapport avec le sang de n'importe quel blessé, alors... il y avait une certaine honte, c'étaient quand même des idées honteuses, comme quand on signe des appels pour la paix...

Here, in other words, the film maker is revealed to be operating on the basis of uncertainty, inadequacy, and inauthenticity, rather than, as with Ivens, from a position of mastery and possession of the truth. In a sense, nothing is represented here, and the problems of representation are demonstrated simply by expressing them directly to camera. This also means that the voice becomes the dominant element, with the function of the images largely reduced to being an illustrative counterpoint to what Godard is saying - and the voice, despite its hesitancy, nevertheless gives an impression of sincerity which provides a very straightforward point of contact with the audience: we are hearing what Godard really thinks.

In *La Chinoise*, on the other hand, the Vietnamese war is presented in a much more distanced and carefully framed fashion, in the context of a seminar held by a group of Parisian Maoist students, in which 'Guillaume' (Jean-Pierre Léaud) presents an analysis of the relationship between America, the Soviet Union, China and Vietnam; his speech is intercut with shots of one of the group, 'Yvonne' (Juliet Berto), acting the part of a Vietnamese woman, first with toy American bombers buzzing round her like wasps, and then pretending to machine-gun the enemy from behind a barricade made out of copies of Mao's *Little Red Book*; there are also intercut stills of comic-strip images of a GI in the jungle, and Batman. Here, in contrast to his presentation in *Loin du Vietnam*, Godard's own position is difficult to locate, because of the characteristically elusive mixture of irony, caricature and sympathy with which Léaud is shown. For instance, his analysis sees the conflict as above all one between Maoism and Soviet revisionism, with Vietnam itself of little more than incidental interest, and as allied with China in a way that is blatantly inaccurate; does Godard share this view or is he parodying it? Léaud's style of speaking is both realistically authoritative, presenting the issues with an over-simplified, pedagogical kind of clarity that brooks no argument, and at the same time a caricature of this 'discours du maître' (for example, he uses different pairs of sunglasses representing the flags of the different nations as a kind of visual aid). A further uncertainty arises from the dislocations between the different types of representation involved. In particular, Léaud's discourse stands in a rather complex relation to the intercut sequences: in so far as he is shown initiating and controlling them, and in so far as they act as illustrations of his analysis, they are subordinate to it, as is the case with Godard's own discourse in *Loin du Vietnam*; but in this instance they simultaneously subvert the authority of his presentation, because what he introduces as 'quelques faits - parmi eux est la vérité' - are clearly not facts at all but comic-strip pictures and Berto's pointedly unrealistic, stylised dramatisations of the war. As opposed to Léaud's logical, but simplistic and authoritarian, discourse, the latter work on a figurative level - as images but also as imagery of the Vietcong and America. They thus discredit his formulations while simultaneously having a force of their own - which, to confuse matters further, in terms of political content is the same as his (i.e., pro-Maoist and pro-Vietcong): as though, perhaps, the target for Godard's irony is not Maoism but academic pseudo-revolutionary discourse.

The meaning of this episode - that is, 'what Godard really thinks' - is therefore not immediately obvious. Instead, the sequence has to be interpreted through these dislocations; and the result is to foreground the central problem of representation, namely the irreconcilable difference between facts and images - as Godard has said elsewhere: 'ce n'est pas une image juste, c'est juste une image'. It is also open to the possible conclusion that, paradoxically, the only relative truth about Vietnam that is accessible to us in the West does lie in images, as long as we do not confuse their status with that of facts. Confronting us with deliberately anti-realist representations, in other words, serves as a warning about the constructed nature of all representations; and, despite the very different treatment, this is of course ultimately the same issue as concerns him in *Loin du Vietnam*.

As the above discussion of their films has tried to demonstrate, there is a clear contrast between Ivens and Godard on the question of the relation between the cinematic image and truth, and between cinema and revolutionary political action. Ivens thinks that the director can reach the truth of the situation he is filming, can demonstrate that truth in his film, can make it intelligible to the audience and can engage the audience on an emotional level as well; that, moreover, he should do this because emotional involvement leads to political commitment. Godard, on the other hand, is suspicious of all these concepts, and concentrates on a questioning of cinematic representation within his films themselves, in order to reveal underlying assumptions of realism, authenticity, and so on, which are seen as complicit with bourgeois ideology.

What is particularly interesting about the differences between Ivens and Godard, as shown in their film-making practice of 1967, is that their respective positions foreshadow a theoretical debate that took place in the years immediately following 1968 in the pages of *Cahiers du cinéma* and *Cinéthique*[8] - as though the problems involved in representing Vietnam forced them to confront issues that elsewhere still remained to be clarified. On one side of this argument were those, often but not always aligned with the PCF or CGT, who saw political cinema in a fairly pragmatic light as putting across a single unambiguous and authoritative message, using genres and styles that would be most effective because they were already familiar to working-class audiences: in practice, this meant the realist genres of commercial entertainment. Against this was the leftist view that cinema would not be politically effective while it remained contaminated by the forms and practices of bourgeois

---

[8] The principal articles in this debate are translated into English and printed in *Screen Reader 1* (London: SEFT, 1977).

cinema; films had to theorise their own conditions of production, and the first priority was to work towards a new materialist cinema with a new 'language' - inevitably not very accessible to mass audiences - and to reject the idealist notion of a pre-existing monolithic truth that could be simply transmitted from director to audience.

The events of 1968, as well as generating theoretical debate, also had a more direct effect on the practice of film makers, including those I have been discussing. For example, the move towards collective work is reflected in Chris Marker's development: he had originally set up SLON just to make *Loin du Vietnam*, but as a result of his experience of filming 'cinétracts' during 68 he decided that in future he would only work collectively, and revived SLON to this end. Equally, from 1968 until 1973, Godard worked entirely with the Maoist *Dziga Vertov* group.

As for Ivens and Loridan, while the events of May were taking place in France, they were working on *Le Peuple et ses fusils* in Laos, and when they returned to France to start editing the film, they decided to do it together with people who had been involved in filming the events there. Ivens said: 'when we returned, the need to pursue this work in common and at the same time to enlarge our collective was felt by everyone. Whilst we had been away there had been the May revolts, the general strike. This had to be taken into consideration. Our film was going to address itself to an audience which came fresh from the experience of a certain type of revolt and also a temporary setback to this revolt. That is why we worked with French militants.'[9]

Le Peuple et ses fusils was in other ways significantly different from *Le Dix-septième Parallèle* - partly as a result of their own dissatisfaction with the latter, but also because they were influenced, they say, by 68 and the redefinitions of cinematic practice that it generated. Ivens comments in another interview:

the audience could have the feeling that they are living with the Vietnamese in *The 17th Parallel*. And perhaps they will feel

---

[9] In an interview in *Cinéma Politique* (November 1978), 70-71, translated and printed in Delmar op.*cit.*, p. 66.

that less with *The People and Their Guns*, but I believe they will learn more from it, because of the treatment. In fact one could sit in an armchair in front of *The 17th Parallel*, and to a certain extent 'enjoy' one's emotions. This isn't possible this time. You are forced to listen.[10]

This implies exactly the move away from identification that is at issue in materialist cinema; and Jean-Pierre Sergent (another member of Ivens' group) adds another key emphasis when he says, in the same interview: 'one could say that...*The17th Parallel* is a narrative, *The People and Their Guns* an essay on theory.'

The idea of film as essay rather than narrative is a familiar one in Godard's later work, and is well exemplified in his and Jean-Pierre Gorin's *Letter to Jane*, which came out in1972. Earlier in the same year, they had worked with Jane Fonda in *Tout va bien*, and *Letter to Jane* consists in an analysis of a photograph taken of her in North Vietnam and released by the Vietnamese to the Western press where it was widely published as a gesture of liberal support for the North Vietnamese. The film is a commentary spoken (in English) by Godard and Gorin over a series of still images, juxtaposing the photograph with other pictures in *L'Express*, where it appeared, and other related images. It thus employs basically the same format as Godard's section of *Loin du Vietnam*, but is formally more radical in its use of a blacked-out screen, and its constant returning to the same photograph.

Equally, they are asking the same question as in *Loin du Vietnam*: 'we are going to use this photograph, then, to go and seek an answer to the following question in Vietnam: how can cinema help the Vietnamese people win their independence?' - that is, using the photograph to explore the relation between their film-making practice, as exemplified by *Tout va bien*, and the war in Vietnam. There is, however, also a marked shift of emphasis in that the separation which in *Loin du Vietnam* was experienced as a personal problem is now taken as a fact of the objective situation, and the starting-point for the analysis. The commentary goes on: 'today's

---

[10] *Cinéma* 70. no. 143.

question about the revolution...should be: how to change the old world? And one can see right away that the old world of the Vietcong is not the same as the old world of a Western intellectual, that the old world of the Palestinian is not the same as that of a black child from Harlem, that the old world of a worker in a Renault factory is not the same as that of his girlfriend.' In place of a simple demand for revolutionary unity, the advancement of the struggle is now seen to require a theoretical articulation of the relations between different situations. In this case, it has to start from the difference that the North Vietnamese decided it would be a positive and useful act to release the photo to the Western press, whereas Godard and Gorin think it does more harm than good, for reasons that they explain in some detail. Thus instead of Godard's pre-68 remarks which, while subjectively very individualist, are also very generalised in their reference to the difficulty of making a film about Vietnam, we have here a more specific analysis of one particular image - in terms of its relation to its caption, and the use of focus, camera angle, and framing, all of which produce an image of 'the militant as *star'*. We are made to look at Jane Fonda rather than at what she is looking at; and her face contrasts significantly with the out-of-focus face of an anonymous Vietnamese man beside her. His, they argue, is an expression of his concrete historical situation, while hers wears an all-purpose expression of tragic pity and a kind of knowing but vacuous self-consciousness. They go on to demonstrate, with considerable virtuosity, that 'this face which says "I know a lot" but doesn't say *what* it knows' recurs throughout Hollywood cinema (Dean, Brando, Henry Fonda, etc.) and throughout the capitalist news media (Golda Meir, Johnson, Che Guevara, etc.). The media, in other words, has its own historically determined force of inertia which obliterates political difference, and so, even when brought to bear on a revolutionary situation, defuses it.

It is perhaps this realisation of the need to analyse the basic processes of representation in the media seen as a capitalist institution that is the most evident effect of 1968 on films about Vietnam, and indeed on political films in general. Conversely, the films about Vietnam perhaps played a part in initiating a wider interest in the Third World after 1968: Godard went on to make films about Palestine and Mozambique, SLON filmed in Cuba, Ivens and Loridan in China; in addition 1969 saw Louis Malle's *Calcutta*, and in 1971 Pierre Kast made a documentary on Brazil, *Macumba* (which was never released). Nevertheless, it seems to me that the importance of the war in Vietnam as an object of representation lies above all in the way that it raises issues of representational 'truth' and identification in a peculiarly clear and urgent form, and articulates them within a political context.

12. THE CONCEPT OF GENERATION AS EXEMPLIFIED BY THE CLASS OF 68

PASCAL ORY

Generation is an issue that is nowadays widely and hotly debated, especially in the field of French historiography. What is a generation? Do generations exist and, if so, of what - or of whom - are they generations? In order to extend these lines of inquiry I will endeavour to 'prove as I go that there are such things as generations' by charting the progress of one of them. In doing so, I will try to adhere to the definition of cultural history as 'the social history of representations' that I have advanced elsewhere. I would be more than happy were this crude exercise in psychology to stimulate both research in this area and comparisons with similar or dissimilar cases from other eras and parts of the world.

Although what follows will be schematised, I am well aware of having adopted a perspective that is wide: perhaps it is too wide. My remaining scientific scruples have caused me to limit my discussion to the concept of an intellectual generation while at the same time wondering whether there are not other sorts of generation ('cultural' or 'political', for example), or whether these are merely derivations of the former, leaving the intellectual dimension as the only indispensable parameter of this concept. On the methodological level, it follows from the decision to emphasise the intellectual aspect that, if an approach of this variety could and should combine the qualitative with the quantitative, it should at least always take as its starting-point the theoretical/practical complex of those actors who claim to speak on behalf of their contemporaries and, at the same time, in relation to a specific conjuncture. My plan will develop from this two-fold temporal starting-point (society on the one hand, events on the other) and draw distinctions between four factors which, as I see it, define an intellectual generation. Two arise out of the contemporary scene (a certain situation, a certain movement), and two from a combination of circumstances (a certain crystallisation, a certain ending). I will present these two modes of the experience of one generation by alternating elements of each.

SITUATION

It seems to me that the basic situation of a given generation is always two-fold, that is demographic and intellectual, comprising - if I may be allowed to use a somewhat risky metaphor - in the former instance 'innate' and in the latter 'acquired' features.

In terms of population, the generation of 68 was wholly involved with a certain condition which was at once qualitative and quantitative. Quantitively-speaking, it was the generation of the baby boom. By this we should understand that, qualitatively, it turned into what I would call the 'university boom' as soon as it reached its twenties. From the first factor stems the importance accorded at that time to the idea of 'youth'. This is recognised today as being recent in political terms. It might also be said that, after the era of the first 'youth movements' (that is before the First World War) and after that of youth politics (that is the period between the wars), the 1950s and 1960s saw the demographic upturn in post-war France that promoted business acumen and social ambition, which were given a great cultural consensus-value. The 'pop-scene' hardly even caricatured the strength of this emergence, but had already provided its two distinctive features: internationalisation (according to British and American models) and 'hedonisation' (systematic pursuit of pleasure).

By 'university boom' I understand the rather violent encounter of these new age-groups with a system of higher education which had become, thanks to them and above all because of the transformation of society's demands on higher education, a system of mass higher education (though not 'of the masses', which is a different question altogether). The university system was all the more unprepared and all the more fragile for the fact that, of the three traditional levels of French education, higher education was undoubtedly the most subject to the influence of intellectual liberalism and, in its structures as in its rhetoric, the most individualistic and élitist.

This gave rise to the theme of 'refusal', whose importance has already been noted by other commentators; not refusal to succeed, as was the case with the ultra-left at the turn of the century, but to 'join' established society, the France whose Thirty Glorious Years were coming to a close without anyone's even suspecting it. In this light, the generation of 68 appears to be in all respects a generation with growing pains (physical, demographic, cultural) as well as pains caused by growth, not so much the problems of how to maintain prosperity as those of what it was for and how it should be divided. On this last point Pompidou and Cohn-Bendit,.however paradoxically, agreed.

From what has already been mentioned there resulted in particular the social structure of the 68 movement, which privileged a small kernel of young workers and a clear majority (of a vanguard...) of 'intellectual workers', if we understand by this stock term what I would sooner call the members of the cultural professions. These can be subdivided into creation: (artists and scholars), and dissemination: (teachers and journalists).

The intellectual genealogy of the class of 68 may be traced back to the dual heritage of Marxism (not Marx's) and Freudianism (not Freud's) which had already dominated the preceding generation (although in different proportions). Its originality on this score lay rather in what it extrapolated from the two lines of thought that had already been marked out and which could, broadly speaking, be described as ethnology (via structuralism) and ethics (via existentialism). The fact that there was already a contradiction between the value accorded by the former to 'relativity' and by the latter to 'commitment' no doubt prefigured the final schism; for the time being, this bipolarisation was experienced as a positive thing, underlying both the popularity and the canonical status of syncretic works such as those of Wilhelm Reich among the forbears, or Herbert Marcuse among the older generation, or of Deleuze and Guattari's *Anti-Oedipe* from among the younger. On the same subject, there is more than one meaning to be gleaned from the fact that the 68 feminist movement, which was at the origin, among other things, of the women's editorial complex, chose as its name

'Psychanalyse et Politique' (called 'Psych et Po' by the generation's initiates).

CRYSTALLISATION

I think that every generation becomes aware of itself because of one seminal event symbolising values; to put it differently, an event and its meaning. The event, May 68, originated in the collision of the generation's political movement not so much with conservatism as with the inflexibility of established authority. It left its stamp on the group's style (a treasure-house of images, inexhaustible as is all real treasure), on its dynamism (hermetic but dense: the event left its protagonists in a state of dissatisfaction that was in itself a beginning) and finally on the protagonists themselves, who must always be split into two groups. These were the veterans of the May troubles - active or passive, revolutionaries or reformers - and the latecomers, initially deprived of the chance to make history and therefore all the more anxious to make up for lost time in their own eyes as well as in history's.

To judge by this, it would be perfectly legitimate to describe this historical configuration, as events, riot or crisis, but not revolution. The Avignon Festival of July 1968, a date of no mean importance in the career of Jean Vilar, the history of the festival and that of the French theatre, acted as the first of those paradoxical 'dress rehearsals' which took place after the play was over and at the same time served to underline its exceptional theatricality.

As for the system of values symbolised in this way, it would no doubt be centred on the word - more ambiguous than it at first appears - 'root'. Root-values indeed were those of the prevailing radicalism, which was the discourse and practice of rupture, of violence. As far as form went, this gave a certain aggressiveness to tone and actions: an undisguised eulogy of lawlessness. On a deeper level, such questions did not spare two citadels which had, up until that point, remained untouched by the revolutionary movement in general: in the theoretical sphere, egalitarianism; in that of action, the sanctity of private life which, for example, served so often to establish a vivid contrast between a militant's 'progressiveness' and his domestic lifestyle. But radicalism was also lived out by way of simultaneous aspiration to liberty and identity - where an echo can be found of the tension between Marxism and psychoanalysis. 'No liberty without identity' was translated into philosophical terms by, in one direction, an original combination of the return to nature (on the individual level) and the primacy of the will (on the collective level). Sexual desire and revolutionary aspiration were equated in the content of works like that, which has been mentioned, by Deleuze and Guattari, which solemnly postulated that 'desire is in essence revolutionary'. In the other direction, the liberty-identity pairing was the driving force and at the same time the common feature of three movements which, though of unequal importance, were clearly linked with each other and with May 68: regionalism, ecology and consumerism (all of them radical).

Such a system of values did not govern only words. It dictated the principles of organisation and of specific forms of action. The former celebrated the active minority, direct action and the rejection of an organic hierarchy. In this light, the MLF, an anti-association as well as the fabric that connected better-defined groups, summed up this wish and was the closest it came to fruition. The latter obviously belonged to the old inheritance of anarchism, revolutionary syndicalism and surrealism. Rather than the Dreyfusard tradition of a petition of intellectuals (the 343 signatures of the abortion statement) it was here a matter of - to sketch a typology - unrest, provocation, masquerade, the harnessing of symbols, physical pressure and collective illegality being pushed to the fore.

The hypothesis could be advanced that it was certainly in this area that 68 leftism showed most clearly what it really was: the last French crisis of prosperity.

MOVEMENT

Perhaps above all else, a generation is that place where contemporaries meet each other. This should be understood in the sense that it forms a network which evolves with roughly the same personnel (though not entirely: some will fall by the wayside) but not necessarily with all going in the same direction.

The typological approach, which is itself two-fold, works best when applied to this network. The simplest approach permits us to distinguish the fairly straightforward system of influences. The class of 68 had its personalities like Jean-Paul Sartre and Simone de

Beauvoir, who were objects of devotion (pilgrimage and patronage, to be precise), its places for hammering out ideas like the seminars of Louis Althusser, Jacques Lacan, Roland Barthes and the University of Vincennes, its typical organs of dissemination, from *L'Idiot International* to Editions Maspéro via the first issue of *Actuel*, and its associations which were sometimes informal, like the MLF (hence the 1979 'trademark' scandal), but most often in obedience to the law of 1901, even if they did from time to time end up in the dock.

Still more interesting, perhaps, is the typology of the actors or, to put it in other, though still somewhat theatrical, terms, the casting. This matter indeed requires that we take into account the concept of a symbolic age. A generation is without doubt bound up with contemporaneousness, but this is a relative term. In this generation as with all others, the *central kernel*, in terms of quality and quantity, was made up of two age-groups: the twenty-year-olds (playing the part, in due course, of students) and the thirty-year-olds (among whom many latecomers - if not converts - were recruited, as has been said above). But every generation elects its own masters. I would distinguish three categories of these: the older generation, or rather the forty- and fifty- year-olds, perhaps at the height of their creative powers, and certainly of their intellectual prestige: a Barthes, or a Foucault. These were the patriarchs, who were distinguished from the latter not just by age (in which case Lévi-Strauss and Lacan would be part of this group, whereas I would include them with the older generation), but by the fact that they had already been masters for one or two generations before (the Sartre-Beauvoir couple, of course); and the ancestors, the honoured dead, all the more warmly resuscitated for this grave-robbing generation, feeling that it was the first to do them justice (for example, Charles Fourier). Finally, I do not think it would be pushing formalism too far to point out in between these categories not only a few borderline cases, rare enough in any event, but above all cases of complicity (an example of such fellow-travellers is Jean Daniel) and, still more noticed at the time, of defectors (for example, Maurice Clavel).

From these common structures every generation evolves with more or less vigour and breadth. The picture that I have just painted so crudely reaches a state of extreme sophistication, guaranteeing a sizeable and growing audience and constituting an excellent prelude to the final stage which every generation comes to: its installation,

generally with the advent of the next generation, in the driving-seat
of cultural power while it awaits, later still, political power. The
ideological ambiguity of the situation in 1981 (see the argument
surrounding the left-wing intellectuals' 'silence') stemmed, in my
opinion, from the fact that the change of majority took place at a
time when the political generation in the ascendant was still the
previous one - that of decolonisation or more exactly UNEF. That of
68 had only attained hegemony in intellectual and media terms albeit
with its content perceptibly transformed from what it had originally
been at the end of the 1960s.

My theory is, in fact, that a generalised leftism, adequately
symbolised by the fate of the *Gauche proletarienne*, was replaced
from about 1970 onwards by a specialised leftism, the latter
rechannelling its militant energies here into 'sexual liberation', there
into 'militant regionalism' and elsewhere into 'alternative press'. A
group like VLR with its review significantly entitled *Tout!*, seems to
me to have been, in this respect, the most representative instance of
this decisive change of direction.

It may however be guessed that such evolution could not in the
long run avoid one fundamental question, bringing up once more the
internal contradictions which had, in the early days, been the
movement's strength. It was as if the May slogan, 'The more I make
love, the more I make revolution: the more I make revolution, the
more I make love', had ended up by being split into autonomous, and
therefore meaningless, fragments.

ENDING

Since everything has an end, so, by definition, has a generation, end
being understood here in the sense at once of completion and of
finality. Like all others, the generation of 68 thus disappeared and
left its mark behind it.

On occasion, the Solzhenitsyn effect has been said to have played
a major role in the collapse of the Marxist frame of reference after
about 1975. This serves only to avoid the question. The essential fact
remains: why was Solzhenitsyn readable at this time when Suvarin
in 1935 or Kravchenko the years afterwards were not? Everything
leads me to think that the ideological shift at the end of the 1970s,
which was indeed striking, was due to the conjunction of two, more

structural factors: the economic crisis and the intellectual movement
of leftism itself.

The economic, and therefore social, crisis could have made
leftism more dynamic, However, besides the fact that it arrived at a
moment when leftism had already reached the stage of
fragmentation, it is clear that it only better demonstrated how much
radicalism partook of 'ideological luxury'. The effects of this
phenomenon were felt in particular by the ecologists, at once
justified and marginalised by the economic crisis. The main
explanation remains, for me, the mixture of the generation's
exhaustion and the wild extrapolation that no doubt characterises any
intellectual movement of a certain duration. The romantic
generation, for example, had experienced this phenomenon, which
had been translated for them into both a crisis of aesthetics and an
ideological evolution away from monarchism and towards
democracy. 68 at once generated its own radicalism, perceptible in
the success of the 'post-modernist' formula, and a return to the
concerns of the West, perceptible in the absence of an even more
exotic successor to the latest batch of exotic political models (China,
Vietnam, Cambodia...).

In intellectual terms, the questioning of established values as well
as the failure of so many concrete actions brought, for a generation
so preoccupied with breaking new ground, a simple decline of
radicalism. It was noticeable in the return to reformism and
established political structures, plus the unexpected rehabilitation of
social democracy, a *paradoxical usage* of the values of rupture,
where provocation veers towards cynicism, libertarianism towards
liberalism (see Foucault's later work). Finally, it is to be seen in real
reversals of opinion, created by introspection and the glorification of
'success'. Such is the fate of hedonism and expressivism.

Still, the trace remains. The trace of what I persist in calling a
cultural revolution. It is enough to look at the field of everyday
social practices to get an idea of the route followed by French
society as a whole between 1965 and 1980. Is this incontrovertible
change attributable to May, by which I mean to the theoretical and
practical actions of an intellectual minority in its rise to media
power? I believe so. For it would be easy to list, case by case, the
decisive role played by such-and-such a group of 68 in such-and-
such a precise change (on the question of abortion, for example), but
above all because the problem is not one of knowing whether the

movement would have developed in the way it did without May: it lies in the indelible colouring that May gave to it. There has been a French modality of cultural change clearly different from, for example, the English or Spanish modalities.

From this comes a chronological hypothesis that will serve as a provisional conclusion to this all-too-cursory interpretation: the entrance and the exit of the generation of 68 appears to me to confirm a minor, though interesting law of cultural succession and periodisation, encapsulated in the decade of the 68 generation. Assuming that every intellectual generation is built around a seminal event, or complex of events, and develops as this event works itself out, France seems to have lived, since the end of the Second World War at least, according to the rhythm of generations of ten years, approximately between the fifth years of each decade. Coming after the 'liberation generation' (formation: the Cold War) and after that of decolonialism (formation: the installation of the Fifth Republic), the generation of 68 occupied a privileged position at the end of a great upward cycle, before the grey period of the generation of 75/85 (event: the economic crisis; formation: the turning away from communism of the intelligensia) and the (bitter-sweet?) period of the present generation. Further definitions must wait another decade.

13. SOUVENIRS, SOUVENIRS....

MARIE-NOELLE THIBAULT

If I can make a contribution to this conference, it is not as a historian, because this is not my period, but as an active witness of the events of May 68. It is hard to place oneself in the picture painted of 68, twenty years on, by this conference. I intend, then, to attempt simply to put some order and clarity into the memories and feelings I have left, whilst at the same time remaining well aware of the fragile and subjective nature of such accounts.

It seems to me that above all, it is important to distinguish the generation involved in the making of 68 from the movement itself.

I am not convinced that the chronological divisions proposed by Pascal Ory are entirely relevant. I think rather that between 1960 and 1968, there was a generation of militants, youngsters and students, whose experience was relatively homogeneous, and who can be found, essentially, visible or invisible, in the entire 1968 movement. These militants were in the UNEF, in the UEC, or in both at once. Their common culture appears to be characterised by three main features.

Firstly there was a strong Marxist influence. These were years of intense ideological debate. The reference to Marxism was both profound and omnipresent: but very different in tone from that of post-May 1968. We read, of course, Marx, Lenin, Trotsky. Khrushchev's initiative resulted in a re-appraisal of Stalinism and the Russian revolution. *Les Tempes Modernes* published several special issues on Italian Marxism, which sold instantly. *Les Editions Sociales* published, not before time, a translation of the manuscripts

191

of 1844, and selected extracts of Gramsci. Rosa Luxembourg was back in fashion. Finally, we read reviews such as *Socialisme ou Barbarie*. Concepts of the new working class were widely discussed. There was a not inconsiderable trend towards self-management and anarcho-communism. The UEC launched Weeks of Marxist Thought which attracted tens of thousands of people.

But for this whole generation, the PCF was no longer the home of orthodox Marxism. Everything and everyone questioned the party. The era of fellow travellers was over. If some intellectuals still chose the PCF, it was no longer a choice of development and movement, it was a choice in favour of order and stability, to fight against protest by the young, intellectuals and students. The left of the UNEF and of the UEC were engaged in open battle with the PCF: in direct contrast to earlier opposition, which had always remained internal. The UNEF and the UEC took a public stand, went into print, took initiatives, called demonstrations, acted and organised.

It is in this context that something must be said about Althusser. He was a perfect example of those intellectuals who defended the communist party out of a concern for order. To go straight to the heart of the matter, the PCF was, for him, the university hierarchy's last line of defence. Similarly, the concepts he devised, such as the technical division of labour, functioned as justification for professorial power. For this generation, therefore, Althusser was first and foremost a political enemy, and his ideological influence was limited to the group of ENS students, future militants of the UJCML, who fought against the movement and supported the PCF, before being expelled from it *in extremis* in 1966.

The Algerian War opened the eyes of this whole generation, and was largely responsible for moulding it. The deep horror felt at the atrocities of the colonial war provoked if not a refusal, then at least a lack of attachment to democratic values: democracies are after all imperialist countries too. The awakening of this generation to the struggles for national liberation and the Third World were seen again in its admiration for Cuba, its support for Vietnam and later on, its fascination with China. But the last feature, which I consider to be perhaps the most important, namely political action, including the support for national liberation struggles, was conceived of as a mass movement. This generation encountered the Algerian war only in its later stages, and hence could support the FLN after it had emerged from the complete isolation in which it had remained for years. The demonstration organised by the UNEF on this issue in 1960 attracted more than ten thousand people. Organised in this same way later on, was the fight against the OAS (University Anti-Fascist Front), the various student struggles and the support for Vietnam. In this respect, this generation was fundamentally different from those who, a few years earlier, between 1955 and 1960 had founded the support networks for the FLN: often outstanding militants, they produced brilliant analyses of France from the very beginnings of Gaullism, but acquired their political experience in a context of such isolation and radical marginalisation that very few managed to recover from it. It is perhaps this widespread attachment to mass political struggle which allowed us to avoid real terrorist outbursts, some years later, when life returned to normal.

These few points, certainly insufficient and too closely linked to my personal experience, seem, at least in part, to account for the culture of a generation, which was above all else a political culture.

But the May movement itself was clearly something other than the product of this generation. It was the demonstration of profound developments in French society which had not necessarily been detected or analysed, much less brought under control, in the preceding years. I think that the movement completely overtook even those who had contributed to its birth, and who threw themselves into it heart and soul.

Two aspects of this movement in particular appear to me to reveal this imbalance:

1. The curious relationship between the May movement and politics. This point has been underlined by many authors: the indifference of many of the demonstrators on passing the National Assembly at the beginning of the month of May prefigures the absence of the movement in the June elections. Throughout this conference, it has been emphasised several times over that this fundamental indifference was later on to nourish the birth of movements whose conception of policy and politics was radically different. The MLF has been quoted as an example. This is true. Today, a movement such as SOS Racisme seems also to have inherited this new way of envisaging politics. But, finally, the main consequence of May, politically speaking, seems above all to be the present destructive crisis in our entire system of political representation. In this context, the distance can easily be measured between the objective of the pre-68 generation, which was the

revolutionary changing of society without any need to question the primacy of the political domain, and the result of the movement, which is precisely the re-evaluation of this issue.

2. The relationship between the May movement and French communism. Certainly, the generation of the sixties protested against the hegemony of the PCF, but if this protest was conducted, politically speaking, autonomously, it developed nonetheless within the same culture. May saw the whole communist culture shaken. One of the elements of this culture, which goes back to the deepest roots of the French revolutionary tradition, is that the PCF is rooted in a working class separated from the rest of society; it speaks for this separation. In May, the closing of the factory gates still symbolised the reality of this separation, and was reminiscent of 36. The reality however, was quite different: within the factories, the firms, the offices, the workers no longer stood alone, as they might have in June 36. This time round, the employees and the managers were just as solidly on strike as the workers. The separation could no longer be made. To acknowledge this is easy enough. In contrast, the analysis of the long-term consequences of the reintegration of the working class into French society seems to me to be more difficult, and constitutes one of the elements of the current crisis in the system of political representation and of the acute (and to my mind definitive) anaemia of the PCF, an anaemia which the militant students of the sixties neither desired nor imagined.

Many other points could be developed as to why one could find both continuity *and* division between the militant experience of pre-68 and that of May 68. In my view, division is predominant. This is probably why it is so difficult for a great number of those who were militants before during and after the movement to conceive of themselves as part of an overall perspective of continuity and coherence.

14. STEPPING STONE AND SHIFTING LEGACY: A FEW CONCLUSIONS AND REAPPRAISALS OF MAY 1968 AND ITS HISTORY

VLADIMIR CLAUDE FISERA

This chapter aims to make a synthesis of the foregoing chapters and also to elaborate, albeit briefly, on the import of May 1968. The latter should emerge by itself, from the critical résumés of the papers read at our conference. What is most striking is the overall dynamic approach shared by the contributors: May 1968 is seen as a staging post, a stepping stone more than a barrier or even a foundation stone. It is a historical 'revealer' and accelerator, and the momentousness of the event had just been recalled to the minds of the present analysts by the no less momentous events of the May-in-December of 1986. This second event quite naturally but with no apparent continuity flowed from the first and helped to locate the historical size, meaning and scope of the former. So that 1986 and the whole generational sequence 1968-1986 provided just as much the focus for our conference as the two miraculous months of May-June 1968 themselves.

The second striking aspect is that despite fleeting references to trendy post-modernist, *revenu-de-tout* and also ferociously pro-liberal moods (in the continental sense),[1] the dominant attitudes

---

[1] On post-modernism, neo-Benda-ism and Europeanism as the pillars of

towards 1968 have been those of a healthy and pluralistic *libre examen*.

In my anthology *Writing on the Wall: France, May 1968, a Documentary Anthology*,[2] I remarked how difficult it is for the 'witness-participant-historian' to speak objectively about 'his war'. This difficulty still remains twenty years on.

I shall refer here mainly to the papers relating to the events as a whole from a political point of view. Furthermore these papers, on their own, already deal with the importance or otherwise of this evanescent Year of Dreams[3] more apparent than real, whose spirit and spiritual and cultural heritage matter more than short term factors and accidents, however real these might be.

Hervé Hamon began. This was totally justified in view of the seminal documentary weight of his and Patrick Rotman's two volume 'documentary' on May 1968 entitled *Génération*. Volume 1 is subtitled *Les Années de rêve* [4] and goes from 1957 to the autumn of 1968. Note here too the resort to the word *dream* as a semantic identifier of the *tout autre*; had May been translated in 1968 or in 1986 by a *political* victory this word would certainly not have been chosen for *analytical* purposes. Their second volume, *Les Années de poudre* [5] continues the tale - the book is subtitled 'récit' - of the overlapping itineraries of the leftist leaders of the movement up to the present day. The (gun)powder of the title echoes the temptation of resorting to minority violence but also, we may add, the reality of the political 'powderisation' of the same alleged political and ideological extremists and of their chiliastic expectations. These individual and collective itineraries of particular actors [6] belonging

---

present-day French thought see Brice Couturier, 'L'intelligentsia française est-elle nulle?', *Globe*, Paris (October 1987), 63.

[2] V.C. Fisera (ed.), *The Writing on the Wall: France May 1968* (London: Allison & Busby), 1978, p. 9. An American edition is published by St. Martin's Press (New York, 1979).

[3] Title of a BBC Radio 4 programme broadcast on 20 and 24 January 1988 (editor David Caute, producer David Levy with my being one of the contributors). The programme is a real gold mine of primary documents, mostly interviews with participants twenty years on.

[4] H. Hamon and P. Rotman, *Génération*; vol. 1, *Les Années de rêve* (Paris: Seuil, 1987).

[5] vol. 2, *Les Années de poudre* (Paris: Seuil, 1988).

[6] There has been criticism of the constant emphasis on a few 'telegenic'

to a specific intellectual age-group are recalled as a multi-voiced novel, a *Bildungsroman*. It takes us from enthusiastic naivety often to defeat, always to isolation but also to a late understanding of the realities of everyday life, to an awareness of the constraints of the *longue durée*, to use a term popularised by the *Annales* school of historians. This is the history of the taking root of a political vocation not unlike a religious one. The historian Pascal Ory, author of a cultural history of France between 1968 and 1981, has also set out for us the landmarks of this route in his group portrait, his *portrait de classe* (school photograph), to use the title of a most beautiful fictionalised history of one such school generation coming from the pen of another member of this same generation, the late Jean-Pierre Énard. It might be judicious to take these two contributions together and to add to them, as an echo, that of Roger Duclaud-Williams.

Hervé Hamon centred his exposé on a group more restricted than the entire intellectual generation which was the subject of Pascal Ory's enquiry. As in volume 1 of his book, Hamon focused on a particular vector of political action, the UNEF (students' union) and more precisely he threw light on its hard core, those among its 1965-68 leaders who came from a unit that had already 'gelled', a group of militants originating from the UEC of the post-1956 period. Actually

---

charismatic political group leaders stemming from the atomisation of the 1962-1965 *Union des Etudiants Communistes* (UEC) with a stress on spectacular events, life stories and on the phraseological, always peremptory language that these heroes would use. Various reviewers noted the lack of coverage of the non-Marxist-Leninist left (PSU, anarchists), of the cultural but non-political alternative and last but not least of the rank and file especially the non-student one, this army of enthusiasts, of doubters and of 'beautiful losers' to paraphrase Leonard Cohen's cult book of the time. See for instance the following significantly entitled reviews: Jean-Paul Gault, 'Allez papi ... raconte-moi la guerre', *Le Monde Libertaire*, 21 May 1987; Jean Bars, 'Les enragés de mai 68', *Autogestion - l'Alternative*, the PSU weekly, 18 May 1987; Michel Contat, 'Le Télé-roman des soixante-huitards', *Le Monde*, 8 January 1988. Sylvie Caster, who used to write in *Hara-Kiri* and *Charlie Hebdo*, the best-selling newspaper of that generation, notes with a somewhat perfidious sharpness that the two authors do confess that they have concentrated on the 'best ... those who came out of the establishment cradle' (see her 'Les parvenus du pavé', *Le Canard Enchaîné*, 13 January 1988).

the UEC was in crisis earlier than that, as early as 1956, especially as regards its 'Secteur Lettres' and particularly the Sorbonne. The scene was already set by that time with fast-learning naive ideologists and leaders such as Jean-François Kahn or Gabriel Cohn-Bendit, Danny's less famous brother. Philippe Robrieux in his autobiographical *Notre Génération communiste 1953-1968* (Laffont, Paris, 1977) alludes to these fore-runners, himself making the link with the 1968 'vintage' of former UEC leaders. The UEC was 'normalised' in 1965 owing to the efforts of its chaperone Roland Leroy, in particular at its Montreuil conference. By that time its cadres had swelled their ranks with youth leaders from the PSU and from religious youth organisations. Like hermit- or soldier-crabs these went together and offered the great empty shell of the UNEF - whose membership is by definition and of necessity young, inexperienced and subject to swift turnover - a whole constellation of older leaders, of seasoned operators who knew the art of management, chiefs looking for Indians and for an ideological/rhetorical if not organisational revenge on the Communist Party (PCF). Hence their rule by speech ('mandarinat de la parole') aptly diagnosed by Danny Cohn-Bendit in his 'spoken memoirs', *Le grand Bazar*. Pulling this particular thread from the May 1968 ball of wool (i.e. the UEC until 1965, the UNEF after that date) Hamon quite naturally concentrates on the more general political dimensions, leaving aside the strictly student trade-unionist ones and those concerned with criticising the education system, on which Antoine Prost throws light in his chapter.

And yet this neglected dimension was truly central for those who called themselves officially *gauche syndicale* and not *gauche politique* and who were stronger than the political sects. By going down that path Hamon underlines how much these youngsters were obsessed by high politics, how this vanguard-by-default would always define itself *vis-à-vis* the PCF and Leninist models, be they exotic ones such as latter-day Cuba and China. This indeed led to an exclusive obsession with politics *le tout-politique*, the excesses of which caused the break-up of what was ostensibly a unified mass political movement of students. That is why Hamon insists on political theory as the stake of conflict between the official PCF exegetists and these youngish non-professional 'renegades'. However, Hamon recognises that the Nanterre case was very different, as the UNEF did not exist there. It could be added that at

Nanterre as in Strasbourg or in Nantes the student body, as in the December 1986 movement, did not tolerate political organisations, insisted on their dissolution and was adverse to all theorising.[7] Similarly, Hamon leaves aside the festive (*ludique*) 'cultural' current which goes from the situationists to the Paris Beaux Arts (Fine Art) students via the Odéon theatre and the Avignon festival.

This precludes any universalisation of the Hamon model. According to him, after the events of May 1968, it was only after a process of sobering up (*dessoulage*) from the excesses of politics, which he sees as theoreticism and masochistic militantism induced by Marxism-Leninism, that some of his characters would find a 'libidinal' way out, others a metaphysical or even a psychoanalytical or religious solution. Actually, those who lived through these events experienced even the pedestrian political activities (meetings, sit-ins, occupations, strikes, demonstrations) mostly as an anxious but exhilarating break with the past, causing premature breaks and realignments in their emotional and personal lives. This is well attested in the novels about 1968 such as those by Robert Merle, Natacha Michel, Nicolas Mansar, Gilbert Cesbron or in Danny Cohn-Bendit's autobiography mentioned above. The central paradox of the May movement was that the means were revolutionary, while - especially among non-students - the aims were rarely so. These means themselves, precisely because they were revolutionary (direct action, street activities, streams of improvised speech exchanged between strangers, change in the framework and the routine of daily life), had self-sufficing virtues which were ephemeral in essence. As Marx, much devalued today, put it,'during a strike what counts for

---

[7] See my contribution to *The Year of Dreams* and the unpublished oral testimony of Jean-Claude Richez, a leader of the *Jeunesse-Communiste Révolutionnaire* (JCR). In an interview with me on 7 November 1987 he stressed that Daniel Bensaid, Alain Krivine's *alter-ego* as JCR national leader was severely challenged in the JCR for having agreed to dissolve the branch at Nanterre into the broader 22 March Movement. On the specificity of Strasbourg see also Jean Claude Mayer's interview for the *Year of Dreams* in which this former JCR leader notes the same post-situationist streak which led the movement to choose as its targets the local daily paper and - for the first time - the military institutions, viz. the soldiers' movement at Mutzig. The fifty to eighty *groupuscule* members could not resist such a trend. See also J.-C. Richez, 'Revolte de mai 1968', *Encyclopédie de l'Alsace* (Strasbourg: Publitotal, 1985), Vol. 10, 6369-74.

the worker is the whole collective aspect of the strike, the association which is being created there and the enjoyment which he can find by stopping work and doing something else'.[8] Intellectuals and student intellectuals, divorced from social roots and even from intellectual professional work, could, in the events of May, as some of them had perceived earlier in their own reading of the Chinese cultural revolution, find the opportunity to overcome the 'cult of the book', the cult of abstraction and even a dessicated form of knowledge. They could at last, as Sartre had advocated, put existence itself, at its most trenchant, in the forefront of things and at the top of their priorities and values [9].

Hamon lists the main misunderstandings about May 1968. First, he distinguishes between a certain tiny intellectual elite and the *yéyé* (pop music-inclined) crowds which in his mind were healthier than the former and whose temporary link with the same *groupuscules* created a favourable relationship of forces and hence produced the event. Roger Duclaud-Williams stresses this same distinction regarding the December 1986 events: a minority student culture and a dominant teenage culture which impregnates the student sub-culture. Hamon draws a good deal on the paradox between the archaism of ideologies (one should qualify it by distinguishing between the Marxist-Leninist type and the libertarian ones which surely remain unaffected by this description) and the novelty of the movement, together with the consensus on the refusal to spill blood. This archaism lasted until about 1974 when the former (the ideology) dissolved into the latter (the movement).

Pascal Ory concentrates rather on the broad cultural values which were common to these ex-youngsters - radicalism, voluntarism, naturism, rank-and-file-ism and direct action. These touched upon politics but could not be limited to it and asserted themselves more fully after 1972. According to him, one cannot talk about a final defeat but about a change in methodological priorities as the cultural took over from the political.

Hervé Hamon on the other hand sees in post-1968 political leftism - with the sole exception maybe of the PSU whom he regards more

[8] See V.C. Fisera, 'France: May 1968, Revolution in our Time', *Labour Leader* (ILP) (Leeds: June 1978).
[9] See interview with Benny Levy (alias Pierre Victor), *The Year of Dreams*, op. cit.

indulgently - a nostalgic and inadequate imitation from which only the movements for educational renovation and for women's rights were worth saving. The ultimate yardstick by which these harsh pronouncements are made is the failure to gain ground in public opinion at large. Almost alone from this meagre harvest the political weekly *Politique Hebdo* emerges with any honour. The modest Hervé Hamon was its mainstay with Paul Noirot and from 1970 to 1979 it managed to be at the same time totally political *and* totally free from Marxist-Leninist cant, open to all winds, especially as regards culture and sexuality, and self-critical in the extreme. This weekly, probably for these reasons, was by far the most widely read newspaper of the New Left, a sort of left alternative to *Le Nouvel Observateur*. Similarly, Antoine Prost's very fruitful work in thinking out a new education system, especially in 1981-1984 when he produced a seminal government report on this subject, should not be overlooked despite his elegant and praiseworthy silence on this major contribution.

A new press and a new education rather than a new society or a new mode of production are indeed the consequence and the example of the trend from a generalised to a specialised leftism which Pascal Ory clearly delineates. Personally, I would favour the expression 'spirit born of 1968' rather than that of 'leftism' which smacks of the political organisations' monolithism and self-marginalisation so decried by Hamon. One could talk here of a voluntary self-limitation by the movement itself after 1974. This is due to an awareness of the ebbing of the open political crisis,[10] to the professionalisation of activism linked with the transition of these youngsters into the so-called 'world of work' and to an expression of the desire to see a concrete incarnation of their radical, egalitarian, critical and ethical vision.

Pascal Ory and Margaret Gibbon too put their finger on two fundamental causes of the fading of the May 1968 generation and of its organisations. The first one is the price to be paid for the dissemination of this same new democratic, localist, egalitarian,

---

[10] This had been diagnosed from inside the New Left, by the late and much lamented Serge Mallet back in 1971 in his communication to the *Praxis* conference of that year. See his 'Movements sociaux et lutte politique de l'après-mai 1968 en France', *Praxis*, Zagreb, VIII, 3-4 (1972), 357.

feminist and liberatarian spirit. Militants and their organisations withered away as ideas which used to be *avant-garde* and were found only in obscure 'think tanks' became assimilated by public opinion or at least by the coming generations and made headway in public opinion on their own. This spirit became self-evident, matter-of-fact, dispensing with instances of stimulation and of prophecy. The danger is to see in this dissolution of the singular into the general *Zeitgeist* a loss of priority - as Margaret Gibbon and Marie-Noelle Thibault have aptly shown - e.g. women's demand for respect and equality of rights. These claims have won the argument but have still not been fully implemented, thus feeding a sort of inertia as if there could be satisfaction with what has been achieved in the 1970s, without belittling these considerable, epoch-making breakthroughs. The same goes for the education system, for civil and sexual freedom, for political and social rights.[11] The second reason for this 'fading' is sheer human fatigue. The journalist and activist Maurice Najman who exemplifies more than anyone else this whole generation,[12] when giving the short biographies of his peers, kept repeating as a *leitmotiv* the sentence 'il a les *bras coupés*', meaning so and so is still around but has lost his pep, his breath and is no longer active.

Broken arms, out of breath! The gods of yesteryear died or failed

---

[11] The balance sheet of the May 1968 movement in the railway industry has been eminently positive according to Henri Bronner, the CFDT leader of the railwaymen's strike in Alsace in 1968 as local unions gained legal recognition, became used to seizing initiatives on their own without waiting for the go-ahead from headquarters and dared to challenge the State at the central level too. All this appeared clearly in the spontaneous railwaymen's strike movement of winter 1987 (see his interview with David Caute and V.C. Fisera, *The Year of Dreams*, op. cit.).

[12] Maurice Najman, one of the first UEC dissidents and *Libération* journalists, was on the staff of *Les Nouvelles Littéraires* and *L'Autre Journal* while leading the *Alliance Marxiste Révolutionnaire* which evolved along with its main theoretician Michel Raptis (better known as Pablo) from strict Trotskyism to *autogestion*. Najman who is one of the editors of the monthly *M* (M for 'monthly, Marxism, movement') coached its leader Pierre Juquin in his presidential campaign. See among other articles M. Najman's '68/86, autre chose' *M*, 7 (January 1987) and ibid., 14, (October 1987) for a round table on the comparison between 1968 and 1986.

before new ones had emerged, mainly because of the sheer exhaustion of the radical logic which was specific to this given generation. Politico-cultural generations in post-war France lasted for anything between six to twenty years (e.g. 1954-1962 according to A. Prost in his oral comment on P. Ory's paper, while the latter talks about a 1955-1975 sequence, both being in agreement as regards the key dates of 1954-1955 and 1974-1975).

Actually it is rather reassuring to see the *soixant 'huitards* fading away no sooner than their predecessors did and with no smaller a balance-sheet to say the least. This balance-sheet must include in any fair verdict the dissemination of the right of free speech, the right to dissent (the right to *witness*, in evangelical parlance), the demand to broaden the spaces in which decisions are taken (wider use of general assemblies, of debates - in this, France is not unlike the Poland of today, after all - between state and institutions as a whole on the one hand and self-designated and self-led organisations on the other) as well as the refusal of any back-tracking on the social, civic and especially cultural and sexual gains of the 1960s and especially of the 1970s.

As regards the more specific studies supplementing the general ones, it is noteworthy that both A. Prost and R. Duclaud-Williams single out the loss-cutting approach of the authoritarian state, which was conscious in the autumn of 1968 as in December 1986 that it had to give way on some degree of modernisation in order to defuse the student revolt, which would otherwise have led to an overall explosion. This happens when the extra-parliamentary challenge has reached a certain threshold of credibility and thus threatens the powers that be. This triggering effect of demonstrations seems to come into play when their participants reach the one million mark and when workers' solidarity strikes and demonstrations make the movement spill over from the education ghetto into society at large. A. Prost also made clear the underlying, vague but deep-seated distrust of the young, be it in 1968 or during the 1983-1984 movement against the Savary schools reform - a distrust of the mighty bureaucratic state as organiser of the citizens' professional and personal destiny.

We can therefore see the functional aspect of extra-parliamentary turmoil which periodically jolts the rigid French system into action through crisis, performing the role of a midwife of social change. However, as emerges from both A. Prost's and J. Charlot's studies, this very turmoil produces at the same time a backlash as it leads to the coalescence of a conservative group. The latter, feeling threatened, resorts then to obstruction of the modernising process which it would have probably agreed to, had there not been this threat and, in retrospect, this unforgettable if shameful shiver of fear. Hence, as soon as the sound and fury have abated in the streets, these same conservatives would start to block the ongoing reforms or promises thereof.[13]

The demand for a broadening of decision-making to all concerned and for modernisation of society is even more central to the preoccupations of the socialist left as described by L. Bell in his paper. Added to this is the socialist left's insistence on the autonomy of political actors and of social groups *vis-à-vis* the state. This latter claim goes together much better with the existence of a market, even if it is a capitalist one than with a state, even if it is a socialist one. In this break of the modernist left with the Marxist and especially with the Guesdist-Leninist heritage lies the whole ambiguity which is at the root of the difficult position of M. Rocard and even of the CFDT in the French political and ideological landscape, which was marked out so precisely and so long ago. The main impact of May 1968 on this modernist left born in the mid-1950s is that of anti-productivism which could be found only in Paul Lafargue or in the pre-1914 CGT. It runs against both the redistributive Keynesianism of the SFIO and the democratic managerialism of the modernist left itself (theories of the new working class). By falling in with this, the socialist left gradually went beyond the horizon of the workplace as the sole *locus* of the mechanism of change and of global social regulation. Social movements were promoted to the very central level as socialist instruments and levers of change, to a place which up to then only the state and the plan - with a little help from 'the Party' - used to share. Pluralism became a common behavioural trait even in the minds of experts in socialist economics who are more than ever aware of the substantial link between the autonomy of social movements and the existence of a market. The latter is seen ultimately as the sole guarantor of the existence of the former and eventually of socialist democracy itself.

To conclude I would like to mention an observation which I made

---

[13] The fate of De Gaulle's catalogue of reforms spelled out in his 24 May 1968 speech is a case in point; see text in *The Writing*, op. cit., p. 15.

in the preface of my anthology on May 1968 to which I referred earlier. I noted then that only three words belonged to all tendencies in May 1968. These were: 'action', 'solidarity' and (priority of the) 'working class'. It is clear that the first two at least have remained at the centre of the social movements of today, even when working-class movements are involved, as in the railwaymen's strike of the 1986-87 winter.

Two other symptoms remain: 'a profound crisis of values', in the 1980s as in the 1960s, only masked by 'superficial prosperity'.[14] This crisis of values and what is more the disappearance of shared values between, on the one hand, a large fraction of the population, especially the young, and on the other, the state and economic elites is attested by the mass circulation *and* establishment weekly *Le Journal du Dimanche* which in an article devoted to the huge Madonna concert in Sceaux near Paris in August 1987 made an analogy with the 'May 68 of last December', diagnosing a 'total lack of communication between the political élite - *la classe politique* - and youth'.[15] As to the message of May 1968 twenty years on, the *contestataires* of today through their movements seem indeed, in the words of educationalist Patrick Boumard of the University of Paris VIII (that lasting creation of the events), to have opted for: either putting local issues before general ones, or, as far as possible, teasing more general implications out of local issues, rather than considering the general issues *per se*.[16]

My thanks are due to the ASM&CF and to the University of Strasbourg Faculty of History for their kind assistance.

---

[14] As formulated by Hendrik Hertzberg, the scholar and former advisor to J.F. Kennedy in his review of James Miller's history of the American SDS, *Democracy is in the Streets* (see his article 'Part of the solution, part of the problem' *New York Times Book Review* (21 June 1987), p. 33).

[15] *Le Journal du Dimanche* 30 August 1987. See also Gabriel Macé 'Les boum-boum de la rentrée', *Le Canard Enchaîné*, 2 September 1987.

[16] See his presentation - 'De l'explosion sociale à la réflexion généralisée' - of the precious dossier on the 1986 student movement, and on French universities today in *Raison Présente*, Paris, 82, (1987), 6.

Index